Attacks on the Press in 1993

330 Seventh Avenue, 12th Floor
New York, New York 10001
Phone: (212) 465-1004
Fax: (212) 465-9568
Telex: 910 250-4794
E-Mail: cpj@igc.apc.org

Second Edition

TABLE OF CONTENTS

Preface

BY CHARLAYNE HUNTER-GAULT,
MACNEIL-LEHRER NEWSHOUR

When my colleague, Jeff Goldman, called me shortly after we
returned from assignment in Somalia in April, I didn't know what
to expect when he said: "Are you sitting down?"

Jeff is a great producer, intrepid, resourceful and creative in the
field, and like all of us who practice this craft, given to occasional
theatrics.

"Yes, Jeff, I'm sitting down," I said, with a can-you-just-get-on-
with-it air.

"Well, Sam's been shot," he said. "And it's not at all clear that
he's going to make it."

Sam was Sam Msibi, a 32-year-old South African cameraman
who had just spent six weeks with us in Somalia. For many
nights, I sat and listened as Sam and Grant Reynolds, a white
South African colleague, debated South Africa's struggling
transition to democracy. They talked about their hopes and fears—
Sam's fears, especially, about the violence in and out of townships.
One dark night, on a rooftop overlooking Mogadishu, I brought Sam
news of such violence. I had just heard on the *BBC* radio that African
National Congress executive Chris Hani had been killed. As I held his
hand, Sam cried for Hani and for his country. Later, in search of a
better mood, he showed me pictures of his twin 3-year-old daughters,
Lumka and Manhlakanipho.

Without giving Jeff a chance to continue, I attacked with a series
of questions, buying time before I had to process the news of Sam's
shooting. I needed time, because it reminded me of a terrible day
seven years earlier.

Back in 1986, the news had come to me in an equally dramatic
fashion. I was about to go on the air when another colleague from
South Africa called. He said that the cameraman who had worked
with me on a series on apartheid had been hacked with machetes
while covering clashes between rival township factions and it was "not
at all clear that he was going to make it." Within minutes, I was on

5

the air, watching his bloodied body being lifted into an ambulance, while Jim Lehrer mercifully narrated the story as I tried to gain my composure long enough to read the next, unrelated item.

That was a Friday, and I spent the next two days waiting for the news that seemed inevitable. And, finally, it came. The man we all in fun had called Dr. Death, because his name was George De'ath, had died—the first journalist to lose his life in the long struggle to bring about a democratic, non-racial South Africa.

Now, another South African journalist, a cameraman, my colleague, my friend, Sam Msibi, was clinging to life, shot on his way home to Katlehong by armed men whose intent, in part, was to steal his camera. Once again, I found myself weeping.

Miraculously, Sam Msibi survived the five bullets that were fired into his body, even the one that passed through his heart and collapsed his lung. Another South African reporter, on assignment in Sharpeville, was not so fortunate. He was brutally hacked to death this year.

In the few short years between De'ath's murder and the attempt on the life of Sam Msibi and others, many of us have cried many more tears. Attacks on the press, once rare, have become almost commonplace, not only in South Africa, but around the world.

The reasons for these attacks vary. Many, though not all, can be traced to the enormous political upheavals and instability that have accompanied the end of the Cold War. Insecure governments of fragile nations are not eager to have their internal struggles opened to public scrutiny when those governments deny their citizens basic human rights.

Many of our colleagues around the world lack the constitutional protection American journalists enjoy, and they are vulnerable. Over the past year, I have come to know many of them through "Rights and Wrongs," the public television human rights news magazine that I anchor. That's how I learned of the work of Black Box, the Hungarian video producers who bravely documented the struggle against communism in their country. When the right wing nationalist forces, opposed to diverse perspectives, took control of "free" Hungarian State Television after a brief period of "glasnost," Black Box found its contributions no longer welcome.

Then there's the case of Omar Belhouchet, the Algerian journalist honored by the Committee to Protect Journalists at its 1993 International Press Freedom Awards Dinner. Omar is the director of a leading French-language newspaper, *El Watan.* He was attacked by extremists **and** thrown in jail by the government, charged with publishing "false information." In truth, there was nothing false about it, it was just information that the government did not want revealed. Since Muslim fundamentalists began a war against the Algerian government, violent attacks against journalists have dramatically increased, leaving nine journalists dead in Algeria in 1993, more than in any other country, more even, than in Somalia.

Two months after I left a relatively peaceful Somalia, Jean-Claude Jumet, a French television soundman, was killed by sniper fire when the television crew's vehicle was ambushed on the road between the airport and the port city of Mogadishu.

A month later, in July, four journalists were killed when a crowd, angered by the death of more than 50 Somalis in an aerial attack on Somali General Mohamed Farah Aidid's command post, set upon them, throwing rocks, wielding clubs and firing guns.

Because Somalia was on our political and media screens at the time, the deaths of these journalists did not go unnoticed. But in places like Algeria and Tajikistan—at least four, and possibly as many as 15 journalists were assassinated in that new Central Asian republic in 1993—these attacks on journalists are symptoms of political upheavals largely ignored by the western press. What is most disturbing about these attacks is that a crackdown on the press is often the first signal of a broader assault on human rights.

That is why the work of the Committee to Protect Journalists is so vital. For the past twelve years, CPJ's mission has been to investigate, protest and publicize attacks against journalists who work in print, on radio, or on television around the world. We carefully monitor press freedom conditions and document attacks on and abuses of journalists—from harassment to detainment to physical attacks and killings.

Once a year a few of these heroic journalists are invited to New York for CPJ's annual International Press Freedom Awards. It is both humbling and inspiring to hear of their triumphs over often unimaginable adversity. But it is also encouraging to hear how vital to their struggle is the knowledge that someone, somewhere out there understands what they are up against and is prepared to defend them.

Each year as I sit at the Awards dinner, I am renewed as a journalist when I hear these incredible stories. And each year, as the attacks mount on them and the death toll goes higher, I rededicate myself to their mission. This report is the result of the Committee to Protect Journalist's investigative efforts over the past year, and it is dedicated to our colleagues in the line of fire all over the world.

Charlayne Hunter-Gault *is a national correspondent for The MacNeil/ Lehrer NewsHour and member of CPJ's Board. She has received numerous awards for her reporting, including the prestigious George Foster Peabody Broadcast Award in 1986 for Excellence in Broadcast Journalism, and the 1990 Sidney Hillman Award. Hunter-Gault's most recent publication is a memoir,* **In My Place.**

Introduction

BY WILLIAM A. ORME, JR.,
EXECUTIVE DIRECTOR, CPJ

Ahmet Sumbul, a reporter for the Istanbul daily *Aydinlik*, was jailed last July by Turkish authorities. His crime? Interviewing members of the outlawed Kurdistan Workers' Party. Sumbul is one of eleven Turkish reporters imprisoned for allegedly sympathetic coverage of Kurdish and other dissidents. In Beijing *Xinhua* staffer Wu Shishen was sentenced to life imprisonment for passing on to a Hong Kong colleague a widely circulated but "classified" copy of a speech by China's president. He joined 21 other journalists in Chinese jails. Many of Kuwait's foreign-born reporters were forced at gunpoint to work for an Iraqi propaganda sheet when Saddam Hussein's troops occupied the country in 1990; Kuwaiti judges later found 18 guilty of "collaboration" and gave them sentences ranging from ten years of hard labor to death.

These are just some of the more than 2,000 cases of press freedom violations that CPJ staffers track every year. In March 1994, as this book went to press, there were at least 125 journalists in prisons around the world. More than half had been detained for more than two years. In almost all cases, authorities readily acknowledge that they were jailed because of their reporting. With few exceptions, the stories of these journalists have received little attention abroad. One of CPJ's main jobs is to investigate and publicize such cases—and to ask journalists everywhere to join our campaigns for the release of these unjustly imprisoned colleagues.

Pressures on press freedom come in many forms: indirect harassment, censorship and self-censorship, bribery and coercion, physical assaults and even murder. But the jailing of a journalist is one abuse that can be quickly rectified. Public pressure from CPJ and other press freedom groups has led to the release of many detained journalists in the past. Even in cases where such protests have seemingly had no immediate effect, we have learned years later that living conditions improved for some prisoners. And by holding governments publicly accountable, we can sometimes prevent further abuses.

In many countries journalists are not jailed, but killed. The assumption common even within the profession is that most of these deaths are tragic but inadvertent combat casualties, and that foreign correspondents—war reporters—are the group most at risk. Yet most of the 56 deaths of news people documented by CPJ last year were deliberate assassinations of reporters working in their own home towns. This has been the consistent pattern around the world since the Committee began investigating the deaths of journalists a decade ago.

What has changed dramatically in recent years is geopolitics. In the 1980s scores of Central American journalists were murdered by government-aligned death squads; in the 1990s we are seeing similar patterns of repression in Central Asia. The most dangerous assignment for war correspondents of this generation had been Vietnam, but Bosnia—a country not even on the map when the decade began—has proven to be even more hazardous. For years the primary fear of independent journalists in much of the world has been retaliation from government forces on the totalitarian left or the authoritarian right; while these remain serious concerns, in many countries the most direct assaults on press freedoms now come from religious fundamentalists and dissident nationalists. In Somalia and the former Yugoslavia, foreign journalists have come under attack from rebel gunmen who consider them every bit as much the enemy as the multilateral military forces in their midst. (Photographers and television camera crews, always on the front lines, continue to suffer disproportionate losses in these conflicts.)

Other forces outside the law are also targeting journalists. Journalists are intimidated against reporting on drug trafficking not just in Columbia, but in Tajikistan and Lebanon and Zambia and Thailand—and in New York City, where cocaine traffickers allegedly ordered the 1992 contract killing of editor Manuel de Dios Unanue. Three of De Dios's killers were tried and convicted last year, an exception to the rule: Most murderers of journalists remain brazenly at large, protected either by local authorities or by the anarchic collapse of local authority. But by documenting and publicizing these cases—and by pressing governments to conduct thorough investigations—we can try to hold the killers and their protectors accountable.

This book contains the most comprehensive and carefully documented record anywhere of press freedom violations around the world in 1993. Yet because of the stringency of our research methods and the difficulty in obtaining reliable information in many of the countries that we cover, it greatly understates the frequency and severity of these problems. Every case listed here was investigated and verified by the Committee's own research staff. Our sources range from phoned-in tips to local press and wire service reports to first-hand accounts from the affected journalists themselves. We never publish an account of an incident based on a single source. In every documented incident, CPJ specialists have also determined that the objects of these attacks were legitimate journalists or news organizations and that their work was the likely motive for the attacks. This is often very difficult to establish. We also often have only the sketchiest information about the most besieged and anonymous members of the journalistic community: the local freelancers and part-timers working in the remote provinces of strife-ridden countries like Peru and Angola and Tajikistan.

There are other gaps in our coverage. We do not systematically monitor press freedom problems in the industrialized democracies—not because such cases are unimportant, but because we choose not to direct our limited resources toward countries that have their own aggressive press-monitoring groups. In the United States, conflicts arising from the abuse of libel laws and restrictions on information and news coverage are watched closely by several well-staffed professional organizations. The Committee limits the scope of its work in the United States to the most egregious cases of direct attacks on journalists, including homicides. But the killing of journalists on American soil is far more frequent than is generally assumed: Since the highly publicized Mafia murder of *Arizona Republican* reporter Don Bolles in 1976, there have been at least a dozen other American reporters murdered for reasons that appear directly connected to their work. Most of these cases remain unsolved, and most of the victims were immigrant journalists working in local foreign-language media (see our Special Report on page 145).

The murder or imprisonment of a journalist is not inherently more significant or objectionable than any other killing or jailing. But when the motive behind these attacks is to silence the reporter, the real target is the reporter's audience. The ultimate issue is not the freedom or safety of individual journalists, but the public's right to uncensored information and analysis.

We take care in our reports not to exaggerate the degree of real danger faced by most reporters and photographers and television producers and newspaper editors. In the industrialized societies of what we still anachronistically term "the West," journalism is hardly a hazardous profession. Only a handful of reporters are routinely dispatched to combat zones, and battlefield casualties among foreign correspondents are thankfully rare. The most acute problems confronting our profession are found elsewhere in those societies that find themselves somewhere along the difficult continuum between authoritarianism and democracy. Our mandate is to use the resources and influence of the American news media on behalf of colleagues elsewhere in the world who do essential and courageous work without our legal, political and economic advantages.

We are also dedicated to the improvement of safety and working conditions for reporters dispatched to war zones and to providing useful, timely information to correspondents and editors covering those conflicts. The services CPJ are now offering to news organizations include:

• **Emergency Assistance** to journalists in trouble

• **Handbooks** and other practical help for reporters covering dangerous situations (Our "Journalists Advisory On the Former Yugoslavia" is now in its third printing)

• **Sources:** We can provide up-to-date names, phones and fax numbers of independent journalists in virtually every country in the developing world

• **Expertise** and advice from staff specialists on access problems and the logistics of foreign news coverage: if visas are difficult to obtain, if certain countries or districts are becoming too dangerous for reporters, CPJ will know

• **Background briefs** on countries and the news media (Is this radio station trustworthy? Is that newspaper aligned with a certain political party? How does censorship and self-censorship affect the news in Zaire or Russia or Mexico?)

Since CPJ's yearly *Attacks on the Press* report began appearing in book form in 1987, the volumes have grown progressively larger and the number of incidents documented annually has more than tripled.

Nations where abuses against reporters were once relatively rare now appear in our reports with long lists of cases of intimidation, harassment and censorship.

Does this mean that things are getting worse? Not necessarily.

The increased number of incidents detailed in each year's report is due in part to the Committee's own expansion. Our permanent staff has doubled over the past five years. We now have full-time specialists covering each of our five main areas of concentration: Asia, Latin America, Sub-Saharan Africa, the Middle East, and Central and Eastern Europe. We also have part-time research associates specialized in Haiti and Turkey, two perennially problematic countries, plus several interns assisting in casework documentation. Equally importantly, we are now linked to other press freedom groups worldwide by the International Freedom of eXpression Exchange (IFEX), an e-mail network through which we exchange breaking news and coordinate international protests.

And the news we gather through these networks is not all bad. In some ways, these often-grim statistics are a tribute to the vibrancy and growth of the news media worldwide. There are more journalists getting into trouble around the world than ever before because there are more journalists than ever before. Dozens of countries where there was virtually no press freedom five or ten years ago now have thriving independent print and broadcast outlets. The change is most dramatic in Eastern Europe and the newly independent republics of the former Soviet Union. Even tragedies—such as the six Russian journalists killed while covering the street battles during October's attempted coup—illustrate how profoundly these societies have changed. Similarly historic transformations are under way in much of Africa, Asia, and Latin America, with the press at the forefront of demands for democratic reform. Despite constant problems of the kind we have chronicled here, this new generation of reporters keeps fighting back. We dedicate this book to them.

William A. Orme, Jr. *was appointed executive director of the Committee to Protect Journalists in August 1993. He covered Latin American economic and political affairs as a journalist for the previous fifteen years, based in Guatemala, Mexico City, and Miami.*

■ = Countries where journalists
were in prison as of March 1994

Imprisoned Journalists

In March 1994, at least 125 journalists were held in prison for their reporting. Governments jailed these journalists under charges such as "separatist propaganda," "treason,""counterrevolutionary activities," or "undermining national security;" sometimes there were no charges. The only crime committed by these journalists, 71 of whom have been in prison for more than two years, was to have written something that their governments disliked.

This is the largest number of imprisoned journalists ever documented by the Committee to Protect Journalists. In last year's report, 90 journalists were in prison.

There are 53 prisoners in the Middle East, more than any other region in the world. In Asia another 42 are in jail. Twenty-two are in prison in Africa, and six in Europe and the former Soviet Union. Two journalists are imprisoned in Latin America. With few exceptions, these journalists were working for local news media at the time of their detention.

Despite China's highly publicized release of six journalists, 22 journalists remain in prison, more than any other nation. Six were released in 1993 as part of Beijing's well-publicized, and failed, campaign to host the Olympics in the year 2000 and its effort to have its Most Favored Nation (MFN) status renewed. Less well known is the fact that three more journalists were arrested in China last year. Kuwait, with a population one-thousandth that of China, has the second largest number of imprisoned journalists. Eighteen journalists have been sentenced to long prison terms in unfair trials, where defendants were denied due process. All were accused of collaboration for having worked for a newspaper published during the Iraqi occupation. Only one of them is a Kuwaiti national, the rest are Palestinians, Jordanians, and Lebanese.

Twelve journalists are imprisoned in Syria. Seven have been detained for eight or more years. Four journalists, arrested in 1991 and 1992, were involved in a human rights group.

Nine Vietnamese journalists, arrested over the last three years, were convicted because of their work on the pro-democracy newsletter *Freedom Forum.* The Ethiopian government is holding 17 journalists in custody who work for Amharic-language opposition publications.

Most of the 11 imprisoned journalists in Turkey work for pro-Kurdish or leftist publications and await trial on charges of disseminating "separatist propaganda." Abdallah Ali al-Sanussi al-Darrat, a Libyan journalist, is the longest held prisoner. He has languished in a Libyan jail for nearly 20 years.

International pressure can help free these journalists. Please write respectfully worded letters to the leaders listed below, urging them to release these prisoners immediately.

Albania (1)

Martin Leka

Leka, a reporter for the independent daily, *Koha Jone*, was **arrested on January 31, 1994,** together with his editor in connection with an article that appeared January 21. The article, written by Leka, was about a message sent by the minister of defense ordering troops to leave their weapons in the barracks when they are off duty. Both men were accused of revealing state secrets and writing "slander" against the Minister. On February 28, Leka was convicted and sentenced to one and a half years in prison. He is appealing the verdict.

APPEALS TO:
Prime Minister Aleksander Meksi
Residence of the Prime Minister
Tirana, Albania
Fax: 335 42 27888

Algeria (1)

Salah Gouami

Gouami, director of *Al-Mounqidh*, Arabic-language organ of the Islamic Salvation Front (FIS), was **arrested on January 28, 1992,** after his paper published a communiqué by FIS leader Abdelkader Hachani calling on soldiers to disobey orders to shoot at demonstrators.

APPEALS TO:
General Lamine Zeroual
Chef du Gouvernement
Palais du Gouvernement
Alger, Algerie
Telexes: 66217/66221

Benin (1)

Edgar Kaho

Kaho, director of the independent newspaper *Le Soleil*, was **imprisoned on May 10, 1993.** In December 1992, President Soglo sued Kaho, for defamation relating to an article published in the October 23-November 5, 1991, issue. The article, entitled "SOBETRAP Affair: Where did the 218,000,000 Francs in excess go? Ministers of Kerekou and Soglo Implicated" implicated ministers serving former President Kerekou and current President Nicephore Soglo in a corruption scandal. Kaho was convicted and received the maximum sentence of one year's imprisonment; he failed to appear in court for his sentencing. He did not appeal the decision nor did he go to jail until months later when he was arrested on May 10. Although the press often criticizes the government, local journalists felt that his arrest coincided with the May 10 issue of *Le Soleil*, which ran several articles critical of President Soglo and his wife. Kaho currently remains in custody.

APPEALS TO:
President Nicephore Soglo
President of the Republic of Benin
La Presidence
Porto Novo, Benin

China (22)

Chen Yanbin

Chen, a former Qinghua University student, together with Zhang Yafei, produced an unofficial magazine called *Tielu* (Iron Currents). The government termed it reactionary and charged Chen with making counter-revolutionary propaganda and incitement. He was **arrested in late 1990** and sentenced to 15 years in prison with four years' subsequent deprivation of political rights. Several hundred mimeographed copies of the journal were distributed.

Chen Ziming

Chen, the publisher of *Jingji Xue Zhoubao* (Economics Weekly), was **sentenced** to 13 years in prison **on February 12, 1991.** He and editor Wang Juntao, arrested in October 1989 while trying to flee the country, were labeled the "black hands" behind the Tian'anmen Square demonstrations and found guilty of counter-revolutionary activities. In August 1991, Chen went on a hunger strike to protest his solitary confinement and was eventually transferred to a shared cell. According to Asia Watch, he suffers from heart trouble, high blood pressure, and a serious skin disorder that developed during his imprisonment.

Fan Jianping

Fan, an editor at *Beijing Ribao* (Beijing Daily), was **arrested sometime after June 4, 1989.**

Fu Shenqi

Fu, a former *Democracy Wall* activist who had just been released from a two-year detention for his involvement in publishing an underground human rights journal, was **redetained on June 26, 1993,** and sentenced without trial to three years in "education through labor" camps for inciting trouble and speaking to foreign journalists.

Gao Yu

Gao, a correspondent for several Hong Kong newspapers, has been **detained** by Beijing security officials **since October 2, 1993.** Though formal charges had not been filed as of February 1994, she was reportedly accused of providing state secrets to persons across the border.

Ji Kunxing

Ji was **tried** in Kunming **in September 1989** on charges of fomenting a counter-revolutionary plot. He and three others had published an underground magazine called *Pioneers*, circulated anti-government leaflets, and put up anti-government posters.

Jin Naiyi

Jin, with *Beijing Ribao* (Beijing Daily), was **arrested sometime after June 4, 1989.**

Li Jian

Li, a journalist with *Wenyi Bao* (Literature and Arts News), was **arrested in July 1989.**

Liao Jia'an

Liao, a People's University graduate student and co-editor with Wang Shengli of the unofficial student journal *Da Jia* (Everyone), received a three-year prison sentence from the Beijing People's Intermediate Court in August 1993. Liao was **arrested on June 8, 1992,** and is said to have been formally charged with counter-revolution on December 1992. He was initially held at the Banbuqiao Detention Center in Beijing, where, according to Asia Watch, a hepatitis infection he contracted was left untreated.

Liu De

Liu, a member of the editorial board of the literary magazine *Jianna Literature and Arts Journal* in Sichuan Province, was **sentenced** to seven years' imprisonment **in February 1987** for "villifying the socialist system." Liu had also been active during the 1979-81 Democracy Wall period. His release was expected in February 1994.

Ma Tao

Ma, editor of *China Health Education News*, **received a six-year prison term in August 1993** for allegedly assisting *Xinhua News Agency* reporter Wu Shishen in providing President Jiang Zemin's "state-classified" 14th Party Congress address to a Hong Kong journalist. According to the *Associated Press*, Ma is believed to be Wu's wife.

Ren Wanding

Ren, a former *Democracy Wall* journalist who founded the underground publication China Human Rights League, actively supported the 1989 student democracy movement in speeches and articles calling for freedom of expression. He was **arrested June 9, 1989,** and sentenced on January 26, 1991, to seven years in prison and three years' subsequent deprivation of political rights. Ren, who previously spent four years in prison, has reportedly been denied proper treatment for his cataracts and is said to be in danger of losing his eyesight. His chronic sinusitis, chest infections, acute gastritis, and severe internal and external hemorrhoids have also gone untreated.

Shang Jingzhong

Shang was **tried** in Kunming **in September 1989** on charges of fomenting a counterrevolutionary plot. He and three others had published an underground magazine called *Pioneers*, circulated anti-government leaflets, and put up anti-government posters.

Shi Qing

Shi was **tried** in Kunming **in September 1989** on charges of fomenting a counter-revolutionary plot. He and three others had published an underground magazine called *Pioneers*, circulated anti-government leaflets, and put up anti-government posters.

Wang Jun

Wang, a *People's Daily Overseas Edition* reporter, was **handed a two-year prison sentence in May 1993** a year after his arrest for allegedly giving state secrets to the international media. Active in the press protests of 1989, Wang had been put on disciplinary probation.

Wang Juntao

Wang, editor of *Jingji Xue Zhoubao* (Economics Weekly), was found guilty of "conspiring to subvert the government" and "carrying out counter-revolutionary propaganda." He was **sentenced** to 13 years in prison **on February 12, 1991.** His wife, Hou Xiaotian, has accused prison authorities of medical negligence in their treatment of her husband.

Wu Shishen
Wu, a *Xinhua News Agency* reporter, **received a life sentence in August 1993,** for allegedly providing a "state-classified" advance copy of President Jiang Zemin's 14th Party Congress address to a Hong Kong journalist. Wu had been arrested in October or November of 1992.

Xi Yang
Xi, Beijing correspondent for the Hong Kong daily *Ming Pao*, was **arrested on September 27, 1993,** for "stealing and espionage of state secrets." The "secrets" in question allegedly included unpublished savings and loans interest rate changes for the People's Bank of China, as well as information on the Bank's international gold transaction plans, provided to Xi in both cases by Bank official Tian Ye. On December 22, Beijing authorities said Xi would be tried in secret, and that he "did not want a lawyer."

Yang Hong
Yang, a reporter for *Zhongguo Qingnian Bao* (China Youth News), was **arrested on June 13, 1989,** in Kunming. He was charged with circulating "rumor-mongering leaflets" and protesting against corruption.

Yu Anmin
Yu was **tried** in Kunming **in September 1989** on charges of fomenting a counter-revolutionary plot. He and three others had published an underground magazine called *Pioneers*, circulated anti-government leaflets, and put up anti-government posters.

Yu Zhengmin
Yu, a journalist with *Fazhi Yuekan* (Law Monthly) in Shanghai, was **arrested sometime after June 4, 1989.** He was later described in an article in *Wenhui Daily* as an "agitator" of the Shanghai student demonstrations.

Zhang Yafei
Zhang, a former student at Beifang Communications University, edited an unofficial magazine called *Tielu* (Iron Currents) about the 1989 crackdown at Tian'anmen Square. He was **arrested in September 1990,** charged with making counter-revolutionary propaganda and incitement, and in March 1991 was sentenced to 11 years in prison and two years' subsequent deprivation of political rights.

APPEALS TO:
His Excellency President Jiang Zemin
His Excellency Prime Minister Li Peng
Office of the Prime Minister
Beijing
People's Republic of China
FAX 86-1-5125810
TELEX 210070 or 22478

Croatia (2) *

Ognjen Tajic and Milovan Pejanovic
Tajic and Pejanovic, journalists with *Serbian Television* in Pale, were **arrested in January 1993** by Croatian police near Peruca Dam for allegedly carrying weapons on Croatian territory. The two were sentenced in April to six and seven years' imprisonment, respectively, by a military tribunal in the Croatian town of Split.
*Both journalists were released in July 1993.

APPEALS TO:
Dr Franjo Tudjman
Predsjednik Republike Hrvatske
Visoka 22
41000 Zagreb
Croatia
Faxes: + 38 41 444 532

Cuba (1)

Yndamiro Restano

Restano, former reporter with *Radio Rebelde*, was **arrested** in Havana **on December 20, 1991,** and accused of having "prepared printed material inciting civil disobedience and actions against the socialist society." He was convicted and sentenced to 10 years in prison on May 20, 1992, on charges of "rebellion." Restano was a veteran reporter with *Radio Rebelde* until he was suspended from his job in 1985, for talking to a foreign journalist. He is a leader of the Harmony Movement, a pro-democracy dissident group.

APPEALS TO:
Dr. Fidel Castro Ruz
President
Havana, Cuba
Telex: 51212 P DESP PRESID

Ethiopia (18)

Tefera Asmare and Iskander Nega

Asmare and Nega, editor and publisher respectively of the Amharic language newspaper, *Ethiopis*, were **detained** by police **in early September 1993** and charged with "incitement to war" in connection with an article which gave credence to rumors of unrest outside the capital. They were eventually granted bail after 53 days in detention only to be **arrested again on November 12** on charges of "inciting people against the government" and "disseminating false rumors." They remain in custody. The case is currently in court.

The following editors and publishers of Amharic newspapers were **arrested in January and February 1994**. The motives for their detention remain unclear.

Daniel Kifle, editor of *Fendisha*, was **arrested on January 15.**
Antensay Tafesse, editor of *Mogad*; **Daniel Tadesse,** editor of *Waqt*; **Nayk Kassaye,** editor of *Beza*; and **Yohannes Abebe,** assistant editor of *Beza* were **arrested on January 22.**
Asrat Damtew and **Tesfaye Berehanu,** journalists with *Muday*, were **arrested on January 28.**
Girmay Gebre-Tsadi, Kinfe Assefa and **Mulugeta Gigo,** also with *Muday*, were **arrested in early February.**
Meleskachew Amha, editor of *Dewol*; **Berhane Mewa,** publisher of *Dewol*; and **Befekadu Moroda,** editor of *Tomar*, were **arrested on February 9.**
Nesanet Tesfaye, Mesele Haddis, and **Kibret Mekonnen,** journalists with *Aimiro* were **arrested in mid-February.**

APPEALS TO:
President Meles Zenawi
Office of the President
Addis Ababa, Ethiopia
Fax: 251-1-514300 (c/o Ministry of Foreign Affairs)

India (2)

Gurdip Singh
Singh, Managing Editor of the Punjabi daily *Aaj di Awaz*, was **detained** by state police officers **on January 11, 1994,** along with seven other newspaper employees. Ten days later, Singh was charged with violating the Terrorist and Disruptive Activities Act (TADA), on the basis of allegedly incriminating statements made by a Kashmiri separatist, Nisar Ahmed, who has been in police custody for two years.

Jasbir Singh
Singh, a proofreader for the Punjabi daily *Aaj di Awaz*, was arrested by state police officers on January 11, 1994.
APPEALS TO:
His Excellency Narasimha Rao
Office of the Prime Minister
South Block, Gate No. 6
New Delhi 110011
India
FAX: 91-11-3016857

Indonesia (1)

Adnan Beuransyah
Beuransyah, a journalist with the newspaper *Serambi Indonesia*, was **arrested on August 16, 1990.** He was tried in March 1991 in Banda Aceh on charges of subversion and sentenced to eight years in prison.
APPEALS TO:
His Excellency Suharto
Office of the President
Istana Merdeka
Jakarta
Indonesia
FAX 62-21-352685 or 62-21-363406

Iran (3)

Salman Heidari
Heidari, a reporter for the Tehran daily *Salam*, was **arrested in late June 1992** and accused of espionage. Some view Heidari's arrest as an attempt by President Rafsanjani to intimidate the hard-line opposition. It is unclear whether he has been formally charged and tried.

Manouchehr Karimzadeh

Karimzadeh, a cartoonist, was **arrested on April 11, 1992,** after a piece of his appeared in the science magazine *Farad.* It depicted a soccer player with an amputated arm and wearing a turban, and the image was interpreted by the authorities to be a caricature of the late Ayatollah Khomeini. An Islamic revolutionary court originally sentenced him to one year in prison, but he was retried in 1993 by order of the Supreme Court and sentenced to 10 years imprisonment.

Abbas Abdi

Abdi, editor-in-chief of the radical daily *Salam,* was **sentenced** by the Tehran Islamic Revolutionary Court **on December 22, 1993,** to one year in prison and a suspended sentence of 40 lashes. He had been arrested in late August. The charges were never made public, but it is believed that they stemmed from a report published in *Salam* about the opposition of government officials to the admission of dissident religious leader Ayatollah Hossein Ali Montazeri to a Tehran hospital.

APPEALS TO:
His Excellency Hojatoleslam
Ali Akbar Hashemi Rafsanjani
The Presidency
Palestine Avenue
Azerbaijan Intersection
Tehran, Islamic Republic of Iran
Telexes: 214231 MITI IR; 213113 PRIM IR
(marked for the attention of President Rafsanjani)

Iraq (1)

Aziz al-Syed Jasim

Jasim, editor of *Al-Ghad* magazine and former editor of the official daily, *Al-Thawra,* was **taken into custody** at a secret police station in Baghdad **on April 18, 1991,** and has not been heard of since. Government officials have denied that he is under arrest. Earlier in the year Jasim had been interrogated by the secret police after refusing to write on behalf of the government during the Gulf War.

APPEALS TO:
President Saddam Hussein
Presidential Palace
Karraddat
Mariam
Baghdad, Iraq

Israel and the Occupied Territories (2)

Ahmad al-Khatib

Al-Khatib, a cameraman from the Gaza Strip city of Rafah working for *Visnews,* was **arrested on September 16, 1992,** because he had shot video of armed activists of the Izz al-Din al-Qassam Brigades (affiliated with Hamas). He was held for about 35 days in Gaza Central Prison and then he was transferred to Ketziot detention center (Ansar 3). Al-Khatib was charged with providing services to an illegal organization for allegedly giving a copy of video tape he shot of Al-Qassam brigades training to the unit. In January 1994 he was convicted and sentenced to two years in prison and a fine of 8000 shekels.

Mousa Qous

Qous, a reporter with the English-language edition of *Al-Fajr* weekly, was **arrested on October 21, 1991.** On November 19, 1991, he was sentenced by the Lod Military Court to four years in prison for membership in the Popular Front for the Liberation of Palestine and for instructing others to write graffiti. His appeal of the sentence was rejected on December 26, 1991.

APPEALS TO:
Yitzhak Rabin
Prime Minister and Minister of Defence Office of the PrimeMinister PO Box 187
Jerusalem Israel
Fax: 972 2 664838

Ivory Coast (1)

Hamed Bakayoko

Bakayoko, publisher of *Le Patriote* and *Le Patriote-Express* was **arrested on February 16, 1994,** and charged with insulting the dignity of the head of state in an unsigned article, which appeared on January 25. The article did not mention the new president by name, but asked how Ivorians could fear "a dwarf" when compared to the "giant Felix Houphouet-Boigny," the Ivory Coast's late veteran leader. Bakayoko was convicted of violating a 1991 press law which criminalizes statements deemed offensive to the dignity of any head of state, domestic or foreign. *Le Patriote* and *Le Patriote-Express* were suspended for three months. Bakayoko was fined 200,000 CFA francs, and sentenced to one year in prison. It is not clear if his sentence will be appealed. He remains in custody.

APPEALS TO:
His Excellency Henri Konan Bdie
President of the Ivory Coast Republic
Presidence de la Republique
Abidjan, Cote d'Ivoire

Kuwait (18)

Fawwaz Muhammad al-Awadi Bessisso
Ibtisam Berto Sulaiman al-Dakhil
Usamah Suhail Abdallah Hussein
Abd al-Rahman Muhammad Asad al-Husseini
Ahmad Abd Mustafa

The five journalists were given **life sentences in June 1991** for working with the Iraqi occupation newspaper *Al-Nida*. They were taken into custody after Kuwait's liberation and charged with collaboration. The trials, which began on May 19, 1991, in martial-law courts, failed to comply with international standards. The defendants were reportedly tortured during their interrogations. Their defense—that they were coerced to work for the Iraqi newspaper—was not rebutted by prosecutors. On June 16, the journalists were sentenced to death. Ten days later all martial-law death sentences were commuted to life terms, following international protests.

Wafa Wasfi Ahmad
Belqiss Hafez Fadhel
Zekarayat Mahmoud Harb
Walid Hassan Muhammad Karaka
Rahim Muhammad Najem
Ghazi Mahmoud al-Sayyed

A martial law tribunal in **June 1991 sentenced** the three men and three women **to 10 years in prison** with hard labor for their "supporting role...in helping to publish the [Iraqi occupation] paper [*Al-Nida*]." The defendants reportedly were tortured during interrogation. The prosecution did not offer direct evidence to rebut the coercion defense of the accused. Four other staffers were also sentenced to 10 years in prison for allegedly working at the paper, though it appears that they did not work as journalists: Riyadh Fouad Shaker Ali; Ahmad Muhammad Hannoun; Zuhra Muhammad Adel Abd al-Khaleq; and Lefta Abdallah Menahi.

Daoud Suleiman al-Qarneh
Hassan al-Khalili
Muhammad Zahran
Nawwaf Izzedin al-Khatib

On **June 20, 1992,** Kuwait's State Security Court **sentenced** four Palestinian journalists convicted of having worked for *Al-Nida*, organ of the Iraqi occupation, **to 10 years in prison.** They are: al-Qarneh, formerly deputy chief editor at the *Kuwait News Agency (KUNA)*; al-Khalili, formerly an editor at *KUNA*; Zahran, accused of translating for *Al-Nida*; and al-Khatib.

Bassam Fouad Abiad
Mufid Mustafa Abd al-Rahim
Ghazi Alam al-Dine

On **July 28, 1992,** the State Security Court convicted Abiad, Abd al-Rahim and Alam al-Dine of working for *Al-Nida*, news organ of the Iraqi occupation. Abiad, a Lebanese citizen, was **sentenced to 15 years in prison.** Abd al-Rahim, a Palestinian, was sentenced to 10 years in prison. And Alam al-Dine, a Jordanian citizen and former editor at *KUNA*, was sentenced to 10 years in prison, although he had only worked a total of 12 hours for *Al-Nida*. Each was also fined KD 2000.

APPEALS TO:
Sheikh Saad al-Abdullah al-Sabah
Crown Prince and Prime Minister
c/o Embassy of Kuwait
2940 Tilden St., NW
Washington, DC 20008
Fax: 202-966-0517

Lebanon (1)

Kazem Akhavan

Akhavan, a photographer for Iran's official *Islamic Republic News Agency (IRNA)*, was **kidnapped** at a Christian militia checkpoint south of Tripoli **in 1982.** Reports that he was killed shortly after his capture have never been confirmed. Iran contends that Akhavan and three other Iranians are still in captivity and requested, late in 1993, that the Lebanese government investigate their fate.

APPEALS TO:
Prime Minister Rafiq Hariri
Beirut, Lebanon
Telex: 923 42 253

Libya (1)

Abdallah Ali al-Sanussi al-Darrat

Al-Darrat, a journalist and writer from Benghazi, was **arrested in 1974 or 1975** and has been held in the interim without trial.

APPEALS TO:
Revolutionary Leader
Col. Muammar al-Qadhafi
c/o Libyan Mission to the United Nations
309-315 East 48th St.
New York, NY 10017
Fax:212-593-478

Myanmar (formerly Burma) (6)

Myo Myint Nyein

Nyein, who was **arrested in September 1990** for contributing to *What's Happening*, was sentenced to seven years in prison under the 1950 Emergency Provisions Act.

Nay Min

Min, a lawyer and *BBC* correspondent, was **arrested in 1988** and sentenced in October 1989 to 14 years of hard labor.

Nyan Paw (aka Min Lu)

Paw, a journalist for *What's Happening*, was **arrested in September 1990** and sentenced in November to seven years' imprisonment under the 1950 Emergency Provisions Act.

Sein Hlaing

Hlaing, publisher of *What's Happening*, a satirical news magazine, was **arrested in September 1990** and sentenced to seven years in prison under the 1950 Emergency Provisions Act.

U Maung Maung Lay Ngwe

Ngwe was **arrested in September 1990** and charged with writing and distributing publications which "make people lose respect for the government." The publications were titled *Pe-Tin-Tan* and *U Wisara Hnint U Ottama Ko-Sarr-Pyu*.

Win Tin

Tin, former editor of two daily newspapers and vice-chair of Burma's Writer's Association, was active in establishing independent publications during the 1988 student democracy movement. He also worked closely with imprisoned NLD leader Aung San Suu Kyi. He was **arrested on July 4, 1989**, and sentenced to three years' hard labor. He is reported to be gravely ill.

APPEALS TO:
His Excellency General Than Shwe
Prime Minister and Minister of Defence
Chairman of the State Law and Order Restoration Council

Ministry of Defence
Signal Pagoda Road
Yangon
Myanmar
TELEX 21316

Peru (1)

Jose Antonio Alvarez Pachas
Peruvian authorities claim Pachas, a reporter with the daily *Cambio*, has ties to leftist rebels of the Tupac Amaru Revolutionary Movement, one of two guerrilla groups fighting the Peruvian government. Pacha was **detained in June 1992.** Peru's National Journalists' Guild (Colegio Nacional de Periodistas), has endorsed Pachas case and is actively seeking his release.
APPEALS TO:
Presidente Alberto Fujimori
Palacio de Gobierno
Plaza de Armas
Lima 1, Peru
Fax: 5114-337020
326535

Rwanda (1)

Janvier Africa
Africa, the editor of the Kigali-based bi-monthly *Umurava* newspaper and a former government informant, was **arrested September 14, 1992,** and convicted of "threatening the head of state." His detention appears to stem from articles published in the August issue of *Umurava*, in which he alleged that individuals close to President Juvenal Habyarimana and leaders of the Coalition for the Defense of the Republic (CDR), a Hutu extremist group, were directly involved in death squad operations. Following the distribution of the newspaper's August issue, two cars drove up to Africa's house and left a leaflet behind stating . . . "You count on publishing more (against the president) in the next issue; if you do it, you will not survive . . ." Africa is said to have chosen to remain in the Central Prison for his own safety, pending an appeal.
APPEALS TO:
President Juvenal Habyarimana
President de la Republique
Presidence de al Republique
BP 15, Kigali, Rwanda
Fax: 250-74583

South Korea (2)

Choi Chin-sop
According to Amnesty International, Choi, a journalist with the monthly current affairs magazine *Mal*, was **arrested on September 14, 1992,** as part of a crackdown on an alleged North Korean "spy ring." Choi was sentenced to three years in prison on **February 24, 1993,** for belonging to an alleged "anti-state" organization—the pro-reunification 1995 Committee—and disseminating

material in support of North Korea. Several of Choi's articles on human rights issues in South Korea were introduced as evidence against him at his trial.

Masato Shinohara

Shinohara, Seoul bureau chief of Japan's *Fuji Television* network, was **sentenced to two years in prison on December 22, 1993,** for illegally obtaining classified military documents and showing them to Japanese Embassy's personnel. Korean officials had detained Shinohara on June 26, and had arrested him on July 13 on charges of violating the country's military secrets law. Shinohara, who contributed to Japanese defense periodicals on a freelance basis, maintained that the had collected the information for his own research purposes.

APPEALS TO:
His Excellency Kim Young-Sam
Office of the President
Chong Wa Dae (The Blue House)
1 Sejong-no
Chongno-ku
Seoul
Republic of Korea

Sudan (1)

Nadir Mahjoub Mohamed Salih

Salih, a reporter for the banned Communist paper *Al-Shabiba*, was **detained** by the authorities **in June 1993.** CPJ was unable to confirm a report of his release in the fall.

APPEALS TO:
His Excellency Lieutenant General Omar Hassan al-BashirHead of State and Chairman of the National Salvation Revolutionary Command Council
People's Palace
PO Box 281
Khartoum, Sudan
Telexes: 22385 PEPLC SD or 22411 KAID SD
Faxes: 249 11 71724

Syria (12)

Ibrahim Habib

Habib, a freelance journalist arrested in 1987, was **sentenced** to three years in prison **in July 1993.** It is unclear whether or not he has been released.

Faisal Allush

Allush, a journalist and political writer held since 1985, was **sentenced in June 1993** to 15 years imprisonment for membership in the banned Party for Communist Action (PCA).

Jadi Nawfal

Nawfal, a freelance journalist, was **arrested on December 18, 1991,** and sentenced the following March to five years in prison for belonging to Committees for the Defense of Democratic Freedoms and Human Rights in Syria (CDF).

Anwar Bader
Bader, a reporter for Syrian radio and television, was **arrested in December 1986** by the Military Interrogation Branch. He was accused of membership in the Party for Communist Action (PCA). His trial began in the summer of 1993. Its outcome was still unknown as of February 1994.

Rida Haddad
Haddad, an editorial writer for the daily *Tishrin*, was **arrested in October 1980** and accused of membership in the Communist Party-Political Bureau.

Samir al-Hassan
Al-Hassan, Palestinian editor of *Fatah al-Intifada*, was **arrested in April 1986** because of his membership in the Party for Communist Action. His trial began in the summer of 1993. Its outcome was still unknown as of February 1994.

Ahmad Hasso
Hasso, a Kurdish writer and freelance journalist whose work has appeared in the Lebanese paper *Al-Safir*, was **arrested March 17, 1992**. His trial began in the summer of 1993. He was sentenced to two years in prison.

Salama George Kila
Kila, a Palestinian writer and journalist was **arrested in March 1992** by the Political Security division in Damascus. His trial began in the summer of 1993. Its outcome was still unknown as of February 1994.

Izzat al-Mahmoud
Al-Mahmoud, a Syrian journalist working in Beirut, was **handed over** to the Syrian government by Lebanese authorities **in 1982**.

Abdallah Muqdad
Muqdad, a journalist with the *Syrian Arab News Agency (SANA)*, was **arrested in 1980** on suspicion of membership in the Ba'ath Party's February 23 movement. His trial began in the summer of 1993. Its outcome was still unknown as of February 1994.

Nizar Nayouf
Nayouf, a freelance journalist who has ccontributed to *Al-Huriyya* and *Al-Thaqafa al-Ma'arifa*, was **arrested in January 1992** in Damascus with several human rights activists from the Committees for the Defense of Democratic Freedoms and Human Rights in Syria (CDF). In March 1992, he was **sentenced** by the State Security Court to **10 years in prison** for "disseminating false information and receiving money from abroad." He was severely tortured during his interrogation.

Ahmad Swaidan
Swaidan, a reporter for *Kifah al-Umal al-Ishtiraki*, was **arrested in January 1982** on suspicion of membership in the Ba'ath Party's February 23 movement. His trial began in the summer of 1993. Its outcome was still unknown as of February 1994.

APPEALS TO:
His Excellency
President Hafez al-Assad
Presidential Palace
Damascus
Syrian Arab Republic
Telex: 419160 munjed sy

Tajikistan (4)

Mirbobo Mirrakhimov and Akhmadsho Kamilov

Mirrakhimov and Kamilov were **arrested on March 23, 1993,** and imprisoned for slandering the former speaker of the parliament. They were charged with "conspiracy to overthrow the government through the mass media."

Khayriddin Kamilov and Khurshed Nazarov

Kamilov and Nazarov were **charged in March 1993** with "conspiracy to overthrow the government through the mass media" and the possession of videotapes allegedly showing human rights abuses by the pro-government National Front.

APPEALS TO:
Chairman of the Supreme Council,
Imamli Rakhmonov
Respubulika Tadzhikistan
g. Dushanbe
Fax: + 3772 22 69 71

Tunisia (2)

Hamadi Jebali

Jebali, editor of *Al-Fajr*, the weekly newspaper of the banned Islamist Al-Nahda party, was **sentenced** to 16 years in prison by the military court in Bouchoucha **on August 28, 1992.** He was tried along with 170 others accused of membership in Al-Nahda. Jebali was convicted of "aggression with the intention of changing the nature of the state" and "membership in an illegal organization." During his testimony Jebali denied the charges against him and displayed evidence that he had been tortured while in custody. In January 1991, Jebali had been sentenced to one year in prison after *Al-Fajr* published an article calling for the abolition of military courts in Tunisia. International human rights groups monitoring the mass trial concluded that it fell far below international standards of justice.

Abdellah Zouari

Zouari, a contributor to *Al-Fajr*, was **sentenced** to 11 years in prison by the military court in Bouchoucha **on August 28, 1992.** He was tried along with 170 others accused of membership in the banned Islamist Al-Nahda party. He had been in detention since February 1991 when he was charged with "association with an unrecognized organization." International human rights groups monitoring the trial concluded that it fell far short of international standards of justice.

APPEALS TO:
President:
M. Zine El Abidine Ben Ali
President de la Republique
Palais Presidentiel
Tunis/Carthage
Tunisie
Faxes: 216 1 744721
Telexes: 14900 prpsa tn 12163 ppsd tn

Turkey (11)

Gurbetelli Ersöz
Ersöz, the editor-in-chief of *Özgür Gündem*, was **arrested on January 12, 1994,** along with other staff members during a raid on the headquarters of the paper in Istanbul. She is being charged with aiding the outlawed Kurdistan Workers' Party (PKK). However, while all the others charged in the case were released, the court has denied pleas to release her. Her trial has not yet started.

Erkan Aydin
Aydin, a former editor of the pro-Kurdish daily *Özgür Gündem*, was **arrested on November 25, 1993,** for articles published in his newspaper. The case against him and the newspaper continues.

Hatice Onaran
Onaran, a journalist with the left-wing magazine *Devrimci Çözüm*, was **detained on November 4, 1993.** She is charged with separatist propaganda based on the Anti-Terror law and remains in custody while her trial continues.

Cemil Aydoğan
Aydoğan, editor-in-chief of *Mezopotamya*, a local newspaper published in Mardin, was **detained on October 22, 1993.** He was formally arrested on November 9.

Zana Sezen
Sezen, editor-in-chief of the left-wing, pro-Kurdish weekly *Azadi*, was **arrested on October 18, 1993,** and charged with "separatist propaganda" for articles published in the magazine. She remains in jail while her trial continues.

Mustafa Kaplan
Kaplan, a reporter for the Islamic daily *Beklenen Vakit*, was **sentenced** to eight months in prison **on September 28, 1993,** for an article he wrote. He has been in prison serving his term since then.

Şadi Etdöver
Etdöver, *Özgür Gündem's* Elazığ correspondent, was **arrested on September 22, 1993.** He is in Erzurum prison while his trial for allegedly aiding the PKK proceeds.

Sakine Fidan
Fidan is the Diyarbakır correspondent of the left-wing weekly *Mücadele*. She was **arrested on July 3, 1993,** and remains in Diyarbakır prison waiting for the conclusion of the trial against her.

Ahmet Sümbül
Detained on July 2, 1993, Sümbül was arrested five days later on charges stemming from articles he had written for his newspaper, *Aydinlik*. He has been in prison while his trial continues at the Diyarbakir State Security Court. Among the charges he faces is talking to the outlawed PKK's members "under the guise of a journalist."

Hayrettin Dündar
Dündar, Siirt correspondent of *Özgür Gündem*, has been **in custody since June 1993.** He is being accused, in a trial that is pending, of aiding the PKK.

Bahattin Sevim
Sevim, Van correspondent for *Özgür Gündem*, was **arrested in May 1993.** He is being charged with aiding the PKK and awaits the conclusion of his trial in jail.

APPEALS TO:
Prime Minister:
Mrs Tansu Çiller
Başbakanlik
06573 Ankara, Turkey
Telexes: 44061/44062/44063 bbmt tr
42099 basb tr
42875 bbk tr
Faxes: +90 312 417 04 76 PRIME MINISTER
+90 312 230 88 96 (attn: Prime Minister)

Ukraine (1)

Alexander Volosov

Volosov, the editor of the newspaper *Orientir*, is serving a two and a half year sentence on charges of libel and slander. **In November 1993, he was sentenced to four years in prison** with an additional four years suspended in connection with an article in which he accused a Public Prosecutor of corruption. After Volosov appealed the court's decision in January 1994, his sentence was reduced to two and a half years.
APPEALS TO:
President Leonid Kravchuk
Kiev Ukraine
Fax: 70-44-291-5333

Vietnam (9)

Doan Viet Hoat

Hoat, editor and publisher of the pro-democracy newsletter *Freedom Forum*, was **sentenced to 20 years of hard labor in late March 1993** for his involvement with the publication. He is currently serving out his sentence, lowered to 15 years on appeal, at the Xuan Phuoc labor camp, 650 kilometers from Ho Chih Minh City. Hoat suffers from kidney stones, a condition that developed during his previous twelve-year incarceration by the Hanoi regime.

Pham Duc Kham

Kham was **sentenced to 16 years in prison in late March 1993** for his involvement with *Freedom Forum*. His sentence was reduced on appeal to 12 years. Kham is presently interred at Xuan Phuoc labor camp with Doan Viet Hoat and Le Duc Vuong.

Nguyen Van Thuan

Thuan was **sentenced to 12 years in prison in late March 1993** for his involvement with *Freedom Forum*. His sentence was reduced on appeal to eight years. Thuan reportedly suffered a stroke, while at Ham Tan labor camp, and was transferred to a military hospital in Ho Chi Minh City.

Le Duc Vuong

Vuong was reportedly **sentenced in late March 1993 to seven years in prison** for his involvement with *Freedom Forum*. Vuong is presently interred at Xuan Phuoc labor camp with Doan Viet Hoat and Pham Duc Kham.

Nguyen Thieu Hung

Hung was reportedly **sentenced in late March 1993 to four years in prison** for his involvement with *Freedom Forum.*

Nguyen Xuan Dong

Dong was reportedly **sentenced in late March 1993 to four years in prison** for his involvement with *Freedom Forum.* Dong, who is in his late sixties and has lung disease, is currently held at Han Tan labor camp.

Pham Thai Thuy

Pham was reportedly **sentenced in late March 1993 to four years in prison** for his involvement with *Freedom Forum.*

Hoang Cao Nha

Nha was reportedly **sentenced in late March 1993 to eight months in prison** for his involvement with *Freedom Forum.* His release, which was expected by the end of 1993, has not been confirmed.

Nguyen Dan Que

Que, **sentenced to 20 years in prison in November 1991** on charges of compiling and distributing subversive literature, had distributed political handbills and sent documents abroad. Que, who suffers from hypertension and a bleeding gastric ulcer, is imprisoned at the Xuyen Moc labor camp in Dong Nai province.

APPEALS TO:
His Excellency Do Muoi
General Secretary of the Central Committee
Communist Party of Vietnam
1 Hoang Van Thu
Hanoi
Socialist Republic of Vietnam

Western Sahara (1)

Bahi Mohamed Ould Deif

Bahi Mohamed, a Moroccan journalist, **disappeared in 1986** while reporting from Tindouf, in western Algeria. An Algerian newspaper reported, after his disappearance, that he had been arrested by the *Polisario,* for plotting the assassination of Mohamed Abdelaziz, general secretary of the *Polisario.* Abdelaziz's claim that Bahi Mohamed is at liberty and free to return to Morocco have not been confirmed. The Moroccan National Press Syndicate wrote to CPJ in 1993, that he is still being held against his will and has not been tried.

APPEALS TO:
Muhammad Abd al-Aziz
Secretary General of the Polisario Front
B.P. 10
El Mouradia, Algiers
Algeria

Where Journalists Were Killed in 1993

= Countries where journalists
were killed this year.

Journalists Killed in 1993

At least fifty-six journalists were killed in the line of duty in 1993. Most of the victims were local nationals working for local and international news media. In many cases, the reporters were deliberately targeted for assassination by ethnic or religious extremists. The deaths of 16 other reporters who were killed last year are still being investigated by the Committee to Protect Journalists.

For the second year, Europe and the republics of the former Soviet Union had 21 fatalities, the year's largest number. In the Middle East and North Africa, 14 journalists were killed, the largest number CPJ has ever recorded in this region. Ten were killed in Africa, eight in the Americas, and three in Asia.

Nine Algerian journalists were assassinated by Muslim fundamentalists who have intensified their campaign to topple the current pro-Western government. Muslim fundamentalists started a war against the Algerian government two years ago after the cancellation of parliamentary elections the fundamentalists were expected to win. In Turkey four journalists were killed, caught in the violent war that Turkey has waged against Kurdish separatists. All but one of the journalists killed in 1993 worked for the pro-Kurdish newspaper *Özgür Gündem*.

In Russia, seven journalists were gunned down last October during the battle between supporters of President Yeltsin and rebellious parliamentarians. A total of eight journalists were killed—the highest number in a single year in Russia's history. Independent journalists in Tajikistan were persecuted by the National Front, a paramilitary group linked to the Communist government which seized power last year. The deaths of four journalists were fully documented, but investigations continue on the murder of reporters who died under suspicious circumstances. In Yugoslavia, the death toll for journalists continued to climb. Four journalists were either killed by sniper fire or in crossfire in 1993. And the deaths of five others are under investigation.

A U.N.-led mission in Somalia turned deadly not only for U.N. troops but for journalists. Four reporters and photographers working for western media were killed by an angry mob in retaliation for a U.N. raid against warlord Mohammed Farah Aidid. The murders brought to a halt the on-going coverage of the conflict. Most western agencies pulled out their correspondents. In Angola, three reporters were killed last year. The press has been targeted by both UNITA rebel forces and troops belonging to the MPLA government. Unconfirmed reports also say that as many as 40 journalists have been killed since the war resumed in 1992 after UNITA challenged presidential election results. These claims are under investigation.

In the United States, where press freedoms are taken for granted, a Haitian radio broadcaster was assassinated in Miami under suspicious circumstances. His murder continues a trend whereby dissident voices in ethnic communities are being killed. He was the third Haitian journalist killed in the U.S. since 1991.

In Latin America the killing of journalists has decreased greatly, as newly instituted democratic governments have curbed army abuses. But journalists continued to be killed in Colombia, where four journalists were assassinated by leftist guerrillas and drug traffickers. Asia ranked as the region with the lowest number of journalists killed in the line of duty. Only three journalists were killed because of their work. The cases occured in India, where two journalists were killed by religious militants, and in the Philippines, where the publisher of a small newspaper disappeared mysteriously and is presumed dead.

Algeria (9)

Religious extremists are suspected of involvement in each of the following murders in Algeria.

JUNE 2
Tahar Djaout, editor-in-chief of the weekly cultural publication *Ruptures*, was shot outside his home near Algiers by Muslim militants on May 26. He died of his wounds on June 2. Djaout, who won the prestigious Prix Mediterranee in 1991 for his novel *Vigiles*, had received several death threats. His magazine, founded in January 1993, expressed views strongly opposed to Islamic fundamentalism.

AUGUST 3
Rabah Zenati, a television journalist, was killed by unknown gunmen.

AUGUST 9
Abdelhamid Benmeni, a journalist with the news weekly *Algérie-Actualité*, was killed in his home.

SEPTEMBER 9
Saad Bakhtaoui, a journalist with *El-Minbar*, organ of a small political party, was kidnapped and shot to death.

SEPTEMBER 28
Abderrahmane Chergou, a former journalist and official of the leftist PAGS party, was stabbed to death outside his home in the Algiers suburb of Mohammedia.

OCTOBER 5
Djamel Bouhidel, a photographer with the weekly *Nouveau Tell*, was killed in Blida, west of Algiers.

OCTOBER 14
Mustapha Abada, former director of Algerian state television (replaced in August 1993), was shot and killed in Ain Taya, near Algiers.

OCTOBER 18
Smail Yefsah, assistant news director of Algerian television, was stabbed and then shot to death outside his home in Bab Ezzouar in Algiers.

DECEMBER 27
Youcef Sebti, a poet and freelance journalist who contributed to *El Watan* and other Algiers-based publications, was murdered at the National Institute for Agronomy where he taught and resided.

Angola (3)

There are uncorroborated official reports that as many as 40 journalists have been killed since the civil war resumed in October 1992. Due to the difficulty of obtaining reliable information, CPJ has been able to confirm only the following deaths in 1993

MAY

Jose Manuel, a reporter with Benguela Province radio station, and Jose Mariados Santos, a reporter with the privately owned *Moreno Commercial* radio station in Benguela, were shot and killed. According to *Luanda National Radio,* witnesses say the victims were taken from a Land Rover to the beach where they were killed by machine gun fire. The UNITA-run *Voice of the Black Cockerel* radio station claimed that the reporters' vehicle was stopped by MPLA security forces and that the journalists were taken to a prison where they were interrogated, beaten and shot.

AUGUST 23

Elpidio Inacio, a correspondent for Angola's state-owned *Televisao Popular de Angola,* was killed in crossfire between UNITA rebels and government forces while covering the siege of Kuito, the site of intense fighting for the previous three weeks.

Bosnia (5 + 4)*

JANUARY 10

Karmela Sojanovic was killed at her home in Sarajevo by a sharpshooter. She worked for the daily *Oslobodjenje.*

JANUARY 30

Milos Vulovic*, a journalist for *Serbian Radio* in Ilidza, and Zivko Filipovic*, a photojournalist with *Srpsko Slovo,* were killed during shelling of Ilidza.

FEBRUARY 2

Zeljko Ruzicic*, a Croatian working for *Muslim Radio* in Sarajevo, was killed. *Muslim Radio* claims he was killed by an exploding grenade; Croatian intelligence sources claim he was assassinated because of his nationality.

MAY 29

Guido Puletti, who freelanced for the Italian publications *Mondo Economico* and *Brescia Oggi,* was killed in Central Bosnia when the relief convoy in which he was traveling was ambushed. Puletti and two relief workers were shot and killed.

JUNE 2

Dominique Lonneux, a Belgian cameraman working for a Mexican television news team, was wounded and later died when a United Nations Protection Force convoy was attacked in western Herzegovina.

JUNE 10

Ranko Elez*, a Bosnian Serb journalist working for *Radio Foca,* was killed by a Muslim sniper during fighting between Muslims and Serbs near Foca.

JUNE 27

Tasar Omer, a Turkish journalist, was killed by a sniper in Sarajevo while attending the funeral of seven young people who died in shelling the day before.

JULY 10

A journalist carrying a British passport and identified by the Guardian as **Ibrahim Goskel,** was shot and killed at Sarajevo airport.

Colombia (4)

MARCH 12
Eustorgio Colmenares, publisher of *La Opinion*, was shot to death by machine gun on his terrace in Cucuta, the capital of Norte de Santander. The National Liberation Army (ELN), a Marxist guerrilla group, claimed responsibility for the killing.

APRIL 19
Carlos Lajud Catalan, a journalist for *ABC Radio* in Barranquilla, was killed by two gunmen riding a motorcycle. Catalan was a tough critic of Barranquilla's mayor, a priest and member of the demobilized guerrilla group M-19.

SEPTEMBER 28
Manuel Martinez Espinoza, a broadcast journalist from Popayan (Valle El Cauca) and host of a radio program called "El Yunque" on the nation-wide *Radio Super*, was killed by unknown gunmen. He was a frequent critic of drug gangs and politicians.

SEPTEMBER 30
Bienvenido Lemus, a 42-year old reporter for the nation-wide network *Radio Caracol*, was shot and killed by a group of unknown gunmen. His colleagues suspect that the murder was related to Lemus' work.

Congo (1)*

NOVEMBER 4
Laurent Bisset*, a reporter for state-owned *Radio Congo*, was killed near his home in Bacongo, a section of Brazzaville in which at least two dozen people were killed in two days of fighting between government and opposition forces. There are contradictory reports as to whether he was targeted for his reporting or killed in crossfire.

El Salvador (1)

LATE JANUARY
Francisco Parada, a well-known radio station owner, was killed in front of his house in San Salvador.

Georgia (3)

SEPTEMBER 22
Alexandra Tuttle, a freelance journalist and contributor to *The Wall Street Journal*, was killed aboard a Georgian military aircraft when it was hit by a ground-to-air missile fired by Abkhazian rebels. The plane crashed as the pilot attempted an emergency landing in Sukhumi. Tuttle had boarded the flight in Sukhumi and was on her way to interview President Eduard Shevarnadze.

SEPTEMBER 27
Andrei Soloviev, 38-year old photo correspondent for *ITAR-TASS*, was killed while photographing battles in the streets of Sukhumi (Abkhazia).

LATE OCTOBER
David Bolkvadze, 24-year old cameraman for *Worldwide Television News*, was killed in Kobi. He was captured on October 28 by Abkhazian rebels and shot. He died of his wounds a few days later.

Honduras (1)

APRIL 26
Carlos Grant, 67, a correspondent for the national daily *El Tiempo*, was killed in the town of El Progreso by a local loan shark who was upset about an article Grant had written.

India (2)

JANUARY 31
Bhola Nath Masoom, a stringer for *Hind Samachar* and president of the Punjab and Chandigarh Journalist's Council, was shot by two suspected militants near his home in the town of Rajpura. He died the same day.

MAY 22
Dinesh Pathak, an editor for Sandesh newspaper in Baroda, was stabbed to death by a group of assailants while entering the newspaper's office. Six months earlier Pathak had been publicly threatened by Raju Risaldar, a political leader he had criticized. After Pathak's murder, Risaldar was killed during a scuffle with police.

Lebanon (1)

JULY 26
Ahmed Haidar, a cameraman for Hizbollah-owned *Al-Manar Television*, was killed by Israeli shelling while covering the Israeli army's massive incursion into southern Lebanon.

Lithuania (1)

OCTOBER 12
Vitas Lingis, 33-year old deputy editor of *Republica* newspaper, was shot to death by unknown gunmen. Lingis, who had written frequently about corruption, had been investigating a story about the Lithuanian criminal underground.

Peru (1)

DECEMBER 10
Maria Carlin Fernandez, former anchorwoman for the local subsidiary of *Peruvian Radio and Television Network*, was shot dead in a restaurant in Chimbote. Fernandez had received threats after she began investigating the death of a cousin who was killed in a barroom brawl that involved an army intelligence officer. The police have claimed that Ms. Fernandez was the victim of a botched robbery, but the fact that she was shot 11 times in the back belies this explanation.

Philippines (1)

JANUARY 11
Romeo Lagaspi, publisher of *Voice of Zambales*, was last seen by his family on January 11, 1993. He had

been charged with criminal libel for a column he wrote on police corruption, and had filed a counter suit, which was pending when he disappeared. Police showed Mr. Lagaspi's family photographs of a charred corpse, which they hinted was that of the journalist.

Russia (8)

APRIL 14 OR 15
Dmitri Krikoryants, correspondent in the self-declared Chechen Republic for the Moscow-based weekly *Ekspresskhronika,* was killed when unknown assailants opened fire on him with an automatic weapon while he was in his apartment. His colleagues fear he was targeted for reporting on alleged Chechen government corruption in oil trading.

OCTOBER 3/4
Seven journalists were killed during the battle between Russian President Boris Yeltsin and his hard-line opponents—two at the parliament building and five at the Ostankino Television Center. They were
Yvan Skopan, cameraman *TF-1,* France
Sergei Krasilnikov, videoengineer, Ostankino TV Center
Alexander Sidelnikov, cameraman, Lennauchfilm Studio (St. Petersburg)
Rory Peck, cameraman, ARD Television Company (Germany)
Igor Belozerov, staff, Ostankino TV Center, *Channel 4*
Alexander Smirnov, correspondent, *Molodezhny Kuriyer*
Vladimir Drobyshev, correspondent, *Nature and Man*

Rwanda (1)

APRIL 6
Callixte Kalissa, a television producer with the state-run *Television Rwandaise* and a former photographer with the state-run *Office Rwandais d'Information,* was shot dead near his home in the neighborhood of Remera in Kigali. According to a witness, his assailant was dressed in a military uniform and was aboard a vehicle bearing a government license plate.

South Africa (1)

APRIL 23
Calvin Thusago, a reporter for the *South African Broadcasting Corporation,* was killed in Sharpeville by a mob of 30 youths who set upon his car.

Somalia (5)

JULY 12
Hansjoerg (Hansi) Krauss, a German photographer with the *Associated Press;* **Hosea D. Maina**, a Kenyan photographer working for *Reuters;* **Dan Eldon**, a photographer working for *Reuters* with both U.S. and British passports, and **Anthony Macharia**, a Kenyan soundman for *Reuters TV,* were killed by an angry crowd of Somalis. The journalists apparently were invited by a spokesman for General Mohammed Farah Aidid to view the results of a United Nations attack on one of Aidid's locations. When they arrived, they were set upon by people wielding rocks, clubs and guns.

JUNE 18

Jean-Claude Jumel, a French sound technician for the Paris-based television station *TF1*, was killed during an ambush at Mogadishu's airport. Jumel had just arrived in Somalia and was driving into the city with other members of the television crew. Their vehicle was ambushed by unknown gunmen.

Tajikistan (4 + 11*)

JANUARY

Saidmurod Yerov, executive director of *Farkhang* magazine, was arrested by members of the pro-government National Front. His body was reportedly found in a mass grave in Dushanbe on February 2. The reason for his killing is unclear.

MARCH

Zukhuruddin Suyari, a correspondent for the government magazine *Todzhikiston*, was found dead in Kurgan-Tiube. It is suspected that he may have been killed by members of the pro-government National Front because he is from the Garm area.

MAY 28

Pirimkul Sattori, a correspondent for the Kurgan-Tiube newspaper *Khatlon*, was arrested in that city by unidentified persons in military uniform. Several days later, his body was found in a cotton field. The reason for his killing is unknown.

OCTOBER 21

Tabarali Saidaliev, editor of *Ba Pesh* newspaper, was abducted on October 21. His body was found three days later. Members of the pro-government National Front are suspected of involvement.

What follows is a list of journalists believed killed in Tajikistan. We are still working on determining the circumstances of each killing:

Tohirjon Azimov
Mukhtor Bugdiev
Jamshed Davliyatmamedov
Tohir Malik
Hushvakt Muborakshoev
Tohir Olimov
Kurbon Tagoev
Usmon Tuichiev
Tavakkal Faizulloev
Filolisho Hilvatshoev
Kishvaroy Sharifova

Turkey (4)

JANUARY 24

Uğur Mumcu, a journalist for *Cumhuriyet*, was killed by a car bomb outside his home. Three Islamic organizations claimed credit. Mumcu was a long-time supporter of the secular principles of Kemal Atatürk and had reported on Islamic fundamentalism, drug and gun smuggling and the Kurdish movement.

FEBRUARY 18
Kemal Kiliç, Urfa correspondent for the newspaper *Özgür Gündem*, was shot and killed by unknown assailants in Külünçe village. According to his newspaper, Mr. Kiliç had been questioned in January by police about a news release he had put out on the difficulties distributors had faced in selling the newspaper in Şanli Urfa province.

JULY 28
Ferhat Tepe, *Özgür Gündem's* Bitlis correspondent, disappeared after he was reportedly forced into a car as he left his father's shop in the center of Bitlis. His body, found in Lake Hazar near the city of Elazığ, was identified on August 9. The cause of death has not yet been determined. Several teams of police were seen patrolling at the time Tepe was abducted, but they deny knowledge of the incident. On July 29, a caller claimed that Tepe was being held by a group called the Ottoman Turkish Revenge Brigade. The journalist is said to have received death threats in the past.

AUGUST 7
Aysel Malkaç, a 23 year old reporter for *Özgür Gündem*, disappeared after leaving the newspaper's main office in Istanbul. Because there was a heavy military presence around the building when she disappeared, her colleagues believe she was taken into custody by the police. However, the police have denied holding her. A person who was in custody at Istanbul police headquarters between August 5 and 17 wrote a letter to *Özgür Gündem*, claiming he saw Malkaç at the headquarters on the nights of August 8 and 9. Malkaç is still missing and is feared dead.

United States (1)

OCTOBER 24
Dona St. Plite, a Haitian-born commentator for radio station *WKAT* in Miami, was murdered at a benefit for the family of a colleague killed two years earlier. His name had appeared on a hit list of supporters of ousted Haitian President Jean-Bertrand Aristide.

Journalists Receive 1993 Press Freedom Awards

The International Press Freedom Awards, bestowed annually by the Committee to Protect Journalists, honor journalists from around the world for courageously providing independent news coverage and viewpoints under difficult circumstances. To defend press freedom, Award winners have risked arrest, imprisonment, violence against themselves and their families, and even death.

The 1993 Awards were presented on November 11 in New York City to the following individuals:

Omar Belhouchet, director of Algeria's *El Watan* newspaper, has been jailed by government authorities and attacked by Islamic fundamentalists. His paper's independent reporting has not been appreciated by either side of a continuing conflict which began when the secular government canceled parliamentary elections after first-round results favored the Islamic Salvation Front. During 1993 Belhouchet was arrested twice and had his car fired at by gunmen as he drove his children to school. Eight Algerian journalists were killed, all apparently by religious fundamentalists. *ABC News* Anchor Peter Jennings, who presented the Award to Belhouchet, praised "the moral, intellectual, and physical courage required by independent journalists like Belhouchet."

Doan Viet Hoat, editor of an independent newsletter called *Freedom Forum*, has been jailed in a detention camp in Ho Chi Minh City since November 17, 1990. He is there serving a 15-year sentence for "having a document used by a reactionary group as their leading vehicle to overthrow the Vietnamese government." The politically neutral *Freedom Forum* published articles representing viewpoints of the Vietnamese government, former South Vietnamese officials, and Vietnamese living abroad. Seven other journalists were sentenced with Doan, whose arrest seemed to be part of a government crackdown on prominent intellectuals from the former South Vietnam. He had been put in a reeducation camp in 1976 and released in 1988 to then be re-arrested in 1990. Newsletters like *Freedom Forum* are the only outlet for independent reporting in Vietnam today.

Accepting the International Press Freedom Award on his father's behalf, Doan's son, Long Doan, heard presenter Terry Anderson remind the audience that for autocratic governments, "neutrality is not good enough, and objectivity is tantamount to treason... Autocratic governments fear [journalists like Doan], as they should. They bring light and truth as true enemies of all repression." Anderson spent seven years as a hostage in Lebanon and did not see his daughter for the first six and a half years of her life. Long Doan has not seen his father since 1976 when he was seven years old.

Editor **Nosa Igiebor,** together with his staff at *Tell* Magazine in Nigeria, have come under attack for exposing official corruption and criticizing Nigeria's military regime, led by Major General Ibrahim Babangida, who annulled the results of a presidential election and later turned over control to a hand-picked successor. The regime has conducted a determined campaign to silence dissent in the press. *Tell*, a prime target of assaults, has remained at the forefront of the battle to defend press freedom and persevered through constant harassment, occupation of its offices by security forces, the beating of its reporters, and the confiscation of its editions. In August, Igiebor and three of his editors were arrested and held for 12 days without charge. Igiebor's Award was presented by *New Yorker* Editor Tina Brown, who praised her colleague's courage while describing the extreme danger he faced to keep publishing independent news.

Veran Matic and his staff at *Radio B92* in Belgrade stay on the air through tremendous adversity, providing listeners with *BBC* news, Western music, and a satiric perspective on the Balkan tragedy. As a result, they are under constant pressure from the Serbian nationalist government and have withstood both threats of violence and actual beatings in their office and at their homes. No one has been charged in the assaults. With a slogan of "Don't trust anyone, not even *B92*," the popular station supports no political party. Through his position, Matic is trying to create a loose-knit network of independent local media in an attempt to offer alternative views to the nationalist government media that predominate. Award presenter Dan Rather, *CBS News* Anchor said "My new favorite saying is one of Matic's: 'You can be sure you are independent only when everyone starts to hate you,' I like that."

For relentlessly investigating and exposing military offenses against civilians, **Ricardo Uceda**, editor-in-chief of the Peruvian magazine *Si*, has faced physical and legal threats without backing down. In a nation where a near-dictatorial President Alberto Fujimori has used his control of the judiciary to punish journalists who provide critical coverage, and where the military is known for "disappearing" journalists who expose corruption or brutality in their ranks, Uceda's accomplishments are particularly noteworthy. This year *Si* revealed new information that implicated military officers in a 1991 massacre in Lima, and Uceda resisted pressure to reveal its sources. After the magazine publicized the existence of clandestine graves containing the remains of nine students and a university professor who had been abducted by the army, the suspended Peruvian Congress voted overwhelmingly to ask the minister of internal affairs to guarantee the safety of Uceda and his colleagues. In honoring Uceda, Award presenter Arthur Ochs Sulzberger, Jr., publisher of the *New York Times*, called the journalist's work "vibrant, independent, and groundbreaking."

R. E. (Ted) Turner received CPJ's 1993 Burton Benjamin Memorial Award in honor of the ways in which he and *Cable News Network* (*CNN*) have changed the world. Reaching into the smallest hamlets and the highest corridors of power, *CNN* has had far-reaching effects that pundits, political scientists and sociologists will analyze for decades. This revolution occurred thanks to the vision and stamina of Ted Turner and the day-to-day courage of *CNN* journalists–from Peter Arnett in Baghdad to Margaret Moth in Sarajevo–who fight fear, censors, and spin doctors to get the story. Presenting the Award to Mr. Turner was Katherine Graham, chairman of the Executive Committee of the Washington Post Company and winner of the 1992 Burton Benjamin Award.

Now in their fourth year, CPJ's International Press Freedom Awards and Burton Benjamin Memorial Award are among the most coveted honors in the field of journalism. These awards recognize the courage of these journalists and show that their struggles are neither isolated nor forgotten.

International Press Freedom Award Winners 1991 & 1992

1991
Pius Njawe, *Le Messager*, Cameroon
Wang Juntao and Chen Ziming, *Economics Weekly*, China
Bill Foley and Cary Vaughan, United States
Tatyana Mitkova, *TSN*, former Soviet Union
Byron Barrera, *La Epoca*, Guatemala

1992
David Kaplan, *ABC News*
Muhammad Al-Saqr, *Al-Qabas*, Kuwait
Sony Esteus, *Radio Tropic FM*, Haiti
Gwendolyn Lister, *The Namibian*, Namibia
Thepchai Yong, *The Nation*, Thailand

Burton Benjamin Memorial Award

1991
Walter Cronkite, *CBS News* Correspondent

1992
Katherine Graham, *The Washington Post Company*

Answers to your Questions

What is CPJ?
The Committee to Protect Journalists is a nonpartisan, nonprofit organization founded in 1981 to monitor abuses against the press and promote press freedom internationally. CPJ is the only organization in America with a full-time staff devoted to documenting and responding to violations of press freedoms.

Who founded CPJ?
A group of American foreign correspondents who wanted to respond to the often brutal treatment of their foreign colleagues by authoritarian governments.

How is CPJ staffed?
CPJ has a 13-member staff. Its activities are directed by a 30-member board of prominent American journalists.

How is CPJ funded?
CPJ is entirely dependent on private donations from journalists, news organizations and foundations. CPJ accepts no government funding.

Where is CPJ located?
The office is in New York City at 330 Seventh Avenue. Journalists and scholars are welcome to visit and to utilize its extensive library and computer database.

The press is so powerful; why does it need protection?
The press in the United States does have great power and enjoys legal protection. But that's not the case in the rest of the world. Nearly every week a journalist is killed on the job because someone wants them silenced. CPJ has documented more than 100 cases of journalists who are in prison around the world because of what they have reported. Hundreds of journalists are routinely subjected to physical attack, illegal detention, spurious lawsuits, and

threats against themselves or their families. Even in the United States the hazards are very real: journalists have died on the job in New York, California, Florida, Virginia, Washington D.C., Colorado and Arizona.

Is CPJ primarily concerned with foreign correspondents and journalists working in countries other than the United States?
CPJ is concerned with press freedom everywhere. The repercussions of losing such freedoms anywhere in the world are resounding for all journalists and for all citizens.

How specifically does CPJ "protect" journalists?
By publicly revealing abuses against the press, and by acting on behalf of imprisoned and threatened journalists, CPJ effectively raises the warning when attacks on press freedoms occur. CPJ organizes vigorous protest at all levels—ranging from local governments to the United Nations—when abuse takes place. When necessary, CPJ works behind the scenes and through other diplomatic channels to effect change.

How does the journalism profession benefit from CPJ's work?
Because it continuously monitors events around the world, CPJ can warn journalists —who are working or planning to travel— about situations before they become dangerous.

CPJ also publishes informational booklets for journalists traveling in dangerous areas; comprehensive accounts on how journalism works—and isn't working—in various countries; and a quarterly newsletter, *Dangerous Assignments*, on CPJ's most recent investigations and activities.

When would an American journalist call upon CPJ?
In an emergency. Using local contacts CPJ

can intervene anytime foreign correspondents are in trouble. CPJ is also organized to notify immediately news organizations, government officials, and human rights organizations. CPJ will wire money or tickets and provide information for emergency legal assistance.

BEFORE TRAVEL
CPJ maintains a database of local journalist contacts. CPJ also publishes practical "safety guides" that offer advice to journalists covering dangerous assignments.

ON ASSIGNMENT
CPJ provides information to American journalists to better protect themselves while covering dangerous situations, and provides contacts and other practical information to foreign editors and correspondents in the field.

How reliable is CPJ's information, advice, and data?

Using stringent journalistic news-gathering techniques, CPJ investigates dozens of new attacks on the press each week. Our computerized database is the most comprehensive source of information about attacks on the press worldwide.

Since its first appearance in 1987, CPJ's annual report—*Attacks on the Press*—has been widely considered the single most comprehensive report on threats to press freedoms worldwide. News organizations, human rights groups, and other researchers rely on the accuracy of CPJ's reports and documentation.

Who compiles this information? How are abuses researched?

CPJ has five full-time program coordinators, monitoring the press in the Americas, Asia, the Middle East, Africa, Eastern Europe. Program coordinators track developments in their regions through independent research, reports from the field, their own travel, and reports from other journalists.

Staff experts organize international protest campaigns, arrange emergency legal counsel, lead fact-finding missions, and find threatened journalists safe refuge abroad.

What else does CPJ do?

When dangerous situations arise—such as a coup or a crackdown—CPJ will send foreign editors and correspondents same-day advisories with practical information.

CPJ reports are transmitted instantly to other press freedom organizations worldwide through IFEX, the global e-mail network.

CPJ also works with universities and other institutions that provide training to foreign journalists and offers current information about foreign news organizations and press conditions in journalists' home countries.

"Safety handbooks" are also distributed by CPJ to foreign editors, journalism organizations, and schools.

CPJ advises local press groups on how to document violations and mobilize international support.

Each year CPJ presents the Press Freedom Awards to journalists who have displayed special courage in defending press freedom. Recipients have provided independent coverage and viewpoints to readers and listeners despite arrest, imprisonment, physical attack, and threats.

How can I help?

IN AT LEAST FOUR WAYS:
- Become a member. CPJ relies on private financial support.
- Call upon us. Let CPJ know when you, a colleague or other journalists need help.
- Cover attacks on the press as news stories.
- Recognize that in many countries attacks on the press signal a coming crackdown on all freedoms and is a barometer of political and social upheaval.

CPJ Investigates Cases Around the World

The cases of press freedom violations described in this volume were investigated and verified by CPJ's research staff. Each account was corroborated by more than one source for accuracy and for confirmation that the attacks were against journalists or news organizations and their reporting was the probable motive. Additional information on individual cases is available from CPJ at 212-465-1004. The cases in this report are classified as follows:

Killed
Killed or missing and believed dead with evidence of retribution for news coverage or commentary, including journalists killed unintentionally in the line of duty.

Imprisoned
Arrested or held against one's will, including kidnapped.

Attacked
Wounded; assaulted; a news facility physically attacked, raided, or searched; non-journalist employees attacked in any way because of news coverage or commentary.

Threatened
Threatened with physical harm or some other type of retribution.

Harassed
Access denied or limited; materials confiscated; materials damaged; entry or exit denied; family members attacked or threatened; fired or demoted (when it is clearly the result of political or outside pressure); harassed in some other way.

Legal Action
Credentials denied or suspended; fined; passage of a restrictive law; libel suit intended to inhibit coverage; sentenced to prison; visas denied or canceled.

Expelled
Expelled or forced to leave a country because of news coverage or commentary

Censored
Officially censored or banned; editions confiscated; news outlet closed.

Journalists are defined as people who cover news or write commentary on a regular basis. Only attacks that relate to the journalists' professional work are included in this report.

Africa

GAMBIA

GUINEA
BISSAU

SENEGAL

MALI

NIGER

CHAD

ERITREA

SUDAN

DJIBOUTI

SOMALIA

GUINEA

BURKINA
FASO

BENIN

ETHIOPIA

SIERRA LEONE

IVORY
COAST

GHANA

NIGERIA

LIBERIA

TOGO

CAMEROON

CENTRAL
AFRICAN REPUBLIC

EQUATORIAL GUINEA

UGANDA

KENYA

GABON

CONGO

ZAIRE

RWANDA

BURUNDI

Cabinda
(ANGOLA)

TANZANIA

MALAWI

ANGOLA

ZAMBIA

MOZAMBIQUE

ZIMBABWE

MADAGASCAR

NAMIBIA

BOTSWANA

SWAZILAND

LESOTHO

SOUTH AFRICA

Africa

Africa

by Eleanor Bedford

A newly independent press continues to champion the post Cold-War call for democratization. While most governments profess to uphold democratic ideals, the promise of political reform remains largely unfulfilled. Where authoritarian rulers maintained control of the money and the military, critical reporting was brutally repressed. Crackdowns on the independent press coincided with elections that often resulted in merely legitimizing repressive regimes. In keeping with the guise of democracy, governments increasingly rely on legal prosecution to silence dissenting voices in the media.

As authoritarian regimes moved to block democratic reform and sabotage elections, the independent press was a frequent target of attack. In Zaire, Togo, and Nigeria, security forces harassed, threatened, and detained journalists. In Gabon and Congo opposition radio stations were destroyed. Numerous publications were seized and suspended for criticizing government corruption and electoral fraud. Nigeria's vigorous independent media proved resilient. Opposition journalists in Zaire and Togo continue to work at great risk. Ironically, one of the most violent events of the year—the coup d'etat

in Burundi in which tens of thousands were massacred when the military assassinated the country's first democratically elected president and briefly seized power—brought news blackouts but did not target the independent press, whose influence is limited.

Nonpartisan reporting is often a rarity in Africa's polarized political climate. Many independent publications must rely on financial support from opposition parties to survive. Legal prosecution can be tantamount to censorship since lawyer's fees and hefty fines can close down independent publications.

Although the media has gained greater latitude in reporting on matters of public debate, the legacy of colonial law is still used to repress criticism of government officials. While elections have not necessarily delivered democracy, they have brought an exponential increase in legal prosecution of independent journalists. Whereas repressive regimes in Cameroon and Kenya once closed newspapers and detained reporters on a regular basis, they now take them to court. Outmoded sedition and libel laws are used to intimidate the independent press. New guidelines, passed in the name of supporting press freedom, have been used to curtail it. In countries like Benin, Chad, Burkina

Faso, and Madagascar, where reform has brought relatively dramatic improvements in press freedom, journalists continue to be charged for libeling public officials. In 1993, at least five journalists went to jail for libel; many more received suspended sentences.

While a plethora of independent publications now exist, radio, by far the most important news medium in Africa, remains firmly under government control on most of the continent. Independent commissions were established to oversee access to state-controlled media in countries like Malawi and South Africa. Francophone West Africa has lead the way in establishing independent and community radio stations. However, the issue of licensing has proved extremely volatile, particularly in South Africa. As more independent stations emerge, so do decisive attacks against them. In Congo, Mali, Gabon, and Somalia, independent radio stations were bombed, destroyed, or consistently jammed.

In many parts of Africa, journalists face extreme conditions of physical danger. Despite UN brokered negotiations, civil wars continue in Liberia, Angola, and Somalia. The fighting claimed the lives of five foreign correspondents in Somalia and at least three local journalists in Angola. Violence threatened to jeopardize news coverage of the war in Mogadishu and South Africa's strife-torn transition. In Liberia publications have closed and journalists have fled. In Angola, the war rendered nonpartisan reporting virtually impossible.

Despite recent reforms and relative openness, the independent press in Africa, like the democratization movement, faces a daily struggle to survive.

Eleanor Bedford, *Program Coordinator for Africa, joined the Committee to Protect Journalists in 1992. A graduate of the University of Virginia in French and Francophone literature, Bedford previously worked for PEN, the international writers' organization. She led a mission to South Africa and Zimbabwe in 1993. She is fluent in French.*

Kim Brice, *former Program Coordinator for Sub-Saharan Africa, continued to provide her expertise and editorial assistance on this report.*

Avner Gidron, *Program Coordinator for the Middle East and North Africa, wrote the Sudan section.*

Suzanne Hopkins, *a freelance consultant on East Africa, contributed to the Kenya, Tanzania, and South Africa sections of this report*

Andy Carroll, Kelly David, Mark Johnson, *and* **Terry Scheller Wolf** *also contributed to this report.*

Africa

Angola

What little press freedom once existed has deteriorated into partisan reporting due to the resumption of civil war. Following Jonas Savimbi's refusal to recognize the results of the September 1992 elections, which President Jose Eduardo dos Santos's Popular Movement for the Liberation of Angola (MPLA) was widely believed to have won, Savimbi's National Union for the Total Independence of Angola (UNITA) returned to arms, plunging the country into chaos. With continued violence despite peace talks, and law and order virtually nonexistent, journalists are in constant physical danger. The conflict makes in-country travel difficult; foreign correspondents rely on the UN's World Food Program for safe transportation. At least three journalists were killed in 1993, and reports indicate that scores more have disappeared, perhaps murdered or detained, including reporter Bela Malaquias, allegedly held against her will by UNITA troops since June 1992. State-controlled radio claimed that since the resumption of hostilities, as many as 45 journalists were assassinated and over 200 media workers were reported missing. UNITA recently released its own list of atrocities perpetrated against reporters working for UNITA's *Radio Vorgan*, but, given the level of propaganda, it is impossible to substantiate these claims. While a few private radio stations and at least one non-government weekly were established in the period before elections, today they are essentially MPLA-controlled. Accounts of government corruption and human rights abuses continued to appear. However, by December, state-run *Radio Nacional* denounced Angolan journalists working for foreign media as unpatriotic because of their coverage of corruption scandals. Declaring that in any country at war, press freedom has limits, *Radio Nacional* reportedly encouraged "measures" to be taken against Angolan journalists who threaten state security.

MAY
Jose Manuel, *Benguela Province Radio*, Killed
Jose Maria dos Santos, *Radio Morena*, Killed
Manuel and dos Santos were assassinated after being beaten by unknown assailants. According to a *Radio Nacional* broadcast, fishermen near the scene said that the victims were taken from a Land Rover at dawn, dragged to the beach, and shot. *The Voice of the Black Cockerel*, UNITA's radio station, reported their version: government forces detained the two journalists and took them to a state security prison where they were interrogated, beaten, and subsequently executed. The bodies were left on a beach in Lobito. Police say they are investigating the murders.

JUNE 11
Televisao Popular de Angola, Attacked
Members of the separatist movement Cabinda Liberation Front (FLEC) ambushed a *Televisao Popular de Angola* vehicle in Cabinda in retaliation for the government media's refusal to publicize their demands. FLEC released the driver unharmed and surrendered the vehicle once its demand for press coverage was met. FLEC is fighting for the independence of Cabinda, a northern Angolan enclave between Congo and Zaire whose oil produces a large percentage of Angola's export earnings.

AUGUST 23

Elpidio Inacio, *Televisao Popular de Angola*, Killed
Inacio, a correspondent for Angola's state-owned television, was killed when caught in crossfire between UNITA rebels and government forces while covering the battle for control of Kuito, the capital of Bie province. Kuito lies approximately 80 miles northeast of Huambo, UNITA's stronghold.

Benin

The press was able to criticize and freely comment on matters of public debate. Since Nicephore Soglo won free and fair presidential elections two years ago, regard for human rights has consistently improved. A large number of libel cases were brought against journalists this year. The most disturbing case involved a newspaper director who was sentenced to one year in prison ostensibly for failing to appear at his sentencing hearing. Local journalists believe that the real reason for the conviction was a story that criticized President Soglo, despite the fact that articles criticizing the government appear on a regular basis.

MAY 10

Edgar Kaho, *Le Soleil*, Imprisoned
Kaho, director of the independent newspaper *Le Soleil*, was arrested in connection with a one-year sentence he received in December 1992 that was never enforced. He was charged with defamation relating to an article published in a 1991 issue of *Le Soleil* entitled "SOBE-TRAP Affair: Where Did the 218,000,000 Francs in Excess Payment Go? Ministers of

Kerekou and Soglo Implicated," which implicated ministers serving former President Kerekou and current President Nicephore Soglo in a corruption scandal. Kaho's arrest coincided with the May 10 issue of *Le Soleil*, which ran several articles critical of President Soglo and his wife. He is currently still in prison.

JUNE 18

François Comlan, *L'Observateur*, Legal Action
Comlan, director of an independent bimonthly newspaper, received a six-month suspended sentence on appeal for an article that raised questions about the financing of President Soglo's 1991 electoral campaign.

Burkina Faso

After the arrests and detention of two journalists in July, local reporters and human rights activists spearheaded a movement to reform Burkina Faso's draconian press laws. Using a provision of the new constitution designed to allow public opposition to laws, the leaders of the movement collected 60,000 signatures in a petition that proposed specific changes in Burkina Faso's press code. Only 15,000 signatures are required by law to force a review of the law. After initially challenging the validity of the signatures, the government voted on the last day of assembly to revise the law. While the new law remains excessively protective of public figures—it still authorizes the government to send journalists convicted of defamation straight to prison pending trial—it does allow journalists charged with defamation

to furnish proof that their reports are accurate. The new press code will make it easier to establish new publications.

JUNE 15

Florent Dofinita Bonzi, *Le Matin*, Legal Action, Imprisoned

Jean-Paul Badoum, *Le Matin*, Legal Action, Imprisoned

Within a day of their arrest, Bonzi and Badoum, respectively director and editor-in-chief of *Le Matin*, an independent weekly, were tried, convicted of libel, sentenced to six months in prison, and fined 100,000 CFA. The charges stemmed from several articles in the Bobo-Dioulasso based weekly that implicated a former local prosecutor and the ministry of justice in a corruption scandal. The journalists were released on August 3 and their sentence was revoked.

Cameroon

The government continued to resort to short-term detention and intimidation in its attempt to silence the independent media. President Paul Biya, who declared himself the victor after fraudulent elections in 1992, ignored his promises of constitutional reform and his executive power remains unchecked. Reporters continued to be arrested and beaten. The government increasingly used legal proceedings to harass outspoken publications rather than banning them outright as it did in 1992. Two journalists served prison terms for libel charges for the first time since independence. Rotoprint, a private printing plant that publishes most of Cameroon's private newspapers, continued to be

harassed and was under surveillance for most of the year. Prior censorship laws remained in force. Radio and television continued to operate under state control and remained saturated with government propaganda.

JANUARY

Prescott Low, International Federation of Newspaper Publishers, Legal Action

Low, President of the International Federation of Newspaper Publishers (FIEJ), was denied a visa from the Cameroonian government. He was scheduled to participate in a joint mission of the FIEJ and Reporters Sans Frontières, an international press freedom organization, to investigate violations of freedom of the press in Cameroon.

APRIL 2

Severin Tchounkeu, *La Nouvelle Expression*, Legal Action

David Nouwou, *La Nouvelle Expression*, Legal Action

Tchounkeu and Nouwou, the director and reporter, respectively, with the weekly newspaper *La Nouvelle Expression*, were charged with defamation, sentenced to six months in prison and fined 1,500,000 CFA. Both were released under appeal on May 6. The sentence was the result of a lawsuit brought by Zogo Andela, head of Camecrus, a shellfish distributor. An article that appeared in the February issue of *La Nouvelle Expression* alleged that Camecrus was avoiding payment of custom duties in complicity with customs officials. The journalists were charged with "abuse and slander." The appeal has since been annulled.

APRIL 15

Larry Eyong-Echow, *SDF Echo*, Legal Action

Echow, the Secretary for Information of the opposition Social Democratic Front (SDF) and a contributor to the party's paper, *SDF Echo*, was sentenced to six months in prison by a military tribunal. He did not serve his entire sentence.

APRIL 29
Lucien Claude Kameni, *l'Opinion,* Legal Action
Willy-Leonard Diappi, *l'Opinion,* Legal Action
Diappi, a contributor to *l'Opinion* newspaper, and its director Kameni, were each sentenced to eight months in prison and fined 500,000 CFA. They were charged by the government with "spreading false information" in connection with an article published in the July 9, 1992, issue of the newspaper. The article stated that during the National Convention of opposition parties in Douala, it was publicly alleged that former Prime Minister Sadou Hayatou bribed Antar Gassagay, State Secretary for Territorial Administration at the time, to gain votes. Hayatou was anticipating running for president in the 1992 elections.

MAY 11
Le Messager, Harassed
Copies of the special edition of *Le Messager,* featuring political cartoons by Popoli, were seized by individuals in civilian clothing. Several newspaper vendors were beaten.

MAY 12
Pius Njawe, *Le Messager,* Imprisoned
Germain Koumyo Ekwe, *l'Opinion,* Imprisoned
Njawe, the director of the weekly newspaper, and his chauffeur and Ekwe, the editor-in-chief of *l'Opinion,* another private weekly, were detained outside *Le Messager's* offices by police in civilian clothing. All three were held overnight. Njawe's arrest is believed to be connected with an article in the May 11 issue of *Le Messager* entitled "While the Economy Dies, 6 Billion Francs Are Spent on Mvomeka'a Golf Course." Mvomeka'a is President Paul Biya's birthplace. A similar report was published in the May 11 edition of *La Lettre du Continent,* a newsletter on African affairs published in

Paris. Reasons for the arrests of Ekwe and Njawe's chauffeur are unclear.

JULY 5
Le Messager, Censored
Number 314 of the weekly newspaper *Le Messager* was banned for "disturbing public order." The issue contained an article that raised further questions about President Biya's golf course.

JULY 9
Pius Njawe, *Le Messager,* Threatened
Njawe received an anonymous phone call warning him that he would soon be assassinated along with Severin Tchounkeu and Benjamin Zebaze, directors, respectively, of *La Nouvelle Expression* and *Challenge Hebdo.* On July 26, an unidentified man approached Njawe outside his office and repeated a similar warning.

JULY 20
Severin Tchounkeu, *La Nouvelle Expression,* Threatened
La Nouvelle Expression, Censored
Copies of the weekly that featured articles about President Biya's golf course were seized from news vendors in Yaounde. The publication's director, Severin Tchounkeu, received an anonymous phone call warning that either he or members of his family would be killed.

AUGUST 13
François Evembe, *Le Messager,* Attacked, Imprisoned
Evembe, the Secretary General of the opposition party l'Union pour le Changement (UPC) and a frequent contributor to *Le Messager,* was detained by police. On August 16, he was taken to his home, which was searched and ransacked. Evembe was released later that day. Police confiscated his identity cards. The following day, police returned to Evembe's home and detained him again. He was shackled and held in solitary confinement for eight days in "Chateau

Americanos," the headquarters of the Groupement Special d'Investigation, the unit in charge of political crimes. He was deprived of sleep and incessantly interrogated about an editorial that appeared in the August 9 issue of *Le Messager* which criticized state management.

AUGUST 17

Pius Njawe, *Le Messager*, Legal Action
Benjamin Zebaze, *Challenge Hebdo*, Legal Action
Martin Waffo, *Challenge Hebdo*, Legal Action
Zebaze and Waffo, the director and a reporter, respectively, for *Challenge Hebdo*, and Njawe, the director of *Le Messager*, were convicted of publishing confidential government documents. Njawe received a six-month suspended sentence. Zebaze and Waffo were sentenced to five months in prison and were released pending an appeal. The newspapers published a letter from Minister of Justice Douala Moutome to President Paul Biya requesting that opposition activists who had been arrested in Bamenda earlier in the year be tried.

NOVEMBER 3

Ndam Maloune, *Le Messager*, Harassed, Attacked, Imprisoned
Jacques Doumbe, *La Vision Hebdo*, Harassed, Attacked, Imprisoned
Julius Wamey, *CRTV*, Harassed, Imprisoned
ean Baptiste Sipa, *Afrique Horizon*, Harassed, Imprisoned
Borgia Marie Evembe, *Le Messager*, Harassed, Imprisoned
At least five journalists were detained, and two beaten, after attending a press conference held by John Fru Ndi, president of the Social Democratic Front, an opposition party banned by the government. Finding the entrance to the press conference blocked by police, Maloune and Doumbe went to Ndi's home. There they were surrounded by police who confiscated their possessions, including tape recorders, identification cards and money, and then beat

them for two hours. The other journalists were detained by police while trying to contact members of the opposition party. Their possessions were also confiscated. All five of the journalists were released later that night. Sipa's identification card was never returned.

DECEMBER 3

Edmond Kanguia, *Le Messager*, Harassed, Imprisoned
Henri Fotso, *Le Messager*, Harassed, Imprisoned
Mathias Glikmans, *Le Messager*, Harassed, Imprisoned
These three reporters were interrogated by police following a student demonstration that became disorderly. They were released from police custody later that day.

DECEMBER 7

Rotoprint, Harassed
Dikalo, Censored
Police surrounded Rotoprint and employees were prohibited from entering or leaving the premises throughout the night. On the same day, a truck distributing the morning edition of the weekly newspaper *Dikalo* was stopped by police who fired gunshot in the air. Six employees of the state news distribution responsible for delivering the newspaper were detained overnight. The issue seized by police included a front page story announcing government plans to lay off 40,000 civil servants. Publication of the story coincided with a country-wide strike that had been called by the worker's union, Confederation Syndicale des Travailleurs du Cameroon.

Chad

After 26 years of insecurity and war, a Sovereign National Conference opened in January to discuss the country's political future. The new transitional government adopted a Transitional Charter as an interim constitutional document, which provides for freedom of the press. While Chad's first democratic elections are promised for 1994, radio and television remain completely under state control. Chad's private media was rarely subject to attacks this year. A handful of independent publications openly criticized the government. Officials are said to point to editions of the most outspoken weekly as proof of their commitment to democracy. Fighting between government troops and insurgent groups in the south continued. No serious investigation was conducted regarding the murders of two of the three journalists who were killed in mysterious circumstances in 1992.

APRIL 8
N'Djamena Hebdo, Legal Action
Chad's most outspoken independent weekly was convicted of defamation and publishing false information for a story that appeared in the April 20, 1992 edition of the paper. The article contained details about President Deby's extensive real estate investments in the capital. *N'Djamena Hebdo* was fined 200,000 CFA and obligated to pay a total of 100,000 CFA in damages.

JUNE 26
Guidingar Berasside, *N'Djamena Hebdo*, Harassed, Censored
Chris MacCarus, *BBC*, Harassed, Censored
Two soldiers prevented MacCarus, a stringer for the *BBC*, and Berasside, a photographer for

N'Djamena Hebdo, from taking photos at the scene of a violent protest over the assassination of the director of army reform. The soldiers pointed their guns at the journalists, threatened Berasside, and took his camera. MacCarus later accompanied Berasside to the police station to retrieve his camera. The film had been removed.

Congo

Broadcast media became a flashpoint in the struggle between the opposition and President Pascal Lissouba, who took power after disputed elections last year. Following accusations of fraud in the May legislative elections, armed conflict broke out between private militias and government troops. By June, the prime minister declared that state radio and television would only broadcast information emanating from state organs, while opposition statements would be ignored. Although opposition newspapers were allowed to circulate, state-controlled media was censored to the point of reporting propaganda. Fighting briefly abated following August negotiations. When the government failed to allow equal access to radio and television during the second round of elections in October, as agreed, the opposition attempted to establish its own radio station. Government troops immediately crushed the clandestine station and several days of fighting ensued. A reporter for state-run Radio Congo was among the many civilian casualties. The only resident foreign correspondent was expelled for her reports on the violence.

Africa

MAY 3

State Media, Censored

Jean Martin Mbemba, Chairman of the National Legislative By-Elections Organization and Supervision Commission, announced that state media reporters were banned from publishing partial and provisional results of the May 2 legislative by-elections. In an interview with *Agence France Presse (AFP)*, Mbemba stated that the partial results were "liable to disturb social peace and public tranquility."

MAY 24

Edmond Philippe Gali, *Radio Congo*, Attacked

Unidentified men threw a grenade at the home of Gali, a political reporter for state-run radio known for his stinging attacks on the opposition. The roof of his building and his car were damaged.

MAY 24

State Media, Censored

State radio and television broadcasts were suspended without explanation. Soldiers were dispatched to the station several days earlier amid mounting tensions following the announcement of results of the contested parliamentary elections. Sources stated that the blackout was due to conflicts between journalists who supported the "Presidential Movement" and those who favored the opposition. Though broadcasts resumed 48 hours later, the struggle for control of the airwaves from within the station continued for weeks.

JUNE 24

State Media, Censored

Prime Minister Yhombi-Opango announced that only information issued by organs of the state would be broadcast on state-run radio and television stations and that broadcasts of information or declarations "by political parties and associations" were strictly suspended.

JUNE 28

Theodore Kiamossia, *Agence Congolaise d'Information*, Censored

Director of the Congolese Information Agency, Kiamossia was suspended by the newly appointed minister of information for authorizing publication of the newly formed "opposition government" in the agency's daily bulletin. Police impounded all copies of the bulletin before distribution.

NOVEMBER 3

Radio Alliance, Attacked, Censored

Government forces destroyed an opposition station that had begun broadcasting four days earlier from Bacango. According to state-run radio, the attack on Bacongo, a suburb of Brazzaville, was a part of an initiative to flush out militants.

NOVEMBER 4

Laurent Bisset, *Radio Congo*, Killed

Bisset, a reporter for the state-owned *Radio Congo* and outspoken supporter of President Lissouba, was found dead outside his home in Bacongo, an opposition stronghold. The neighborhood was besieged for days when fighting broke out between government troops and opposition forces. At least 25 people died and scores more were wounded. According to a state-run radio broadcast, Bisset was abducted by "armed bands" from the main opposition party.

NOVEMBER 12

Frédérique Genot, *Radio France Internationale*, Expelled

Genot, a correspondent for *Radio France Internationale*, was notified by the ministry of information of her immediate expulsion from the country. Congolese authorities apparently took exception to her coverage of the violent events in and around Brazzaville. According to Genot, a military officer said, "You are telling them we are all savages." She was held under guard in a hotel until her flight to Paris two days later.

Ethiopia

Following the transitional government's Press Proclamation at the end of 1992 which purported to support press freedom, numerous independent publications appeared. In 1993, the government used the proclamation to curtail press freedom, prosecuting journalists for reporting on a long list of subjects that were established as off-limits, including: criminal offenses against the "safety of the state"; false accusations against individuals, nations, or organizations; and incitement of "conflict between peoples." Although there are now as many as 64 independent weeklies and monthlies circulating in the country's capital, authorities harassed the more polemic publications, questioning journalists on a regular basis. More than 14 journalists were detained for various periods of time; legal proceedings were initiated against a number of publications. The intimidation of independent media resulted in a high degree of self-censorship.

APRIL-DECEMBER
Girma Lemma, *Aphrodite,* Imprisoned
Messele Haddis, *Aimiro,* Imprisoned
Nesanet Tesfaye, *Aimiro,* Imprisoned
Kibret Mekonnen, *Aimiro,* Imprisoned
Getachew Mekonnen, *Feleg,* Imprisoned
Nigussie Ayele, *Lucy,* Imprisoned
Girmaye Tsadik, *Muday,* Imprisoned
Belete Abebe, *Muday,* Imprisoned
Mesafe Sirak, *Muday,* Imprisoned
Tesfaye Berehanu, *Muday,* Imprisoned
Kifle Mulat, *Zena Adams,* Imprisoned
Mintesinot Zena, *Zena Adams,* Imprisoned

Independent journalists, editors, and publishers were questioned, detained, or arrested for periods of time ranging from a few hours to several weeks. The circumstances of these arrests are under investigation. At year's end, none remained in prsion, although a new wave of arrests began after the new year.

SEPTEMBER
Tefera Asmare, *Ethiopis,* Imprisoned
Iskander Nega, *Ethiopis,* Imprisoned
Asmare and Nega, editor and publisher, respectively, of the Amharic language newspaper *Ethiopis,* were detained by police in early September and charged with "incitement to war" in connection with an article giving credence to rumors of unrest outside the capital. They were eventually granted bail, only to be arrested again on November 12 for "inciting people against the government" and "disseminating false rumors."

Gabon

After 16 years of authoritarian rule, Gabon was hoping for change this year. Instead, President Omar Bongo declared himself the victor of the December 5 election, the results of which were strongly contested. Prior to the elections, the government used intimidation and extrajudicial measures to silence criticism by the local media. It enforced a 1960 press law in retaliation for outrageous stories that were being published about the President. The law effectively banned all newspapers except for a small number controlled by President Bongo for nearly two months prior to the elections. One private radio station's broadcasts were constantly jammed; another was destroyed after the election.

APRIL 5
Radio Liberté, Censored
In early April, broadcasts from the Libreville transmitter of *Radio Liberté*, an opposition radio station, were jammed. The Minister of Communications, Patrice Nziengui, accused the station of undermining public order and operating without a license. *Radio Liberté* was granted authorization by the National Council on Communication to operate in 1993. The station, owned by the Rassemblement National des Bucherons, Gabon's largest opposition party, believed the government was responsible. The interference subsided for a brief period preceding the December 5 elections and resumed immediately thereafter.

SEPTEMBER 9
All Media, Censored
The prime minister and communications minister announced the rigorous application of a 1960 press code that effectively banned the publication of all but a handful of newspapers. Independent journalists banded together to produce *Le Bâillon Dechiré: The Voice of the Silenced Press*, a satirical underground publication that decried the restrictive press law and the government. On October 7, President Bongo issued a comprehensive press decree that contained several unconstitutional provisions, including requirements that newspapers submit copy to government authorities before publication and register as commercial entities. Rejected by the Constitutional Court, the controversial articles were deleted when the National Assembly voted the decree into law. The final form of the law remains unclear.

SEPTEMBER 23
Richard Memiaghe, *Le Scorpion*, Legal Action
Brice Levigot, *Le Scorpion*, Legal Action
Memiaghe and Levigot, the director and editor, respectively, of *Le Scorpion*, one of the banned newspapers, were fined and received a two-month suspended sentence for defaming the president's family in an unflattering article following the death of President Bongo's daughter in May. The case is currently being appealed.

DECEMBER 16
Radio Fréquence Libre, Attacked
Ten men in army fatigues and face masks broke into the headquarters of *Radio Fréquence Libre*, an independent station that had been on the air for little over a month. Security guards were tied up, the radio's office was ransacked and acid was poured over equipment. The station has not resumed broadcasting.

Kenya

President Daniel arap Moi employed a strategy of economic warfare and ongoing harassment against the independent press, forcing several publications to suspend operations temporarily, and driving at least one out of business. Police raided printing houses, impounded equipment, and confiscated publications from news vendors and distributors. Authorities continued to arrest journalists and publishers on sedition charges. Lengthy legal proceedings have crippled them financially. Coverage of ongoing violence in the Rift Valley, widely believed to be government instigated, was restricted. At least one editor was arrested for attempting to go to the area. The government refused to license private radio stations, maintaining its monopoly on both television and radio, Kenyans' primary news source. The KANU-controlled *Kenya Television Network* bowed to government pressure and stopped broadcasting news in March. Although Western donors cut off aid in

(continued on page 68)

Kenya's Shackled Press

by Suzanne Hopkins

Many foreigners still imagine Kenya to be Africa's land of milk and honey, but President Daniel arap Moi's mark, at least in terms of the press, is closer to guardian of failing dictatorship than overseer of Africa's success story.

The ruling party, the Kenyan African National Union (KANU), legitimized by elections last December, has mouthed change about its dismal human rights record. But behind the scenes, President Moi's government continues its blatant disrespect for freedom of expression.

Police have impounded weekly magazines and newspapers from vendors, distributors, and printers. Reporters have been attacked, threatened, and jailed. Opposition newspapers cannot get businesses to advertise because they are afraid to be associated with criticism of the president's rule. And printers, intimidated by government repression, won't take on jobs for the weeklies.

In one of the more publicized cases this year, police completely dismantled one printing operation. In addition, the government, together with a judiciary clearly not independent of KANU, is handing out sedition charges without inhibition.

"The problem here is that we have, to a very large extent, developed a police state," said Blamuel Njururi, editor in chief of the Nairobi *Weekly Observer*, one of a number of weekly newspapers that has cropped up in Kenya in the last several years. "Police informers are in every aspect of Kenyan life. You've got them in almost every newspaper," he said.

As in many African countries that struggle with the legacy of colonialism, part of the problem is lack of a culture of democracy. Legislative or electoral mechanisms don't necessarily translate into civil liberties. Without the guarantees of freedom of expression and association that allow for an effective opposition, as in Kenya, any talk of democracy is deceptive. The daily press, generally considered to be less bold in its analysis of government woes, has not been immune to government repression, but it is the weeklies that bear the brunt. And that has put many editors and publishers in court facing sedition charges.

"Sedition laws still exist which say the journalism profession shouldn't cause disaffection within the government," said Mitch Odero, deputy editor of *The Standard*, one of Kenya's main daily newspapers. "The media, which interprets a multiparty system as checks and balances therefore, go all out with criticism. Then that amounts to causing disaffection against the government and has landed many editors in court."

This has meant extra-legal methods of repression as well as detentions and lawsuits. In 1992, at least 16 reporters were detained and more than 100,000 magazines were confiscated. The office of one magazine was firebombed, becoming the first incident of an arson attack against a publication in Kenya. In 1993, attacks on the press have continued unabated.

On August 1, armed police raided the printing operation Colourprint, confiscated magazines, beat up a watchman, and threatened another employee that they would "spray him with bullets" if he didn't hand over artwork.

When *Daily Nation* reporter Ken Opala arrived to cover the story, police told him to "disappear with that pen immediately or we [will] come for you. You have no business being here."

Colourprint is not the only printing business police have harassed. In one of the more publicized cases this year, Dominic Martin's Fotoform Press, printer of *Society*, *Finance*, and *The People*, was raided at the end of April. Armed police forcibly entered the premises, confiscated equipment, and rewired machines, warning staff that any attempt to restart the presses would land them in coffins.

A recent ruling failed to return impounded equipment and delayed decision on the issue of legality of the raid until sedition charges against Martin and *Finance's* Editor Njehu Gatabaki were brought before the court. The judge ruled that returning the equipment might "prejudice" the sedition case. This delay was part of the government's strategy of financial warfare—silencing the press by running up expenses of publishers and editors who spend their time racing back and forth to court. According to a recent report by Maina Kiai, a Harvard-educated lawyer and executive director of the Kenyan Human Rights Commission, this has cost independent magazines close to $150,000 in lost issues, not to mention the losses incurred in suspending publication. Although the sedition charges were dropped, *Finance* was eventually forced to close.

In the case against *Society*, the government filed sedition charges last year in Mombasa—310 miles from Nairobi. *Society's* editors, Pius and Loyce Nyamora, and their staff were detained for five days in filthy prison cells. After their release, they had to travel to Mombasa every two weeks for more than a year to appear in court. Finally, the sedition charges were dropped. But the ordeal cost them dearly.

As far as prospects for the future, the Nyamoras and others are worried that without alternative sources of news, democracy is doomed. "That is what is going to kill freedom of the press in Kenya because most of us will not see the use to fighting for democracy when we are suffering," said Nyamora.

Suzanne Hopkins, *a freelance writer, worked for the Committeee to Protect Journalists in Zimbabwe, South Africa, and Kenya during the summer of 1993. A copy of this article appeared in the **Christian Science Monitor** on September 30, 1993.*

SPECIAL REPORT: Kenya

1991 to pressure President Moi to enact democratic reforms, they resumed funding at the end of 1993, diminishing prospects for improved press freedom.

FEBRUARY 2
Njehu Gatabaki, *Finance*, Legal Action
Plainclothes policemen seized Gatabaki, editor and publisher of an outspoken independent magazine, outside the Nairobi Chief Magistrate's Court. He was charged with sedition in connection to an editorial critical of the election process and an article, published in *Finance's* January 31 issue, entitled "Moi and Family Has KSh 150 Billion Abroad," and detained for 23 days. Though the state withdrew the charges in October, under Section 87(a) of the Criminal Procedure Code which allows police to reinstate charges at any time.

FEBRUARY 13
The People, Censored
Police confiscated issues of *The People* magazine and detained two of its distributors. They were released the next day.

FEBRUARY 16
Reverend Jamlick Miano, *Watchman*, Imprisoned, Legal Action
Peter Ndekei Kihumba, *Watchman*, Imprisoned, Legal Action
Police detained Miano, the editor of *Watchman* magazine, and his editorial assistant Kihumba, and charged them with seven counts of sedition. The charges concerned several articles critical of President Daniel arap Moi. On February 13 and 14 issues, police seized copies of the magazine, detained two news vendors and confiscated artwork and plates from the magazine's printer, Lengo Press. In late June, the government withdrew 1992 sedition charges against Miano.

FEBRUARY 23
Society, Censored
Plainclothes policemen confiscated copies of the February 22 and March 1 issues of *Society* magazine from Nairobi streets, according to news vendors. No explanation was given.

APRIL 8
Musyoka wa Kyendo, *Finance*, Attacked
Finance, Attacked, Harassed
David Njau, *Finance*, Attacked
Several men forced their way into *Finance's* offices. They smashed equipment and furniture, stabbed editor wa Kyendo and beat Njau, the computer and production manager. They also stole artwork and KSh 250,000. A source considered reliable by *Finance* staff reported that the assailants were members of state security forces.

APRIL 28
Fotoform, Attacked
Finance, Harassed
A contingent of plainclothes and uniformed police officers stormed Fotoform's printing plant in Nairobi and seized 30,000 copies of *Finance* magazine. Police gave no explanation and did not present a warrant. However, the raid appeared to be in response to an article critizing the government entitled "Moi's 100 Days."

APRIL 30
Fotoform, Attacked, Harassed
Dominic Martin, Fotoform, Legal Action
Police officers accompanied by an electrical technician raided the premises of Fotoform and, without a warrant, removed machine parts, completely disabling its operations. Fotoform printed leading independent magazines critical of the government, including *Finance*, *Society* and *The Economic Review*. The owner of Fotoform, Dominic Martin, was eventually charged with publishing seditious material. Charges were later withdrawn. On July 22, the High Court ruled against a request to

prevent further government interference and refused to order the release of Fotoform's machine parts. The plaintiffs appealed. As a result of the raid, *Society* stopped publishing for more than two months; *Finance* was later forced to cease publication.

JUNE 14

Njehu Gatabaki, *Finance*, Imprisoned, Legal Action

Plainclothes police arrested Gatabaki, publisher of *Finance*, outside the Chief Magistrate's Court in Nairobi where he had gone to request the release of his passport to attend the United Nations human rights conference in Vienna. The court rejected his request. That same afternoon the government charged Gatabaki with sedition in connection with the article entitled "Moi's 100 Days." He was held in Nairobi Remand Prison and released on bail three days later. The state withdrew charges in October, under Section 87(a) of the Criminal Procedure Code.

AUGUST 1

Colourprint, Attacked

Society, Censored

Finance, Harassed, Censored

The Economic Review, Censored

Ken Opala, *Daily Nation*, Harassed

A group of at least 35 armed police officers forcibly entered the printing house Colourprint and confiscated 20,000 copies of *Finance* as well as its artwork and negatives. They seized 100 copies of *Society* magazine and two covers of *The Economic Review*. Bushan Sanju, the son of Colourprint's Chairman, was detained for 10 hours and warned that if Colourprint continued printing the magazines, their press would be dismantled. Police beat Colourprint's watchman, Edo Hussein, and threatened another employee that they would "spray him with bullets" unless he handed over the plates for *Finance*. When *Daily Nation* reporter Ken Opala

arrived to cover the story, police warned him to "disappear with that pen immediately or we [will] come for you. You have no business being here."

SEPTEMBER 10

Bedan Mbugua, *The People*, Imprisoned, Legal Action

Government authorities arrested Mbugua, editor of the weekly newspaper *The People*, near Elburgon while he and two clergymen were en route to Molo, the site of the worst ethnic violence since independence. The government declared the area a "security zone" and forbade journalists to investigate the allegedly government-instigated violence. Mbugua and the ministers were charged with organizing an illegal procession and going to a "security zone." Authorities denied all three access to lawyers until September 13, when they were released on bail. Mbugua and the ministers have had to travel to Nakuru every month to appear in court. The government continues to delay the case.

Liberia

The Liberian press, like the country itself, remained paralyzed by war between the West African peacekeeping forces and rebel groups. The fighting stabilized following the signing of a new peace accord in June, but was reinvigorated by the emergence of a new armed faction in September. Recently established independent newspapers collapsed from financial difficulties brought on by the four-year civil war. New press laws and public statements by the interim government and rebel leaders warned the remaining publications to be responsible, and the government declared that all "war-related"

stories must be submitted for clearance. Under pressure from the national press union, the declaration was revoked and mutually acceptable guidelines for war coverage were issued. Although Decree 88A, a law promulgated by Samuel Doe which criminalized criticism of the government was repealed, a similarly restrictive law remains on the books.

FEBRUARY 8
John Vambo, *BBC,* Attacked
Two Nigerian soldiers with the Economic Community Cease-Fire Monitoring Group (ECOMOG) assaulted Vambo, a contributor to local papers and a stringer for the *BBC,* in Monrovia after a taxi overtook his car. The soldiers threatened him, denigrated his reporting, and shot at his tires as he attempted to get away. One accused him of "trying to destroy us." When Vambo flashed his press card, the soldiers grabbed it and beat him with a rifle butt, severely injuring his eye. Civilians eventually intervened and accompanied Vambo to a hospital. He believed the soldiers targeted him in retaliation for a *BBC* report on January 12 that the soldiers may have viewed as both inaccurate and critical of the peacekeeping force.

JUNE 1
All Media, Censored
Minister of Information Lamini Waritay announced that all war-related news would have to be submitted to the information and justice ministries before publication or dissemination. The government complained that some news coverage of the war had jeopardized the effectiveness of security forces. On June 5, following objections from the Press Union of Liberia, the government and the union released mutually acceptable guidelines for coverage of the country's armed conflict.

JULY 12
Gabriel Williams, *The Inquirer,* Harassed
A group claiming sympathy with the United Liberation Movement for Democracy in Liberia (ULIMO) threatened the life of Williams, Managing Editor of *The Inquirer,* apparently for activities unfavorable to ULIMO. A letter delivered to the newspaper's offices said Williams's days would "be numbered" if he did not halt his "anti-ULIMO" activities. Williams had indicated at a meeting of the Press Union of Liberia and on a *BBC* interview that ULIMO was obstructing the peace process by refusing to turn over territory in western Liberia to ECOMOG and the interim government. He also said on the *BBC* broadcast that both Charles Taylor's National Patriotic Front of Liberia and ULIMO shared responsibility for atrocities committed in Lofa County.

Madagascar

The media in Madagascar flourished after 18-years of military rule gave way to democracy. Nevertheless journalists remained fearful that expressing themselves too freely would result in retaliation by the new government. Two journalists were taken to court for articles they wrote; one spent nearly a month in jail for libeling a former public official. Through the violence-plagued transition from Lt. Commander Didier Ratsiraka to the current administration of President Albert Zafy, journalists freely criticized both the government and the opposition. In one instance, they published complaints about a statement made by the minister of culture warning them not to investigate property owned by government officials.

The state radio-television network continued to air reports on public policy subjects; however, they were urged to run more eulogistic coverage of the president's public appearances. Five independent radio stations tackled political subjects, occasionally criticizing the government. While the new constitution guarantees the right to freedom of expression, communication, and the press, most Malagasy journalists remain afraid to use their real names, pursue investigative stories or cite sources for fear of government retaliation.

OCTOBER

Yvonne Razanamazy, Imprisoned, Legal Action
A former public official filed a libel suit against freelance journalist Razanamazy for an article that appeared in the independent daily *Midi-Madagascar*. Razanamazy was arrested in late October and was promptly tried, convicted of libel, sentenced to one month in prison, and fined 100,000 FMG. The decision was appealed. Razanamazy remained in custody until late November.

NOVEMBER

Victor Otonia, *Madagascar Tribune*, Harassed, Imprisoned
Otonia, a regional correspondent for an independent daily, was summoned by a regional court and ordered to reveal his sources for an article that accused local officials of colluding with cattle thieves. He was detained overnight. The case is pending.

Malawi

In the June 14 national referendum, Malawians rejected the authoritarian rule of Life President Dr. H. Kamuzu Banda, calling for an end to the one-party state.

The advent of multiparty democracy gave birth to an aggressively independent press. Although the media faced restrictions prior to the referendum, including detention, censorship and banning, more than 20 independent publications appeared, breaking the culture of silence that dominated Malawi for decades. A shortage of independent printing presses was an ongoing problem. While the *Malawi Broadcasting Corporation* remained under state control, a panel was established to ensure fair coverage and equal access leading up to elections scheduled for May 1994. There is no private or state television in Malawi. Although the parliament has repealed some restrictive press laws, transitional reforms are incomplete and repressive laws remain on the books. Carrying information "harmful to the good name of Malawi" is still prohibited.

JANUARY 2

Felix Mponda, *New Express*, Imprisoned
Police arrested Mponda, cofounder of *New Express*, at Lilongwe airport as he returned from Zambia, where the first issue of the paper had been published. The cover story criticized the Malawian government's treatment of Martin Machipisa Munthali, Malawi's longest-serving political prisoner. It also condemned the government for sentencing Chakufwa Chihana, a trade union official, to two years in prison for sedition. Mponda was charged with importing an unauthorized newspaper and possessing several thousand copies of *Nkhani za ku Malawi*, the party newspaper of the opposition Alliance for Democracy (AFORD). He was released after 14 days in detention. All charges were dropped.

MARCH-APRIL
Weekly Mail, Censored
The Guardian Weekly, Censored
At least four issues of the *Weekly Mail* and
The Guardian Weekly, two South African newspapers, were censored by the Malawian government. Authorities held up shipments of the
paper for several days, while articles pertaining
to Malawi were removed. The weeklies were
distributed to news vendors with holes where
the items had been. The newspapers were told
that any story critical of Malawi's Life President
Ngwazi Dr. H. Kamuzu Banda, the official
hostess M. Kadzamira, or any cabinet minister,
was considered "undesirable for readership"
in Malawi.

MARCH 18
UDF News, Censored
Malawi Democrat, Censored
The government banned *UDF News* and the
Malawi Democrat, respectively owned by the
opposition United Democratic Front and the
Alliance for Democracy (AFORD), on March
18 or 19. About one week later, the High Court
ruled that the ban was unlawful and the newspa-
pers were allowed to circulate.

JUNE 5
The Independent, Harassed
The son of Janet Karim, editor of *The
Independent*, was driving away from Montfort
Press, where he had gone to pick up a new issue
of the newspaper, when he saw a group of men
blocking the road. As he tried to pass them,
an oncoming car forced him into a ditch.
Guards from Montfort Press heard the crash
and rushed to the scene, but by the time they
arrived, the assailants had fled. Karim believes
that the incident was meant as a threat; she later
reported receiving threatening phone calls.

Mali

In a remarkably smooth transition from a military, one-party authoritarian regime, Alpha Oumar Konare took office as Mali's first democratically elected president in June 1992. In the first year of his presi-dency, the press enjoyed a short reprieve from attack and a rapidly expanding inde-pendent press evolved. The circulation of small independent papers is believed to have overtaken that of the official press. Mali has also proved to be one of the most progressive countries in West Africa in independent broadcasting. More than 13 private and community radio stations exist.

By mid-1993, however, the new presi-dent faced mounting pressure from dissat-isfied supporters who had helped him win the election. The press suffered from his increasing insecurity. In reaction to protests by university students, the gov-ernment issued a public statement accus-ing the media, particularly radio, of fomenting backlash against the govern-ment. A new press law was passed, carrying stiff penalties for the slander of government officials, heads of state and foreign diplomats. Several journalists have already been prosecuted under the new law, prompting a call by media organi-zations and government officials for the National Assembly to conduct a review of all press laws.

MARCH 3
Adama Traore, *Les Échos*, Legal Action
Boubacar Sangare, *Les Échos*, Legal Action
Traore and Sangare, journalists at the pro-government newspaper *Les Échos*, were convicted
of libel and sentenced to three years in prison
for an article that questioned the competence
of a medicine chief in Koulikoro. The case was
appealed and the sentence was later revoked.

APRIL 5
Jamana, Attacked
Les Échos, Attacked
Siaka Diarra, *Radio Kayira*, Threatened
Almamy Toure, *Radio Liberté*, Threatened
In early April, the government accused certain political leaders and media of "calling for civil disobedience, a rebellion of the armed forces, and inciting and justifying the use of violence." These accusations refer to acts of violence that took place in Bamako on April 5, mainly perpetrated by university students who set fire to the offices of the ruling party and the homes of the secretary-general and education minister. That same day, *Radio Kayira* and *Radio Liberté* broadcast a communiqué from the Association of Students and Pupils of Mali (AEEM) that criticized the government for mismanaging the education crisis. Students ran through the city pillaging and destroying "everything that represented the state" including the Jamana printing cooperative and the offices of *Les Échos* newspaper, which were managed by Alpha Konare until he was elected president in 1992. Following these events, Siaka Diarra, program director at *Radio Kayira*, was questioned by police while Almamy Toure, director of *Radio Liberté*, was interrogated on three different occasions in relation to the AEEM communiqué. Both stations subsequently began receiving anonymous threats.

JULY
Boubacar Kaïta, *La Roue*, Legal Action
Kaita was fined for libeling the governor of Bamako for an article published in *La Roue*, an independent newspaper, which criticized him for allegedly expropriating land from a private citizen.

OCTOBER 25
Toumani Diallo, *Le Démocrate*, Legal Action
Diallo, editor of *Le Démocrate* as well as *La Nation*, both independent newspapers, received a three-month suspended sentence and fined 150,000 CFA for insulting the institution of the Supreme Court in a July 9 article.

OCTOBER 11
Radio Bandenga, Attacked, Censored
Following a broadcast accusing the military of corruption, a group of government soldiers attacked *Radio Bandenga* in Sikamo, a town 400 kilometers south of Bamako. Although station employees escaped unhurt, the independent station, which had only been operating for a few months, was completely destroyed.

Nigeria

Before resigning in August, military leader General Ibrahim Babangida waged a relentless campaign to silence an increasingly vocal press. In the months leading up to the June presidential elections, culminating an eight-year transition to civilian rule that Badangida manipulated every step of the way, the regime regularly arrested journalists. Police seized thousands of news magazines that criticized the regime and the transition process, and often harassed and detained news vendors for carrying them. Early in the year, security forces closed down the outspoken newspaper *The Reporter*. In May, Babangida promulgated the Treason and Treasonable Offenses Decree, which made any statement deemed disruptive to the "general fabric of the country or any part of it" punishable by death. The decree was later "set aside." Attacks on the press intensified amid popular outcry over the annulment of the June elections, widely believed to have been won by Moshood Abiola. Publications either owned by Abiola or based in the southwest, where

Abiola's Social Democratic Party enjoyed wide-spread support, were first forcibly closed then formally suspended. Two young magazines, *Tell* and *The News*, paid a price for predicting what *The Reporter* termed earlier in the year "Nigeria's Prevailing Mess." *The News* was banned and its editors declared wanted by the police. *Tell* suffered constant harassment, raids and arrests. When Babangida stepped down in August, he installed his hand-picked successor, Ernest Shonekan, to head an Interim National Government. Although arrests abated, Shonekan did not repeal the repressive decrees, and the media houses remained closed. In Nigeria's seventh coup d'état in 33 years of independence, the military forced Shonekan to resign in November. Upon seizing power, General Sani Abacha abolished all democratic institutions. Although he allowed banned publications to reopen, he warned the press to be careful about what it published.

MARCH 1

The Reporter, Censored

Mallam Aliyu Hayatu, *The Reporter*, Imprisoned, Legal Action

In an act of harassment against the independent press, State Security Service (SSS) officers and police closed down *The Reporter*, a newspaper in Kaduna; occupied the premises; and arrested Hayatu, the newspaper's editor. He was formally charged with sedition and accused of inciting disaffection against the government with a March 1 editorial titled "Nigeria's Prevailing Mess—Babangida to Blame?" Scores of journalists turned out at the magistrate's court hearing in Abuja in a show of support. Hayatu was released after 17 days in detention. One month later, the government formally banned the paper. It has not resumed publication.

MARCH 3

Martin Oloja, *Newsday,* Imprisoned

Bukar Zarma, *Newsday,* Imprisoned

Oloja, the editor of *Newsday*, and Zarma, the newspaper's editor-in-chief, were detained because of an article titled "IBB Campaign Kicks Off" that implied that General Ibrahim Babangida was promoting a billboard campaign in Abuja that called for four more years of military rule under his control. The government denied having any connection to the campaign. Oloja was released the same day and Zarma was held overnight.

MARCH 12

Bayo Onanuga, *The News*, Imprisoned, Legal Action

Dapo Olorunyomi, *The News*, Imprisoned, Legal Action

Akin Adesokan, *The News*, Imprisoned, Legal Action

Seyi Kehinde, *The News*, Imprisoned, Legal Action

Chiedu Ezeanah, *The News*, Imprisoned, Legal Action

Justice Moshood Olugbani issued an order for five members of *The News* to report to court after the newly-founded weekly magazine published a story about legal proceedings against the civilian head of the National Electoral Commission titled "Dirty Humphrey—NEC Boss in Deep Scandal." Four of the journalists who appeared in court—Onanuga, editor-in-chief; Olorunyumi, deputy editor; Kehinde, editor; and staff writer Adesokan—were detained. Ezeanah, a correspondent in Port-Harcourt, Rivers State, was unable to appear. Judge Olugbani initially did not allow arguments in their defense to be heard and set prohibitively high bail which was later increased. The journalists remained in detention for close to a week until they could meet bail. Several sources suggest that Olugbani may have been biased in the matter since *The News* had previously ignored a request by his office not to publish an interview with him. The interview raised questions about the independence of the judiciary in Nigeria, causing embarrassment to the government.

MARCH 21
The News, Attacked, Censored
Thirty armed security officials raided the offices of *The News*, seizing 30,000 copies of the week's edition which featured an interview with former Minister of Defense Domkat Bali, and later impounded more than 150,000 copies of four different editions. On May 22, State Security Service (SSS) agents and police stormed the premises of the Lagos printers, Academy Press, confiscating more copies of the magazine before forcibly closing *The News's* offices. SSS officials continued to occupy the magazine's headquarters for several months, despite a Lagos High Court injunction in late May ordering them to withdraw. The government formally proscribed the weekly in late June and declared its editors wanted by police. Despite constant threat *The News's* staff continued to publish from hiding and the magazine appeared under the title *Tempo* for several months. Security officials regularly seized copies from the newsstands.

APRIL 1
McNezer Fasehun, *Prime People*, Imprisoned
Jide Shofowora, *Prime People*, Imprisoned
Olumide Orojimi, *Prime People*, Imprisoned
Police arrested Fasehun, editor of *Prime People* magazine, and two journalists, Shofowora and Orojimi, for publishing an embarrassing story about a police officer's wife. All three were held for several days without charge.

APRIL 1
Innocent Okoye, *Daily Satellite*, Imprisoned
Security officials arrested Okoye, editor of the *Daily Satellite*, for a story on the alleged removal of government subsidies on petroleum products. Okoye was held without charge for three weeks.

APRIL 6
Chris Okolie, *Newbreed*, Imprisoned
Iro Ibe, *Newbreed*, Imprisoned
Omotara Idowu, *Newbreed*, Imprisoned
Chijoke Aguiyi, *Newbreed*, Imprisoned
Okolie, editor-in-chief of *Newbreed*, was arrested along with staff members Ibe, the assistant editor, Idowu, the circulation manager, and Aguiyi, a reporter. Ibe, Idowu, and Aguiyi were briefly detained; Okolie was held incommunicado for more than two weeks. He was eventually charged with "publishing false and malicious information," "attempting to incite disaffection against the government," and "causing hatred among classes of people with the intention to endanger public peace." According to authorities, the charges relate to an article published in an April edition of *Newbreed* alleging that General Ibrahim Babangida and other prominent political and religious leaders were members of the Reformed Ogboni Fraternity. Other sources suggest, however, that the arrests concerned an article *Newbreed* proposed to publish, which would have revealed new information about the murder of Dele Giwa, the founding editor of *Newswatch* magazine who was assassinated by a parcel bomb in 1986. On May 12, Okolie was rearrested by agents of the Federal Intelligence and Investigation Bureau and flown to Abuja where he was again detained for several weeks. Okolie was eventually released, although the charges against him have not been formally dropped.

APRIL 26

Tell, Harassed, Censored

Tell, Nigeria's largest-circulating weekly newsmagazine, came under fire after publishing an interview in the April 26 edition with former head of state General Olusegun Obasanjo which criticized Babangida's reluctance to hand over power. Beginning in April, more than 300,000 copies of six different issues of *Tell* magazine were impounded by security officials. Police seized entire print runs directly from Academy Press and confiscated issues from the *Tell* office or directly from news vendors, many of whom were harassed, beaten, and even arrested for carrying the magazine. By August, repeated confiscations forced the magazine to print underground for several weeks.

APRIL 29

Concord, Attacked

Nsikak Essien, *Concord*, Imprisoned
Akin Ogunrinde, *Concord*, Imprisoned
Ben Okezie, *Concord*, Imprisoned
Titi Okorie, *Concord*, Imprisoned
Isiaka Aliyu, *Concord*, Imprisoned
Thomas Adejo, *Concord*, Imprisoned
Rosemary Kadiri, *Concord*, Imprisoned
Jubril Miachi, *Concord*, Imprisoned

In a sudden sweep, police raided the offices of *The Concord Group*, searching the premises and arresting editors and staff. Essien, Ogunrinde, Okezie, and Okorie were held in Lagos while Aliyu, Adejo, Kadiri, and Miachi were arrested at the paper's office in Kaduna. They were briefly detained and released. No reason was given for the raid. *The Concord Group*, owned by presidential candidate Moshood Abiola, is Nigeria's largest media house.

MAY 3

Tell, Attacked

Ayodele Akinkuotu, *Tell*, Imprisoned
Dayo Omotoso, *Tell*, Imprisoned
Paul Akhalu, *Tell*, Imprisoned

SSS officers, searching for *Tell's* editors, invaded the office and sealed off the premises for several hours while police ransacked the office, ostensibly looking for copies of the May 2 edition. The entire print run and plates for the week's edition had been seized from the printer the previous day. Police arrested three staff members in lieu of the editors they were looking for: Ayodele Akinkuoto, senior associate editor; Dayo Omotoso, assistant editor; and Paul Akhalu, chief photographer. All three were released five hours later. The following week, SSS officials ransacked *Tell's* offices again, despite Justice Fatai Adeyinka's May 5 injunction restraining the SSS and the Attorney General from harassing, intimidating, and arresting the publication's editors and staff.

MAY 6

All Media, Legal Action

General Babangida promulgated the Treasonable Offenses Decree, which stated that anyone judged disruptive of "the general fabric of the country or any part of it," in speech or writing, is liable to be sentenced to death. Three weeks later, under domestic and international pressure, the government announced it would "set aside" the decree. At least three other censorship laws still remain on the books.

JUNE

All Media, Legal Action

The Federal government promulgated the broadly worded Offensive Publications Decree No. 35 which empowered it to ban or seize any publication containing articles likely to disrupt the transition to democracy.

JUNE 13

All Media, Legal Action

The news media were banned from publishing partial results of the June 12 presidential elections. Tonnie Iredia, the spokesman of the National Electoral Commission, explained that the ban was necessary "to be sure that nobody announced different versions of the results that can create chaos and anarchy."

JUNE 21
Yinka Tella, *The News,* Imprisoned
Tella, Abuja bureau chief of *The News,* was arrested following the proscription of the magazine. He was held without charge for two months, in what many felt was an attempt by police to coerce the editors of *The News* to turn themselves in.

JUNE 28
Rasak El-Alewa, *The Herald,* Imprisoned
R.K. Yusuf, *The Herald,* Imprisoned
Chief Afolayan, *The Herald,* Imprisoned
Measures against the press extended to government-controlled media when El-Alewa, editor of *The Herald* newspaper based in Kwara State, Yusuf, its general manager, and Afolayan, the chief executive, were arrested in connection with an article on the military government's transition program. They were detained for several days without charges. No reason was given for their arrest.

JUNE 29
Dapo Olorunyomi, *The News,* Harrassed
SSS officers went to arrest Olorunyomi, deputy editor-in-chief of *The News,* at his home. Finding him gone, they took his wife and three-month-old baby instead. They were released within 24 hours when the child became ill.

JULY 16
Bala Dan Abu, *Quality,* Imprisoned
Ade Alawola, *Quality,* Imprisoned
Academy Printers, Attacked
Quality, Harassed
Abu and Alawola, editor and assistant editor, respectively, of *Quality* magazine, were arrested by security agents and detained for two days without charge in connection with a story pub-

lished in the previous week's edition. The article alleged that the daughter of General Babangida was having an affair with the son of opposition candidate, Abiola. Previously, on July 10, police raided Academy Printers and impounded copies of the magazine.

JULY 22
National Concord, Censored
African Concord, Censored
The Sketch, Censored
The Punch, Censored
Abuja Newsday, Censored
Ogun State Broadcasting Corporation (OGBC), Censored
Armed security agents closed *OGBC* for a day and, over the course of two days, occupied the offices of six newspapers, shutting them down. A retroactive decree was later promulgated to formally ban these and all other publications owned by four media houses. The papers remained closed for five months.

JULY 23
Emman Udoka, *The Nigerian Observer,* Imprisoned
Stanley Oppah, *The Nigerian Observer,* Imprisoned
The Nigerian Observer, Censored
The Nigerian Observer, an *Edo* state-run newspaper, published by Bendel Newspaper Corporation, was the sixth publication to be closed down as part of the federal government's sweep. Udoka and Oppah were arrested, held without charge, and released a few days later.

JULY 31
Dele Momodu, *Fame,* Imprisoned
Columnist and contributing editor Momodu was arrested by security agents in Lagos and detained for a week. An outspoken supporter of opposition candidate Abiola,his arrest was probably in reaction to several articles he wrote that vehemently opposed Babangida's annulment of the June 12 presidential elections.

AUGUST 15

Nosa Igiebor, *Tell,* Imprisoned
Onome Ofifo Whisky, *Tell,* Imprisoned
Kolawole Ilori, *Tell,* Imprisoned
Ayodele Akinkuotu, *Tell,* Imprisoned
Tell, Harassed, Attacked
Eighteen armed SSS operatives and police
stormed the offices of *Tell,* broke doors and
windows, ransacked desks, seized documents,
and roughed up reporters. They arrested four
of the magazine's editors: Nosa Igiebor,
editor-in-chief; Onome Ofifo Whisky, managing editor; Kolawole Ilori, executive editor;
and Ayodele Akinkuotu, senior associate editor.
Police confiscated various documents, as well as
copies of two previous editions of the magazine,
featuring stories titled, "Stolen Presidency—
IBB Wages Wars on the Nation" and "Nigeria:
Waiting for the Worst." The *Tell* editors were
taken to Abuja and charged with possession
of secret documents. They were granted bail
on August 27, the day after General Babangida
relinquished power. Charges were later
dropped.

AUGUST 16

All Media, Legal Action
In a bid to regulate the independent press,
the Federal government announced the
Newspapers Decree No. 43 of 1993 by which
all existing and new newspapers were subject
to annual registration guidelines, retroactively
to June 22. The guidelines required payment
of fees totaling $10,000 and approval by a
Newspaper Registration Board, whose chairman would be appointed by the president.
The decree set harsh prison terms and fines
for circulation of unregistered newspapers
and the publication of false statements. It also
demanded that each publication display the
names and addresses of its owners, publishers,
and printers. The decree effectively prohibited
banned publications from appearing under dif-

ferent titles. At the time, *The News* was appearing under the title *Tempo* and *Punch* was publishing *Toplife,* a weekly tabloid. On November
19, a Lagos State High Court declared the
decree unconstitutional.

AUGUST 16

The Concord Group, Censored
Punch Newspapers Ltd., Censored
Sketch Press Ltd., Censored
Bendel Newspaper Corp., Censored
The federal government announced the pro-
mulgation of Newspapers Decree No. 48
(Proscription and Prohibition from Circulation)
of 1993. Retroactive to July 22, it banned all
publications that were closed in the July 22 raid
with the exception of *Abuja Newsday.* The list
was comprised of newspapers either owned by
Moshood Abiola, such as *The Concord Group,* or
based in southwestern Nigeria where local governments were controlled by Abiola's Social
Democratic Party. The premises of these publications were occupied by security forces for
188 days. General Sanni Abacha reversed the
proscriptions the day after he seized power
on November 17.

AUGUST 19

Idowu Awoyinfa, *Tell,* Attacked, Imprisoned
Ayodele Akinkuotu, *Tell,* Imprisoned
Durosinmi Meseko, *Tell,* Imprisoned
Chuks Onwudinjo, *Tell,* Imprisoned
Tell, Harassed, Attacked
Security officials again raided *Tell* offices and
demanded the whereabouts of remaining editors and the magazine's printing press. When
Awoyinfa, *Tell's* librarian, was unable to answer
their questions, police ordered him to the floor
and beat him severely. Awoyinfa was detained
with three other staff members: Akinkuotu,
senior associate editor; Meseko, reporter, and
Onwudinjo, assistant head of graphics. They
were interrogated for several hours and
released. Two days later, police impounded

30,000 copies of *Tell* and arrested two members of *Tell's* marketing staff.

NOVEMBER 15
Sola Odunfa, *BBC,* Attacked
SSS officers went to Odunfa's home and, in his absence, arrested his wife. She was told to produce her husband and detained for several hours. Odunfa is also a contributor to the *Nigerian Tribune,* one of Nigeria's oldest independent newspapers, which was critical of the military-appointed interim government.

Rwanda

The media was able to work more freely this year than in the recent past. For the most part, authorities did not punish private newspapers or their reporters for openly criticizing government policies. One journalist working for the state-controlled television station was shot dead outside his home and another, imprisoned in 1992, remains in custody. It is unclear whether the killing was connected to his work; no arrests have been made. The interim government and the rebel Rwandan Patriotic Front signed a peace accord in August, but it still had not been implemented by year's end. Sporadic violence occurred throughout the country, and reporting in these zones remained dangerous for journalists who might be perceived as sympathizers of either side.

APRIL 6
Callixte Kalissa, *Télévision Rwandaise,* Killed
Kalissa, a television producer with the state-run *Télévision Rwandaise* and a former photographer with the state-run Office Rwandais d'Information, was shot dead near his home in the neighborhood of Remera in Kigali.

According to an eyewitness, his assailant was dressed in a military uniform and was in a vehicle bearing a government license plate. Several days before the attack, Kalissa had found a grenade at the front doorstep of his home. The motive behind his murder remains unknown.

MAY-JUNE
Marcellin Kayiranga, *Kanguka,* Threatened
Kayiranga, an editor with the bimonthly *Kanguka* newspaper, went into hiding after three men in civilian clothing began searching for him. The motive was unclear. The men were believed to be agents of the Center for Criminal Research and Documentation.

MAY 3
Ignace Ruhatana, *Kanyarwanda,* Attacked
Armed men attacked the home of Ruhatana, editor of *Kanyarwanda,* a newsletter published by a Rwandan human rights organization that goes by the same name. They injured Ruhatana in the arm and allegedly attempted to kidnap his sister. The perpetrators seemed to want to steal documents belonging to the newsletter.

JUNE 2
Martin Adler, Freelance, Attacked
Peter Strandberg, Freelance, Attacked
Rwandan Army soldiers fired on Adler and Strandberg, two Swedish freelance journalists, at a checkpoint north of Byumba, situated between army, and rebel-held territory. At the time of the shooting, the reporters were wearing civilian clothing and carrying a white flag and were accompanied by rebel soldiers. The journalists were on assignment for several European print and broadcast media. Neither were wounded, and it is unclear whether the journalists were the intended targets.

Africa

Sierra Leone

The National Provisional Ruling Council (NPRC), comprising a group of young officers who took power in a military coup in April 1992, moved to silence dissenting voices. Finding itself increasingly overwhelmed by economic crisis, rebel insurgencies along the Liberian border, and reports of human rights abuses and official corruption, the NPRC consolidated its power in a series of decrees and public notices. Where there was once a multitude of independent voices—at least 30 weekly papers—there are now only 10 publications, two of which are government controlled. In February, most of Sierra Leone's independent newspapers were suspended for failing to meet restrictive registration guidelines. Over the course of the year, at least nine journalists were arrested; one was beaten. In October, following the publication of an editorial in an independent weekly asking government officials to account for allegations of corruption, authorities quickly jailed anyone remotely connected to the paper and filed sedition charges. This incident had a chilling effect on the remaining independent publications. While NPRC Chairman Valentine Strasser announced the repeal of a repressive press law on the occasion of the NPRC's first anniversary, their commitment to a recently unveiled democratization program remains to be seen.

JANUARY 11
Chernoh Ojuku Sesay, *Pool*, Attacked, Imprisoned

Vice Chairman Solomon Musa summoned Sesay, editor of the *Pool* newspaper, to report to the Criminal Investigations Department. Angered by an article that Sesay reprinted from *West Africa* magazine alleging that Musa recently travelled to Belgium to buy arms, the vice chairman kicked Sesay in the head with his boot, knocking him out for a few seconds. Sesay was taken to Pademba Road Prison and held for several days without charge. The motives for his detention were unclear. In addition to the article concerning armaments, Sesay may have incurred the wrath of the military commander by denouncing, in the January 8 issue of the newspaper, the execution of more than 20 alleged coup plotters in late 1992.

FEBRUARY 8
All Media, Legal Action

In an attempt to silence a vociferous independent press, the National Provisional Ruling Council passed a restrictive press regulation that required all newspapers to meet reregistration guidelines by February 8. Some did; some did not. At least 19 independent newspapers were effectively banned. To date, not one of the papers has been allowed to reregister.

FEBRUARY 15
Pool, Censored

Two armed soldiers entered the office of *Pool*, a Freetown-based independent newspaper, and asked to speak with editor Chernoh Ojuku Sesay. Told that Sesay was out of town, the soldiers ordered the staff to leave and padlocked the office. The office remained closed until Sesay returned two days later. The closure may have been linked to an article that appeared in *Pool* describing Sesay's beating and detention by Vice Chairman Musa. Sesay subsequently issued an apology for the article. The government called a press conference and circulated copies of his letter.

AUGUST 4
New Citizen, Attacked, Harassed
I.B. Kargbo, *New Citizen*, Legal Action

Security officials raided the offices of the *New Citizen* and brought editor I.B. Kargbo to the Criminal Investigations Department for questioning. He was charged with failure to print his name and address in the August 2 issue of *New Citizen*. Under pre-independence law, failure to publish an imprint constitutes a crime punishable by a fine of five pounds, or 4,500 leones, per copy. Kargbo maintains that the imprint did not appear due to a printing error. However, the plates for the August 2 edition were confiscated by the Criminal Investigations Department. The action against the *New Citizen* was widely thought to be linked to an editorial critical of former Attorney General Arnold Gooding, now Secretary of State for Transport and Communication. Charges were dropped several months later.

OCTOBER 13

Dr. Julius Spencer, *The New Breed*, Imprisoned, Legal Action
Donald John, *The New Breed*, Imprisoned, Legal Action
Mohamed Jal-Kamara, *The New Breed*, Imprisoned, Legal Action
Alfred Conteh, *The New Breed*, Imprisoned, Legal Action
Mohamed Bangura, *The New Breed*, Imprisoned, Legal Action
Alusine Kargbo Basiru, Atlantic Printers, Imprisoned, Legal Action

The New Breed, one of the few remaining independent newspapers that has criticized the government, published an editorial entitled "Redeemers or Villains?" It asked the government to account for an article recently published in the Swedish newspaper *Expressen* that alleged that NPRC President Captain Valentine Strasser flew to Antwerp to sell $43 million worth of diamonds. Instead of issuing a rebuttal, the government arrested anyone associated with the paper. They were detained for 10 days before being released on bail. Spencer, the managing editor; John, acting editor; Conteh, business manager; Bangura,

a reporter; and Basiru, their pritner, were charged with 10 counts of sedtion. The paper's proprietor, Alusine Fofanah, named Secretary of State in August, resigned from *The New Breed* and issued a statement disassociating himself from it. Under the Business Registration Act, the paper must register a new proprietor in order to publish. According to the newspaper's staff, they have not been allowed to do so.

NOVEMBER 27

Paul Kamara, *For Di People*, Imprisoned
Salieu Kamara, *For Di People*, Imprisoned
For Di People, Harassed, Attacked

Officials from the Criminal Investigations Department (CID), accompanied by three armed men in uniform, arrested editors Paul Kamara and Salieu Kamara, both of whom are officers of the National League of Human Rights. CID officials searched their offices and residence, confiscating documents, photos, and notebooks. Both were held without charge for three days. According to one report, an official told Paul Kamara that his arrest was related to his work as a journalist.

Somalia

On December 9, 1992, U.S. Marines waded ashore to find themselves blinded by a sea of camera crews and anchormen eager to capture the first moments of Operation Restore Hope. Nine months later, most foreign correspondents had fled. What started as a humanitarian operation and international media event turned into a deadly confrontation when the United Nations took on the task of disarming warring Somali subclans. On June 5, following a weapons search in and around General Farah Aidid's *Radio Mogadishu*, 24 Pakistanis were ambushed and killed.

The UN struck back the following week with a series of aerial assaults, blowing up *Radio Mogadishu,* formerly the *National Radio Network.* The station was accused of broadcasting anti-UN sentiment and was viewed as a flash point for violence. As American troops sought unsuccessfully to hunt down Aidid, journalists became targets of growing resentment. In July, four were stoned and hacked to death by a mob after more than 50 Somalis were killed in an attack on Aidid's headquarters. By late summer, it became impossible for American reporters to walk on the street and dangerous even to drive down "Death Wish Road" to daily news conferences in the UN compound. Major news organizations pulled out foreign correspondents amid threats that Aidid might take Western journalists hostage. Despite the risk, a handful of reporters, primarily freelancers, remained. Both Aidid and Ali Mahdi currently broadcast programs such as the "Voice of the Great Somali People" from mobile radio transmitters. The UN operates its own radio station, *Mantaa,* and publishes a newspaper by the same name. Gunmen killed six Somali distributors of *Mantaa* at the height of the conflict. The UN plans to set up a $2.5 million radio station, *Radio Somalia,* to replace the ruins of *Radio Mogadishu.* Broadcast is scheduled to begin in early 1994.

JANUARY 20
Liu Jiang, *Xinhua,* Attacked
Jiang, head of *Xinhua News Agency's* African regional bureau, was shot in the legs when four unidentified men halted his taxi. As the driver tried to accelerate to get away, the gunmen opened fire on the vehicle. The driver was killed instantly but Jiang and his assistant were able to escape.

JUNE 5
Radio Mogadishu, Attacked
Admiral Jonathan Howe ordered a contingent of Pakistani troops to conduct a weapons search at *Radio Mogadishu,* the former *National Radio Network* controlled by General Mohamed Farah Aidid. Official reports stated that the troops were conducting a routine search of the area, but other reports indicated that the troops opened fire on the station before seizing the studios and transmitters. Aidid's supporters ambushed them and 24 Pakistanis were killed. The United Nations vowed retribution for the attack.

JUNE 12
Radio Mogadishu, Attacked
In the early hours of the morning, U.S. troops led a United Nations attack on *Radio Mogadishu,* striking back for the deaths of the Pakistanis the week before. American AC-130 "Specter" gunships blasted the station, blowing up the building. Kofi Annan, the U.N. undersecretary general in charge of peacekeeping, said that the U.N. forces had begun "a decisive action to restore security in Mogadishu" which would focus on destroying illegal weapons caches and "neutralizing radio broadcasting systems that contribute to the violence and attacks."

JUNE 18
Jean-Claude Jumel, *TF-1,* Killed
Jumel, a French soundman for *TF-1,* was killed by sniper fire when his television crew's vehicle was ambushed on the road between the airport and Mogadishu. He had flown in on assignment moments before.

JULY 12
Hansi Krauss, *Associated Press,* Killed
Hosea Maina, *Reuters,* Killed
Dan Eldon, *Reuters,* Killed
Anthony Macharia, *Reuters,* Killed
Mohamed Shaffi, *Reuters,* Attacked
Four journalists were killed when a crowd,

angered by the death of more than 50 Somalis in an aerial attack on General Mohamed Farah Aidid's command post, set upon them, wielding rocks, clubs, and guns. Hansi Krauss, a German photographer with the *Associated Press;* Hosea Maina, a Kenyan photographer working for *Reuters;* Dan Eldon, an American photographer working for *Reuters* and Anthony Macharia and Mohamed Shaffi, both Kenyan soundmen for *Reuters Television,* had been escorted to the scene of the aerial attack when the crowd turned on them. Shaffi, who had begun filming the carnage while Somalis were searching for their dead and wounded in the wreckage, was roughed up, and shot by gunmen as he fled. He managed to escape when an unknown Somali told him to get in his truck and drove him to El-Sahafi hotel where reporters stay. Shaffi was treated for two bullet wounds and released.

AUGUST 13
Peter Jones, *Associated Press*, Attacked
American journalist Peter Jones, a freelance photographer for *Associated Press,* suffered minor knife wounds when a refugee at a camp outside Mogadishu tried to steal his equipment. Jones's escort fired shots into the air, and the assailant fled. Jones was treated at the Swedish field hospital and released.

SEPTEMBER 10
CNN Drivers, Killed
Five Somalis, hired as drivers by *CNN,* were shot in what began as an attempt to steal their Toyota Land Cruiser, rented by the network. The men stealing the car were from a different subclan from those who had been hired to drive it. A three-hour gun battle ensued outside the El-Sahafi hotel, ending with machine-gun fire from U.S. Blackhawk helicopters.

SEPTEMBER 18
Peter Northall, *Associated Press*, Harassed
Abdelhak Senna, *Agence France Press*, Harassed
A U.S. Blackhawk fired stun grenades on British photographer Northall, on assignment for *Associated Press,* and Moroccan photographer Senna, working for *Agence France Press,* as they photographed U.N. forces in action. Officials said they wanted the journalists out of the area for their own safety. According to Northall, the aircraft continued to fire from 30 or 40 yards away, even after he pointed to his camera to identify himself as a journalist. The blast of one grenade blew out the windows of the journalists' car; no one was injured.

SEPTEMBER 22
Jean-Louis Melin, *France 2*, Attacked
Melin, a soundman for the state-owned *France 2* television network, was shot in the chest five times when his television crew was stopped at a makeshift roadblock outside Mogadishu. Melin survived the assault. His Somali driver was wounded in the shooting, but the other members of the crew escaped unharmed.

NOVEMBER 11
CNN Driver, Killed
A Somali driver working for *CNN* was shot and killed in southern Mogadishu when unidentified gunmen opened fire on a Toyota Land Cruiser rented by the network. There were no *CNN* journalists in the car at the time.

South Africa

In a year of monumental change and sweeping reform, the new South Africa called for a new media. The transition process brought both euphoria and bloodshed. As right-wing resistance to negotiations grew, so did the level of violence. Reporters were literally caught in the cross-fire. *The South African Broadcasting*

Corporation (SABC), long the mouthpiece of apartheid, underwent profound changes. Following months of public hearings and debate over SABC's future, a black woman was chosen to chair its new board of directors. Swelakhe Sisulu, the former editor of the pro-ANC newspaper The New Nation, who was frequently detained in the 1980's for his anti-apartheid reporting, was appointed to a prominent position. The Sowetan, a black newspaper, became the largest circulating daily. Despite guarantees of freedom of expression in the interim constitution, journalists, and black journalists in particular, are concerned that they will come under subtle pressure to, at the very least, delay criticizing the new government.

Laws impinging on press freedom, though rarely enforced, remained on the books. After a reporter was sentenced to one year in prison for refusing to reveal his sources under Section 205 of the Criminal Procedures Act, an amendment was proposed and debated in response to popular outcry; it has yet to pass into law. An Independent Media Commission was established to monitor media coverage, and an Independent Broadcast Authority (IBA) bill was enacted to oversee allocation of frequencies to all broadcasters including the SABC. However, at year's end, the IBA still had not come into force and the issue of licensing proved explosive. The same government which confiscated the transmitter of a left-wing community radio station for broadcasting without a license in the spring, balked at taking action against the armed right-wing Radio Pretoria which refused to shut down when its temporary license expired in December. Clearly, details regarding licensing and legislation remain to be worked out. Meanwhile, a vigorous independent press is bursting at the seams.

JANUARY 10
S'bu Mngadi, City Press, Harassed, Threatened
Members of an alleged protection racket syndicate headed by KwaZulu sergeant Siphiwe Mvuyane repeatedly harassed and threatened City Press Durban Bureau Chief Mngadi after a December 1992 report in the paper on drug trafficking. One member of the alleged syndicate tried to hit Mngadi over the head with a bottle and then, along with about seven other aggressors, threatened him with a gun. Mngadi reported that they said he "deserved to be killed." A few days later, he found his tires slashed. Some of Mvuyane's cohorts threatened another City Press reporter last year.

JANUARY 18
Xoliswa Swarts, Radio Ciskei, Harassed
Zoliswa Sigabi, Radio Ciskei, Harassed
Radio Ciskei suspended Swarts and Sigabi for broadcasting ANC and Transkei government criticism of comments made by Brigadier Oupa Gqozo, military ruler of the Ciskei Homeland, during a press conference at Jan Smuts Airport.

JANUARY 27
Daily Dispatch, Harassed, Attacked
Fifteen members of the Pan Africanist Congress (PAC) forcibly entered and occupied the Umtata offices of the Daily Dispatch, shutting down operations for six days in retaliation for what the PAC said was a news blackout on their activities that amounted to a "campaign of silence." On the first day of the occupation, unknown assailants believed to be linked to the PAC hijacked one of the paper's delivery vans and prevented another from delivering papers. On the second day, Zingisa Mkabile, Transkei PAC Secretary, threatened to "crush" the newspaper and warned vendors and distributors not to sell the paper.

(continued on page 88)

From Government Repression to Endemic Violence

by Eleanor Bedford

Reporting the truth in South Africa has always been difficult. The National Party that has ruled for more than 40 years enacted more than 100 laws curbing the press. While many restrictions still remain on the books, they are rarely enforced. Today, journalists fear violence more than government repression. During a CPJ mission to South Africa in July to investigate the soaring figures—more than 70 journalists were physically harassed, beaten, threatened or shot in the first seven months of the year—and speak with local journalists, everyone agreed that attacks are more likely to come from township youths and opposition parties than government forces. Some attacks are motivated by charges of political bias; others are purely criminal violence.

Reporters who used to write about the evils of apartheid now write critically about anti-apartheid personalities and parties who, until recently, enjoyed their unmitigated support. But as one black reporter said, the struggle against apartheid was also a struggle for a free press. And they're not about to compromise.

Pressure to portray political parties favorably is by no means limited to black political parties. "In the last six months, we've received more death threats than ever before. There are pretty desperate people out there, particularly the far right," said Linda Vermaas, Executive Producer of *MNET's* weekly newsmagazine *Carte Blanche*.

During the June armed take-over of the multi-party negotiation chamber at the World Trade Center in Johannesburg by the right-wing organization AWB, television crews had their camera equipment smashed and electrical cords cut. Reporters were roughed up.

"If you're white the AWB attacks you for being a traitor; if you're black, you're accused of being biased one way or another," a photographer at the *Star* said.

Historic distrust of journalists in South Africa fuels charges of political bias. In extremely volatile situations, journalists are not necessarily seen as impartial observers. In fact, they're considered

85

suspect. On July 6, during the height of the violence in Transvaal townships, Mbuzeni Zulu, a photographer for the *Sowetan*, was kidnapped by members of the Inkatha Freedom Party and accused of being a spy for the ANC. He was held in Kwesini hostel for more than two hours.

"Four hundred angry men couldn't care less that I worked for the *Sowetan*," he declared the following day. "One of their comrades had just been arrested and they wanted their fury released."

By all accounts, photojournalists take the bulk of the abuse. "There is this fear that you'll catch them doing something on film that they could get in trouble for later," several photographers said.

This is not totally unjustified. The South African government has historically used film footage to provide evidence for prosecutions. In fact, in early July, the government obtained a search warrant to obtain copies of the *Weekly Mail's* footage of the AWB invasion of the World Trade Center.

In the escalating criminal violence, cars, cameras, and expensive equipment mark journalists as targets, too. On April 23, *SABC* reporter Calvin Thusago was stabbed to death and cameraman Dudley Saunders was badly wounded when a mob surrounded their car outside of Sharpeville where they had gone to report on the desecration of graves by white fascists.

Three days later, *WTN* cameraman Sam Msibi was shot five times by gunmen in Tokoza township as he travelled from work to his Katlehong home. His car and camera were stolen; Msibi miraculously survived.

"The violence in the townships is different now," Msibi says. "People are well armed...I used to feel it was important to live in the townships, to be near the story. Now, all my friends and contacts in Katlehong have died. I don't think I can stay much longer."

Publicly, every major political party supports a free press. Appeals to supporters to let journalists do their work have had noted success, such as when Thusago and Saunder's assailants were turned over to police by members of the ANC youth league. Yet many reporters told CPJ in July that there was a disparity between the official recognition of the need for open debate and lack of tolerance of criticism at the local level which led to grassroots intimidation. Some called it a lack of understanding of the role of a free press in a democratic society.

Although it remains to be seen to what extent a new government will support a free press, prospects have improved with recent political reforms. Intimidation of journalists has waned as political parties at every level court the press for favorable coverage and media organizations mount campaigns to educate the public about the importance of a free press in sustaining a democracy. At the same time, the new era seems lost on the Afrikaner right-wing, Buthelezi, and the PAC, but by disavowing the press and the public, they may be contributing to their own obsolescence.

The real threat to the press no longer comes from government repression but from the endemic violence. As the international press corps converges on South Africa to cover the elections, more journalists will undoubtedly be caught up in the bloodshed which shows no sign of abating.

Eleanor Bedford *traveled to South Africa in July 1993. A version of this article was published by the **Pacific News Service** on August 2, 1993.*

FEBRUARY 1
Joao Silva, *The Star*, Attacked
Herbert Mabuza, *Sunday Times*, Attacked
Nick Van der Linde, *The Citizen*, Attacked
Steve Hilton-Barber, *Saturday Star*, Attacked
Angry mobs injured four photographers during a violent taxi protest against traffic authorities in Johannesburg. Unidentified protesters hit Silva in the head with a brick, shot Mabuza in the arm, and kicked, beat and robbed Van der Linde. An assailant also hit Hilton-Barber with a tear gas canister.

FEBRUARY 3
David Hendricks, *Daily Dispatch*, Threatened, Imprisoned
Daily Dispatch, Harassed
Two gunmen, claiming affiliation with APLA, the armed wing of the Pan Africanist Congress, briefly abducted delivery van driver Hendricks, as he delivered papers in the Transkei Homeland. After forcing him at gunpoint into the van and driving through Ilitha, they dragged him out and ordered him to light a match to a bundle of newspapers. As Hendricks fumbled to ignite the papers, the gunmen ordered him to leave. They fired two shots at him as he fled and ignited the newspapers and the vehicle.

FEBRUARY 16
Jacques Pauw, *The Sunday Star*, Harassed
Peta Thornycroft, *The Sunday Star*, Harassed
Chief Mangosuthu Buthelezi, leader of the Inkatha Freedom Party (IFP), harassed Pauw and Thornycroft by claiming they had colluded with the National Intelligence Service to prove that Inkatha was smuggling weapons from Mozambique into South Africa. Pauw and Thornycroft had written a story at the end of 1992 indicating that a former IFP official had said in an affidavit that he had smuggled weapons for Inkatha.

MARCH 15
The Star, Attacked
M-NET Television, Attacked
South African police searched the offices of *The Star* and *M-NET Television* for documents pertaining to corruption in the Department of Transport. *Star* reporter Jacques Pauw had written a story on alleged corruption, theft and bribery, and *M-NET* had produced a profile on the official who had uncovered the corruption. A warrant was issued to South African Police in connection with the Protection of Information Act. No documents were confiscated and charges were never filed.

MARCH 24
Journalists, Attacked
A group of student protesters marching through Johannesburg verbally threatened and physically harassed several journalists.

MARCH 28
Ronnie Peters, *Sunday Times*, Threatened
Sunday Times, Harassed
Three gunmen ambushed a *Sunday Times* delivery van, pumping it full of bullets and targeting it with a grenade as it traveled between Durban and East London. The grenade exploded at the roadside and the driver escaped uninjured, though the van sustained damage. During April, the Pan Africanist Congress Transkei Region called a boycott on the *Sunday Times* to protest, the paper's editor said, an editorial that criticized the PAC for failing to condemn the murder of civilians. The editor said it was not known whether the two incidents were related.

MARCH 28
Business Day, Attacked
Armed assailants hijacked a *Business Day* delivery van on the Natal north coast. They stole the truck with 5,000 papers. The paper did not view it as a politically motivated event.

Africa

APRIL 12
Juda Ngwenya, *Reuters*, Attacked
During mass rallies and protests following
the assassination of South African Communist
Party leader Chris Hani, journalists throughout
South Africa faced violent attacks. Outside
the stadium in the East Rand township of
Katlehong, *Reuters* photographer Juda
Ngwenya and other journalists got caught
in the crossfire between police and the crowd.
Angry youths stoned the vehicle of a *Reuters*
television crew and shot at journalists who
attempted to film a burning car.

APRIL 14
Lee Edwards, *BBC*, Attacked
Glen Middleton, *BBC*, Attacked
George Galanakis, *Daily Dispatch*, Attacked
Mkhululi Bolo, *Daily Dispatch*, Attacked
Angry crowds threatened, attacked and harassed
at least two dozen journalists on a national
day of mourning of Chris Hani's death. Among
them were *BBC* soundman Lee Edwards and
cameraman Glen Middleton, who were shot
and wounded when police opened fire on a
crowd of marchers gathered outside the Protea
Police Station in Soweto. In Umtata, during
a rally at the South African Embassy, protesters
stoned George Galanakis and Mkhululi Bolo;
neither was injured. From Durban and
Pietermaritzburg to Cape Town, numerous
others faced intimidation and threats.

APRIL 22
Fred de Lange, *The Citizen*, Attacked
Ilse de Lange, *The Citizen*, Attacked
Nans Gericke, *The Citizen*, Attacked
The Citizen, Harassed
Piet (Skiet) Rudolph, head of the right-wing
Orde Boerevolk, marched in to *The Citizen's*
Pretoria offices and assaulted Bureau Chief de
Lange and his wife Ilse and verbally threatened
and harassed *Citizen* administrative clerk
Gericke. Rudolph apparently attacked de Lange

after he wrote an article making reference
to Rudolph's role in the arrest of Clive
Derby-Lewis, a Conservative Party member,
in connection with Chris Hani's assassination.

APRIL 23
Calvin Thusago, *SABC*, Killed
Dudley Saunders, *SABC*, Attacked
A mob of youths killed Calvin Thusago, a
reporter for the *South African Broadcasting
Corporation*, and seriously injured *SABC* cameraman Dudley Saunders as they returned from
filming the desecration of black graves by
right-wing extremists in Sharpeville. The mob
set upon Thusago and Saunders's vehicle as it
travelled between Sharpeville and Sebokeng.
Thusago got out of the car in an attempt to
reason with the crowd. He was stabbed to
death. Saunders managed to escape although he
sustained knife wounds in his hands, arms, and
back. His left arm was severed. Members of the
ANC Youth League turned over suspects in
the killing to police the following day.

APRIL 26
Sam Msibi, *WTN*, Attacked
Armed men shot and seriously injured Sam
Msibi, cameraman for *Worldwide Television
News*, on his way home to Katlehong. The gun-
men stopped his vehicle and shot him five times
in the chest.; he miraculously survived.

APRIL 27
Bush Radio, Attacked, Harassed
Edric Gorfinkel, *Bush Radio*, Legal Action
Mervyn Swartz, *Bush Radio*, Legal Action
On April 27, officials of the Department of Post
and Telecommunications came to the offices of
Bush Radio in Cape Town and searched the
premises. They warned the staff that police
would confiscate equipment and fine, prosecute
or imprison them under the 1952 Radio
Broadcast Act for operating without a license.
The radio station had applied for a license but
was denied. In protest, the radio station had

gone on the air April 25 and had planned to do so again on May 1. On April 30, officials of various government agencies, including police, entered the station offices and confiscated transmission equipment. They charged *Bush Radio* members Edric Gorfinkel and Mervyn Swartz with "illegal broadcasting; illegal possession of broadcast apparatus, and obstructing the course of justice." All charges were dropped on December 10.

MAY 5
John Woodroof, *Daily News*, Attacked
KwaZulu police, attending the funeral of slain KwaZulu sergeant Siphiwe Mvuyane, warned Woodroof, a reporter for the *Daily News* who was covering the event, to leave. Woodroof criticized Mvuyane in his articles on several occasions. The KwaZulu police proceeded to attack him, punching him in the jaw and kicking him in the back and ribs. Woodroof managed to escape into a building. His pursuers redirected traffic outside, demanding Woodruff to come out of the building and turn over his film. The South African Police force eventually intervened and, threatening to use force if necessary, disbursed the crowd.

MAY 13
The Sowetan, Attacked
Members of the Congress of South African Students (COSAS) assaulted Sowetan newspaper vendors after an innocuous advertisement by the Department of Training and Education had appeared in the paper. According to *The Sowetan*, COSAS had previously showed hostility toward *The Sowetan* for its editorial stance against a teachers strike and assaulted the vendors because of the paper's apparent support of the Department of Education and Training.

MAY 18
Esther Waugh, *The Star*, Threatened
Workers found a mortar bomb and grenade placed in garbage bags on the pavement outside the home of Waugh, *The Star's* political correspondent, in Melville. Police found no suspects, but *The Star* suspected it was the work of right-wing extremists.

MAY 26
Tsale Makam, *The Sowetan*, Harassed
Several defendants in the Boipatong Massacre trial threatened *Sowetan* reporter Makam at the court in Delmas. They apparently objected to an article in which Makam mentioned that they were bused to the court from the Kwa Madala Hostel. One of the accused objected to Makam's report that he was serving a six-year sentence for kidnapping and assault, saying it had endangered his life. However, Makam's report mentioned neither his name nor the prison in which he was serving his term.

JUNE 10
Mariola Biela, *The Citizen*, Attacked, Threatened, Harassed
Piet Rudolph threatened and roughed up Biela, a photographer for *The Citizen*, after he left the Magistrate's Court in Pretoria where Rudolph faced charges of assaulting *Citizen* reporters Fred and Ilse de Lange on April 22. Rudolph damaged Biela's camera.

JUNE 10
Saira Essa, *M-NET TV Premiere*, Threatened, Harassed
Wayne Raath, *M-NET TV Premiere*, Threatened, Harassed
Lawrence Khumalo, *M-NET TV Premiere*, Threatened, Harassed
Essa, a reporter for *M-NET's* "Premiere" news program, and two members of her television crew, Raath and Khumalo, were in Alexandra Township shooting the last segment of a documentary on the right-wing element in South Africa, when they were held up at gunpoint. The assailants broke into the car and stole more than R80,000 worth of camera equipment, all of the film footage from previous shoots, including

the interviews of key political leaders, and personal valuables. Essa said that the men were unknown, but that she suspected the hold-up was premeditated. The assailants, she said, made insinuations that they knew the nature of the story.

JULY 6
Mbuzeni Zulu, *The Sowetan*, Imprisoned
Katlehong Kwesini hostel-dwellers kidnapped *Sowetan* newspaper photographer Zulu and held him hostage for more than two hours. Zulu was on assignment in the East Rand township when marchers accused him of being an ANC spy and took him prisoner. Inkatha members had kidnapped and threatened Zulu with death twice before, in 1990 and 1991.

JULY 15
Johan de Waal, *Beeld*, Attacked
Gunmen armed with AK-47s shot and wounded *Beeld* newspaper reporter de Waal while he did a story on township violence in Katlehong. De Waal had gone into the township with a police captain.

JULY 15
All Media, Harassed
Numerous reporters and photographers were verbally assaulted while waiting outside the Johannesburg Regional Court where AWB members were on trial in connection with the occupation of the World Trade Center.

JULY 21
John "Dinky" Mkhize, *Reuter*, Threatened, Harassed
Bruce Sofutu, *Reuter*, Threatened, Harassed
A gang of armed youths threatened Mkhize and Sofutu in Daveyton, east of Johannesburg, where the two *Reuters* television reporters had gone to investigate police reports of mutilated bodies found near a Zulu hostel. The youths stole the reporter's bulletproof vests, but didn't harm either of them.

JULY 30
Jennifer Turner, *The Citizen*, Attacked, Harassed
Dennis Goddard, *SABC*, Imprisoned
Members of the AWB, a right-wing paramilitary group, assaulted Turner, a *Citizen* photographer, and stole her camera equipment outside the Witwatersrand University. Turner was taking photographs of the AWB members as they protested the Weekly Mail/Anti-Censorship Action Group Film Festival. Turner was hospitalized with back injuries. Police arrested Goddard because they objected to his camera's bright light.

AUGUST 4
Andries Cornelissen, *Beeld*, Legal Action
Beeld reporter Andries Cornelissen was sentenced to one year in prison for refusing to answer questions in connection with an investigation into African National Congress Youth League leader Peter Mokaba. Mokaba allegedly used the slogan "kill the Boer, kill the farmer" at a political rally at Witwatersrand University in May, which Cornelissen covered. The day after the rally, Cornelissen's article appeared in *Beeld*. Authorities subpoenaed him under Section 205 of the Criminal Procedure Act, which stipulates that a journalist must provide information to police. This is the harshest sentence imposed under Section 205. Cornelissen is free pending an appeal.

AUGUST 28
Ponko Masiba, *Imvo*, Attacked
Phila Ngqumba, *East Cape News Agency*, Harassed
Mike Knott, *Daily Dispatch*, Threatened
A bodyguard of PAC President Clarence Makwetu assaulted *Imvo* reporter Masiba as Makwetu arrived at a rally in Mdantsane township near East London. Masiba was taking photographs of bodyguards beating an armed PAC member who had burst through the crowd toward Makwetu. At the same rally, PAC

supporters verbally assaulted Ngqumba, of the *East Cape News Agency*, and threatened *Daily Dispatch* photographer Mike Knott by shouting "one settler, one bullet" at him. The PAC had invited journalists to cover the rally.

SEPTEMBER 21
Mike Proctor-Simms, *SABC*, Attacked
Right-wing AWB supporters assaulted Proctor-Simms, an *SABC* television reporter, at an ANC meeting in Algoa Park, Port Elizabeth. The AWB members, protesting the ANC meeting, punched Proctor-Simms and knocked him to the ground as he tried to keep them from assaulting his cameraman.

NOVEMBER 16
Bronwyn Wilkinson, *The Star*, Attacked
Wilkinson went to report on an incident of sniper fire that critically wounded a motorist at a four-way stop between Phola Park and Eden Park. As she approached the area of the shooting, three snipers in the trees began firing at her car with AK-47 rifles, grazing her arm with a bullet.

NOVEMBER 17
Richard Somlota, *SABC*, Attacked
Taxi drivers assaulted Somlota, an *SABC* cameraman, while he videotaped drivers assaulting several women near Cape Town. The drivers stole his equipment and damaged a tape.

Sudan

Press freedom and human rights continued to deteriorate under the regime of Lt. General Omar Hassan al-Bashir. Since the June 1989 military coup that brought his fundamentalist-backed regime to power, independent journalism has ceased to exist. Of the approximately 40 papers, magazines, and periodicals that had sprung up under the democratically elected government of Sadiq al-Mahdi, only a handful survive. These, along with a few publications launched since the coup, are under close supervision by fundamentalist bureaucrats and must slavishly toe the government line.

A new Press Code was adopted in July 1993 that allows the creation of privately owned newspapers and calls for the privatization of existing papers. But no new private newspapers were established, nor had existing ones been privatized, by the end of the year. Sudanese journalists complain that the new code restricts coverage of many important issues.

In 1993 at least three journalists were detained in so called "ghost houses," clandestine detention centers where prisoners are held without charge and routinely tortured. At the end of the year one remained in detention.

In its ongoing war against the Christian and animist Sudan People's Liberation Army (SPLA) in the south, the Arab Muslim regime has committed serious human rights abuses. And the two SPLA factions, who are fighting each other as vigorously as they fight the government, are also far from blameless. In 1992 the SPLA killed a Norwegian journalist working with a relief agency, and reportedly attempted to murder a journalist and an international relief worker in the spring of 1993.

JANUARY 28
Mohamed Abd al-Seed, *Al-Sharq al-Awsat*, Imprisoned
Al-Sharq al-Awsat, Attacked, Censored
Abd al-Seed, Khartoum bureau chief for the London-based Arabic-language daily *Al-Sharq al-Awsat*, was arrested after security forces

raided and searched the newspaper's Khartoum offices. He was held in solitary detention and released on March 22. According to a report in *Al-Sharq al-Awsat*, which is published by the Saudi Company for Research and Marketing, the paper was informed, in a letter from the director of Sudan's foreign media department on February 1, that its Khartoum offices had been closed and that the press cards of its employees in Sudan were no longer valid. The order affected all the Sudan-based employees of the company's publications which include *Al-Majalla*, a weekly newsmagazine, *Sayidati*, a weekly women's magazine, and *Al-Muslimoun*, a weekly newspaper. The letter accused these publications of publishing "fabricated lies and pure propaganda."

JUNE

Nadir Mahjoub Muhammad Salih, *Al-Shabiba*, Imprisoned

Salih, a reporter for the banned Communist publication *Al-Shabibah*, was detained by authorities in June. The reasons for his detention are unclear, and his whereabouts are unknown. It is feared that he has been held in a ghost house, a clandestine detention center where prisoners are routinely tortured. There are unconfirmed reports that he was released in the fall.

JULY

Taha al-Nouman, *Al-Ittihad*, Imprisoned

Al-Nouman, Khartoum bureau chief for the Abu Dhabi-based newspaper *Al-Ittihad*, was detained in July for unknown reasons. He was released in the fall.

Tanzania

Since Tanzania joined the ranks of converts to multiparty politics in 1992, a burgeoning independent press has emerged. However, democratization has not come without efforts by government stalwarts to retain power. Old tactics of control and repression continued. Privately owned newspapers and magazines flourished, with editors running previously unpublishable material. Although the state maintained control over mainland radio and television stations, a National Broadcasting Commission was set up in November to oversee licensing of private broadcast outlets. Repressive press laws, like the Tanzania News Management Act and the Newspapers Act, remained on the books. A proposed Media Council Act would have given government the power to license journalists, impose fines and imprison offenders of the law. Journalists vigilantly opposed it as an attempt to control the newly independent press; the proposed legislation was withdrawn. Tanzanian journalists continue to keep a watchful eye on government interference.

JANUARY 26

Cheka, Censored

Michapo, Censored

The government banned two private Swahili-language newspapers, *Cheka* and *Michapo*, under the 1977 Newspaper Regulations Act, for allegedly containing material offensive to the morals of Tanzanians. According to *Radio Tanzania*, the government objected to the January 1 and 10 issues of *Cheka* and a December 1992 issue of *Michapo*. The Newspaper Regulations Act allows the govern-

Africa

ment to ban any publication deemed "unwholesome." Media critics in Tanzania believe the government banned the two papers in retaliation for their coverage of sensitive political issues.

AUGUST 26
Canadian Broadcasting Corporation, Harassed
The Tanzanian government arbitrarily revoked permits for a *Canadian Broadcasting Corporation (CBC)* crew that planned on producing a documentary on Canadian-assisted wheat farms in Hanang. The Tanzanian government and the *CBC* crew had been in negotiations since April and the government granted visas to the crew in June. The day before their departure, Tanzanian authorities canceled the visas and notified the airlines that the *CBC* was not welcome in the country. No explanation was given.

Togo

It was a devastating year for Togo's opposition media. The government and its security forces attempted to silence opposition papers and radio partly because of political instability caused by several armed attacks aimed at toppling President Gnassingbe Eyadema. Early in the year, an opposition newspaper editor, who is also a member of the Collective for Democratic Opposition, was shot and severely injured. Several popular opposition newspaper offices and printing plants were destroyed by arson and explosives. As a result, papers began publishing in neighboring Benin to avoid further attacks and financial losses. Street vendors selling these publications were frequently beaten and detained. Local human rights groups believed the security forces were largely responsible for these attacks. In August,

President Eyadema was reelected in an election filled with irregularities. Since that time, at least five journalists have been imprisoned and several newspaper directors charged with libel.

FEBRUARY 26
Leopold Ayivi, *Ablode*, Attacked
Ayivi, the founding editor of *Ablode* newspaper and the press attaché for the opposition Togolese Union for Democracy, was shot as he pulled into his driveway, by two men on mopeds, who were identified as army soldiers by witnesses. Ayivi received two bullet wounds and fell into a coma for several weeks. He is still recuperating from his injuries. Ayivi was undoubtedly targeted for his work as a journalist and his membership in the opposition.

FEBRUARY 28
Rico Tettekpoe, Threatened, Expelled
Tettekpoe, a freelance reporter and press attaché for the government's Human Rights Ministry, received an anonymous phone call at his home. The caller stated, "It is the journalist's turn now; we are going to kill you one by one. You should know you are on the list." Then, on March 8, two unidentified individuals on mopeds were seen parked outside Tettekpoe's home. They left after a neighbor questioned them. Tettekpoe has since fled the country.

APRIL 15
La Tribune des Démocrates, Attacked
Three Staff Members, *La Tribune des Démocrates*, Imprisoned, Attacked
Uniformed soldiers, along with unidentified civilians and members of the presidential guard, circled *La Tribune des Démocrate's* offices and *Libuto*, the newspaper's printing plant, for several hours. They invaded the premises, set it on fire and confiscated files, an attack that caused approximately 70 million CFA in damages. Three staff members were detained and driven

to Lome II, where they were beaten, threatened, and asked to compile a list of the newspaper's staff. That evening, the three men were dropped off in a deserted area outside the capital and stripped of their belongings. Reasons for the attack were unclear.

MAY 10
Selom Gbanou, *Kpakpa Désenchante*, Harrassed
Gbanou, an editor of *Kpakpa Désenchante*, a private newspaper critical of President Gnassingbe Eyadema, was followed on three separate occasions between May 10 and 16 by unidentified men on a moped. Gbanou may have been targeted because of his critical reporting.

MAY 12
Newspaper Vendors, *Kpakpa Désenchante*, Imprisoned, Attacked
Street vendors selling the private newspaper *Kpakpa Désenchante* were detained by security forces in Lome on March 12 and 13 and beaten. They were held in the Gendarmerie Nationale overnight and never charged.

MAY 26
Imprimerie des Grandes Éditions, Attacked
An explosion erupted at the Imprimerie des Grandes Éditions printing plant, which publishes *Kpakpa Desenchante* and *La Tribune des Democrates*, two private newspapers. An offset printer and other equipment were destroyed. The explosives were planted under a street-view window in the printing plant. According to *Kpakpa Désenchante's* staff, an Army jeep was seen 50 meters from the plant moments before the explosion.

OCTOBER
Ibannou Express, Imprisoned
A newspaper vendor known as Claude was detained and held for two weeks in Lome's national police station in October for selling and distributing the opposition newspaper *Ibannou Express.*

NOVEMBER 17
Moudassirou Katakpaou-Toure, *La Lettre de Tchaoudjo*, Legal Action, Imprisoned
Toure, the director of the private opposition newspaper *La Lettre de Tchaoudjo*, was detained without a warrant by six plainclothes police officers at his home. During his detention, Toure was informed that he had been charged with defamation by Minister of Defense Inoussa Bouraima and President Gnassingbe Eyadema in connection with articles published in 1992 and 1993. One article, published in November 1993, alleged that the President was illegally serving as head of state. Toure was freed on December 22 after being sentenced to a total of 24 months in prison, 23 of which were suspended, and being charged a fine totaling 5,500,000 CFA francs. Toure, who had already served one month in prison, was released.

NOVEMBER 19
Baba Coli Razak, *La Lettre de Tchaoudjo*, Imprisoned
Tampoundi Derman, *La Lettre de Tchaoudjo*, Imprisoned
Razak and Derman, two workers in the social affairs department in Sokode, were detained by police for allegedly submitting seditious articles to *La Lettre de Tchaoudjo*, a private opposition newspaper.Razak was convicted for defamation and released on December 28. Derman was released on December 31.

DECEMBER 18
Ali Akondo, *La Lettre de Tchaoudjo*, Imprisoned, Attacked
Akondo, a professor and contributor to *La Lettre de Tchaoudjo*, was detained by police and his home was searched. Several documents including letters from readers of *La Lettre* were confiscated. Seventeen days after his arrest, he was transferred from a police station to Kara prison. He was released on December 31.

Uganda

Despite the relative openness of Uganda's media, the increase in reporting on official corruption proved unsettling for government ministers facing the specter of constituent assembly elections in March 1994. In July, President Museveni's cabinet issued a ban on all government and parastatal advertising in independent newspapers; the ban was subsequently rescinded for all publications except *The Monitor*, Uganda's largest circulating newspaper, known for exposing corruption among government ministers. The government also used sedition to put pressure on its critics, arresting three journalists for articles that accused government officials of corruption. At year's end, a proposed bill seeking to create a media council to monitor and discipline journalists was withdrawn by the government for further review after it was strongly opposed by the press. While restrictions on political party activities continued, Uganda is one of the few countries in sub-Saharan Africa where even the government newspaper, the *New Vision,* openly debates public policy and occasionally criticizes the government. Broadcasting remained under state control, although at least one private radio station is slated to open in 1994.

AUGUST

The Monitor, Harassed

In August, the cabinet lifted its July 14 ban on government and parastatal advertising in all independent newspapers except *The Monitor*. Several sources suggest that the singling out of *The Monitor* signals an attempt by cabinet ministers to penalize Uganda's largest circulating weekly for its reporting on corruption among government officials. The ban remained in effect at year's end.

OCTOBER 1

Teddy Seezi Cheeye, *Uganda Confidential,* Imprisoned

Sseezi Cheeye, editor of the independent weekly *Uganda Confidential,* was arrested at his office by Criminal Investigation Department officials and taken to the Central Police Station in Kampala. He was charged with sedition for running a front-page editorial accusing the Ugandan Revenue Authority of "politically inspired nepotism." On October 5, he was released on bail. The case is pending.

OCTOBER 1

Haruna Kanabi, *Shariat,* Imprisoned

Hussein Musa Njuki, *Shariat,* Imprisoned

Kanabi, sub-editor of the Muslim newsletter *Shariat*, was arrested at his office by Criminal Investigation Department (CID) officials in lieu of the paper's editor-in-chief, Njuki, who was absent at the time. He was charged with four counts of sedition for publishing a letter to the editor in which the authors expressed their opinion that "Museveni and his gang of thieves are destroying the country." The letter also criticized statements made by the minister of information and the minister of labor and social welfare. Kanabi was released on bail after 19 days in prison. On October 2, CID officials arrested Njuki who had evaded police for several weeks. He was similarly charged and detained for eight days.

DECEMBER 4

Teddy Seezie Cheeye, *Uganda Confidential,* Legal Action

The Government added two new charges of sedition against Editor Cheeye for articles published in August which alleged that the president's wife played a role in the murder of her cousin over a family land dispute.

Zaire

The media continued to be caught in the middle of a bitter power struggle between two forces: President Mobutu Sese Seko's authoritarian regime which has ruled Zaire for 28 years; and the popular movement for multiparty democracy led by Prime Minister Etienne Tshisekedi, elected by the sovereign National Conference in August 1992. Following Mobutu's 1990 announcement of democratic reform, an independent press briefly flourished and several dozen publications appeared. However, as Mobutu blocked the transition process and challenged Tshisekedi's authority, Mobutu's troops moved to silence pro-democracy journalists. Reporters for the state-run broadcasting network, swept up in the euphoria of the early days of democratic reform, pushed the limits of press freedom, reporting on opposition political parties and openly supporting the National Conference. They were soon suspended, threatened, and fired. Forces loyal to Mobutu detained journalists, raped female reporters and bombed opposition printing presses.

Three years after Mobutu declared the advent of multi-party democracy, hopes of reform have been dashed. Mobutu maintains control of the state coffers and security apparatus, undermining the transition process, inciting inter-ethnic violence, and plunging the country into economic chaos. It has resulted in a total breakdown of law and order and unprecedented attacks against the press. Mail service into and out of the country has not functioned for more than two years; phone lines no longer work.

In April, following months of political deadlock, looting sprees and violence by government troops in which hundreds were killed and the transitional parliament briefly held hostage, Mobutu illegally dismissed Tshesekedi, in violation of the transitional charter, and named another Prime Minister, Faustin Birwindwa, to head a parallel government. A clampdown ensued. In the first wave of political detentions since 1990, opposition politicians and independent reporters were arrested. Newspapers were suspended, and many journalists were forced to work in hiding, never staying in one place too long. Reporters were constantly threatened. The editors of two independent newspapers were detained for three months; one journalist, Kalala Mbenga Kalao, spent 27 days in prison for an article demonstrating the ethnic imbalance in the armed forces. CPJ has been able to document only a fraction of the alarming number of attacks on the press that have occurred over the past year.

JANUARY 18

Mikiti Nkombe, *Office Zairois de la Radidiffusion et de Télévision*, Harassed

A group of 40 soldiers arrived at the Nkombe residence with a list of people "they had to visit who were enemies of Mobutu." They asked to speak to "Mme Mikiti, head of Tshisekedi's journalists." Finding her absent, they forced her brothers and children to flee, after threatening them with hand grenades, and proceeded to loot and demolish her house. After presenting a program on press freedom in 1989, Nkombe, one of Zaire's few well-known female broadcasters, was detained, repeatedly raped by soldiers, and twice suspended from the *OZRT* for her outspoken reporting and role as president of the *OZRT* union in the late 1980s.

JANUARY 28
La Reference Plus, Attacked

The offices of the Kinshasa-based *La Reference Plus*, an independent newspaper, were attacked by arsonists and looted during the riots when government troops went on a rampage after receiving pay in bank notes issued by President Mobutu Sese Seko. Many merchants would not accept the bank notes because the interim government, made up of opposition members, had declared them worthless. The violence left hundreds dead.

FEBRUARY 3
Voix du Zaire, Attacked

The state-run broadcasting center, *Voix du Zaire*, came under gunfire during an outbreak of looting. The looting seemed to come from Kokolo military camp. The violence began the previous week when angry soldiers looted homes and businesses, mainly for food. No journalists were injured.

MARCH 6
Livia Montana, *Africa News Service*, Imprisoned
Tony Avirgan, Imprisoned

Montana, an editor with *Africa News Service*, along with assistant producer Avirgan and their guide, Floribert Chebeya, head of the human rights organization The Voice of the Voiceless, were detained by plainclothes police while filming a street scene in Kinshasa. They were taken to a police station and held for several hours.

APRIL
L'Interprète, Censored

Citing "grave professional malfeasance," the government banned the new bi-monthly for two months. It did not resume publication.

APRIL 23
Kenge Mukengeshayi, *Le Phare*, Imprisoned, Legal Action

Mukengeshayi, editor-in-chief of the weekly opposition newspaper, *Le Phare*, was arrested by armed agents of the Service National d'Intelligence et de Protection (SNIP) and held in a secret detention center before he was transferred to Makala prison where he was held for three months. Despite the Supreme Court ruling that there were no grounds for his arrest, Mukengeshayi went on a hunger strike to gain his release in late June. Although the charges against him were never made public, it is believed that he was arrested in connection to an article which accused Mobutu of plotting to assassinate Tshesekedi.

APRIL 28
Celestin Kandolo Mulumba, *Le Potentiel*, Imprisoned, Legal Action

Kandolo, editor of the bi-weekly *Le Potentiel*, was arrested and taken to Makala prison when he responded to a court summons for publishing a letter from the public prosecutor's office to the minister of justice. The letter demanded that Nguz a Karl-i-Bond, Mobutu's Minister of Defense, return four government vehicles. On May 5, a lower court judge granted him provisional release. The order was denied. Kandolo remained in prison with Kenge Mukengeshayi while the case was appealed. He was released in late June only after observing a weeklong hunger strike to protest his prolonged detention despite a Supreme Court ruling that there were no grounds for his arrest. Mulumba went into hiding in late September.

JUNE 16
Nicaise Kibel Bel'Oka, *Umoja*, Imprisoned, Legal Action

Bel'Oka, a reporter for the daily newspaper *Umoja*, was arrested on the orders of the Minister of Primary and Secondary Education, Ndolela Sikikonde. Bel'Oka was charged with libel by Sikikonde for an article that alleged that he stole money from his ministry. Bel'Oka was released in late July after the Supreme Court ruled that he was innocent.

JULY 4
Chantal Safou, *Elima*
Safou, a reporter for the independent newspaper, *Elima*, was covering an opposition meeting when she was brutally attacked and severely beaten by three men in uniform.

AUGUST 4
Le Palmarès, Censored
Michel Labi Luya, *Le Palmarès*, Attacked
Le Palmarès was suspended for three months for publishing a caricature of President Mobutu Sese Seko that was reportedly deemed offensive by Zairian authorities. The government stated that the newspaper had been suspended for publishing " offenses against recognized institutions" in its recent issues. Luya, *Le Palmarès's* editor, was assaulted by two military officials outside the ministry of communication building after he was informed of the newspaper's suspension.

AUGUST 25
Kalala Mbenga Kalao, *La Tempête*, Imprisoned
Kalao, editor of "The Nation" column in the outspoken independent weekly, *La Tempête des Tropiques*, was arrested by two military officials outside his home following the publication of a series of articles that he wrote concerning the Zairian Armed Forces. In its August 21-24 issue, *La Tempête* published a list indicating the educational background and training of military generals that demonstrated the ethnic imbalance in favor of those from President Mobutu's region. He was held without charge for 27 days.

NOVEMBER
Umoja, Censored
La Renaissance, Censored
Elima, Censored
Salongo, Censored
In early November, the Ministry of Information suspended four newspapers citing an outmoded press law. The daily *Umoja*, and its weekend edition *La Renaissance* published statements by

opposition leaders that called on the people to boycott the introduction of a new national currency. *Salongo* is financed by President Mobutu. Several sources suggested that the latter was included so that the ban could not entirely be viewed as a crackdown on the opposition press. The papers continued to publish despite the ban.

Zambia

Although Zambia's relatively free press increasingly reported on allegations of corruption and drug trafficking among government officials, it was not without reprisal. Two years after President Chiluba's Movement for Multi-Party Democracy won a landslide victory in Zambia's first freely contested elections in decades, old patterns of repression and corruption returned. *The Weekly Post*, Zambia's leading independent newspaper, was harassed on several occasions for critical coverage. Broadcasting remained under state control. The Media Reform Committee, comprised of 17 representatives from news organizations, academia, and government, made specific recommendations to amend the Legal Code, citing 26 sections which violate press freedom. By year's end, however, the Cabinet still had not approved their recommendations.

JUNE 3
Fred M'Membe, *Weekly Post*, Legal Action
Police summoned Managing Director M'Membe for questioning after the paper ran a story alleging that the Drug Enforcement Commission had asked the President to arrest Princess Nakatindi Wina, Minister of Community Development, on drug trafficking

charges. The story alleged that the president stopped the arrest. The government wanted the *Weekly Post* to disclose its sources but did not press charges against the paper.

SEPTEMBER 17

Weekly Post, Harassed, Attacked

Assailants associated with the Youth Wing of the Movement for Multi-Party Democracy, the government party, ambushed a *Weekly Post* delivery vehicle containing more than 11,000 copies of the paper. Although the charred remains of some of the papers were found, the van was never recovered. The newspaper's managing director said the motive was intimidation; the newspaper regularly criticizes the government.

SEPTEMBER 18

Elias Chitenje, *Weekly Post*, Legal Action

Police called Chitenje, a reporter for the *Weekly Post*, in for questioning in connection with a September 11 story about an investigation into the dealings of a German businessman, Fred Leker. Former police commissioner Mwenda Muyunda, Leker's business partner, apparently requested the summons.

DECEMBER 17

Weekly Post, Harassed, Attacked

Members of the Youth Wing of the Movement for Multi-party Democracy (MMD) attacked the offices of the *Weekly Post* and demanded to see Fred M'Membe, the paper's managing director. That morning, further reports appeared in the paper concerning allegations of Princess Nakatindi's involvement in drug trafficking. The youth apparently viewed the story as antigovernment. When the paper's staff told the youth to leave, they became violent. They verbally abused the receptionist, threw newspapers around, threatened staff and warned they would come back in the afternoon. When they later tried to re-enter the paper's offices, the police arrested seven individuals, charged them

with public disturbance, and fined them a small fee. The MMD Youth leadership later condemned the attack.

Zimbabwe

Zimbabwe is often upheld as an example of a post-independence success story. Yet while Zimbabwe enjoys a vigorous free press, journalists complain about government intimidation tactics. Radio and television are entirely state-run; two of the country's three daily newspapers are owned by the state-controlled Mass Media Trust. The ruling party continues to suppress what President Robert Mugabe once termed journalistic "overzealousness." Two of Zimbabwe's leading journalists were prosecuted for articles criticizing the government; another was fired for asserting that the state news agency was linked to central intelligence. Zimbabwe's libel law continues to be used as a method of harassment and a means of discouraging investigative reporting. Following the publication of articles exposing a government corruption scandal in 1989, the Minister of Information said Zimbabwe could not "afford investigative journalism." In 1993, President Mugabe stated that the country could "not afford" independent broadcasting either, due to "the danger of sabotage and subversion." Despite the relative openness of print media, it is unlikely that the government will relinquish control of the airwaves anytime soon.

MAY

Geoff Nyarota, Legal Action

Nyarota, one of Zimbabwe's leading journalists, is being sued for libel by the Minister of

Foreign Affairs, Nathan Shamuyarira, for a series of investigative articles Nyarota published in 1989 while editor of the *Bulawayo Chronicle*. The articles implicated Shamuyarira in a large-scale cars-for-profit scam, known as the Willowgate scandal. The investigation eventually resulted in the conviction of more than a dozen ministers and high-ranking government officials; it also cost Nyarota his job. Nyarota was threatened with contempt of court for refusing to reveal who leaked the story. The case is pending. Zimbabwean law does not entitle journalists to protect their sources.

JULY

Andrew Moyse, *Horizon*, Legal Action
Former Army Commander General Solomon Mujuru filed a libel suit against Andrew Moyse, editor of the independent magazine *Horizon*. Mujuru is claiming $40,000 in damages for a factual report on his far-flung business empire. The case is currently pending.

NOVEMBER 12

Vincent Chikwari, *ZIANA*, Harassed
The *Zimbabwean Inter-African News Agency (ZIANA)* dismissed Chikwari following a lengthy suspension. Chikwari accused the agency of being "in cahoots" with government intelligence in a November 1992 interview that appeared in the *Sunday Times*. Chikwari is appealing the decision.

The Americas

CANADA

UNITED STATES

MEXICO

CUBA

DOMINICAN REPUBLIC

HAITI

GUATEMALA

HONDURAS

EL SALVADOR

NICARAGUA

COSTA RICA

PANAMA

VENEZUELA

COLOMBIA

PERU

BRAZIL

BOLIVIA

PARAGUAY

CHILE

ARGENTINA

OVERVIEW
OF
The Americas

by Ana Arana

A decade ago, the Latin America press was shackled by the pressures of guerrilla wars, military dictatorships and the economic duress caused by a huge foreign debt. In countries like Argentina and Chile, scores of reporters were assassinated by rightist hit squads. In Guatemala and El Salvador, journalists were intimidated by raging guerrilla wars and repression by government death squads. In Nicaragua, the opposition press was lashed at by a suspicious Sandinista National Liberation Front, as the country fought a U.S.-backed Contra war, and all critics were seen as the enemy.

In the 1990's, political turmoil has ended in most countries; economies have improved and press freedoms have gained ground. Except for Cuba, Haiti and Peru, the hemisphere has a more vigorous and aggressive press than before. In former dictatorships like Argentina, Chile and Brazil, investigative journalism has blossomed, much to the chagrin of new democratic governments. Scandalous press reports of official corruption in Brazil, for example, led directly to the resignation of former President Fernando Collor de Mello in 1992.

Even in El Salvador and Guatemala, where the press has been traditionally pro-government, new independent media outlets have appeared, challenging the army and politicians.

With the end of the Cold War outside forces that polarized Latin American societies were eliminated. Violence still occurs, but governments are being forced to look at the internal problems that cause it, rather than blame it on an international communist conspiracy. Additionally, the tally of violence suffered by the hemisphere over the last 20 years remains stamped on the minds of most Latin Americans, who don't want a return to military regimes and civilian dictatorships.

Those states that ignore the new order, like governments in Peru and Haiti, where an authoritarian leader and a corrupt military grabbed extra power recently through violence, are being shunned by most states. Most countries in the region also isolate Cuba, where a Marxist government struggles to survive its worst economic crisis by muzzling free expression.

A benefit of the changing politics in Latin America is that fewer journalists are being assassinated or disappeared. Reporters were killed in Colombia this year, where a combination of guerrilla forces, paramilitary groups and drug traffickers, retaliate against the press. But only six journalists were killed in the entire region this year, a big improvement, considering that between 1980 and 1986, the region led the world with 109 dead journalists.

Violence broke out in Guatemala, Venezuela and Argentina. But the problems ended quickly. In Argentina, where the press suffered a wave of attacks by thugs connected to the government of President Carlos Menem, the unthinkable occurred: President Menem apologized for the attacks.

But just as new governments in the region are not interested in killing journalists, they still want to control the press. The new trend is to shackle journalists with defamation and libel lawsuits. Countries throughout the region have introduced restrictive laws that can send journalists to jail for writing on corruption and abuses.

Judges in Mexico and Colombia are prosecuting journalists for soiling "the good name" of a politician or influential citizen, even if the story is true. In Honduras, the courts are safeguarding the morals and good customs of the nation. In Brazil, even an innocuous report on the life story of a popular singer was banned by the artist through a court injunction.

Ana Arana, *Program Coordinator for the Americas, is a former foreign correspondent who covered Latin America for the last six years. She was senior foreign correspondent for the Ft. Lauderdale Sun-Sentinel, staff reporter for the San Jose Mercury News and a newswriter for* **CBS News** *and* **KCET** *(PBS) in Los Angeles. She was a highly respected freelance correspondent for* **The Miami Herald, The Baltimore Sun** *and* **U.S. News & World Report** *in Bogota (1990-91) and San Salvador (87-90). Arana, a native speaker of Spanish, is an alumnus of Columbia Graduate School of Journalism and a graduate of San Francisco State University.*

Kim Brice, *Research Associate, wrote the Haiti section of this report.*

The Americas

Argentina

For the first time since military rule ended in 1983, the Argentinean press was subjected to a series of threats and attacks. Some journalists were beaten, others were threatened, and radio stations were fire-bombed. The attacks came as the press continued to grow bolder in its scrutiny of the government of President Carlos Menem. Journalist groups did not accuse the president of direct involvement in the attacks, but press critics said his combative attitude toward the press contributed to the violence. The Argentinean press has fought with President Menem since he assumed power in 1989, but miraculously under his leadership, press freedoms have flourished, not diminished. *Página 12,* an inquisitive opposition daily started and boomed during his presidency. Argentinean journalists who had grown shy during the military regimes learned to be critical of the government again. And Menem has retracted legal restraints that have become fashionable in Latin American countries in recent years. In May 1993, his government repealed a right-to-reply law that would have shielded government officials from press investigations. But the November disappearance of Mario Bonino, a former journalist who worked for the Buenos Aires Press Workers Union, brought fear to the journalism community. Bonino's body was found floating in a Buenos Aires river. His murder remains a mystery, which is extremely disturbing in a country where 93 journalists were killed by military death squads in the 1970s.

JANUARY
Radio and Television, Legal Action
President Carlos Menem sent a controversial radio and television bill to Congress that would regulate the contents of news programs and commentaries. The bill will also create a government watchdog group, the Committee for the Defense of Freedom of Expression.

JANUARY
All Media, Legal Action
President Carlos Menem is expected to back a Congressional bill that introduces the right to reply. Article 117 of the bill will allow any individual who feels he or she has been wrongly affected by false or harmful information to have a reply published by the same publication.

APRIL 1
Carmen Elsa Miranda, *Eco del Norte Salta,* Imprisoned, Attacked, Threatened
Miranda was arrested, beaten and threatened on the orders of Cristina Rossi, a defender in the Attorney General's Office. An attempt was made to confiscate a tape from Miranda with an interview with Rossi. The government official accused of assaulting the journalist was later acquitted by a local court.

JULY
Kuo Jen Lee, *El Semanario Taiwan,* Harassed
Lee received about 10 threatening telephone calls from members of the Taiwanese community in Buenos Aires after he published a series on corruption in Taiwanese language schools in Argentina.

JULY 10
Santo Biasatti, *Radio del Plata,* Threatened
Biasatti, a radio journalist with *Radio del Plata* and well-known critic of the Menem government, received telephone death threats. An unidentified caller warned Biasatti he could be kidnapped and "disappeared" because of his radio programs on national politics.

JULY 10
Santo Biasatti, *Radio del Plata*, Threatened
Horacio Verbitsky, *Página 12*, Threatened
Ana Guzzeti, *Revista Humor*, Threatened
Luis Bruschtein, *Página 12*, Threatened
Ana Guzzeti, a reporter with the magazine *Humor*, received a note saying the above four journalists were going to be kidnapped and would disappear in the near future.

JULY 21
Marcelo Bonelli, *Clarin*, Attacked
Bonelli, a columnist for the newspaper *Clarin* was assaulted by unidentified men on his way to *Radio Mitre*, where he also hosts radio programs. Bonelli is a well-known critic of the Menem Administration. He also writes for the Buenos Aires daily *El Clarin*, and works for a local television channel.

AUGUST 25
Hernan López Echague, *Página 12*, Attacked
Unidentified men attacked López Echague twice within a period of two weeks. On August 25, two men roughed him up in front of his home in Buenos Aires, slashing his right cheek. Two weeks later, on September 8, he was assaulted for a second time by three men, who forced him into a car and beat him as the car was driven around the city. They stated that the next time he would be killed. In both attacks, the assailants warned López Echague to stop investigating the relationship between leading members of the ruling Peronist party and hired thugs, called *patotas*, who attacked journalists.

AUGUST 27
Lally Cobas, *Telefe*, Attacked
Cobas was assaulted in broad daylight while she was trying to get an interview with Hernan López Echague, another journalist who had previously been beaten by thugs. Her assailant was identified and is pending trial.

AUGUST 28
Jorge Jacobson, *Radio Continental*, Harassed
Jacobson received the first of two threatening phone calls on August 25, when an anonymous caller claiming to be a member of an unknown group named "Capt. Evita" threatened Jacobson and his two daughters. Three days later, on August 28, another anonymous caller told one of Jacobson's daughters that her father "would end up in a ditch."

NOVEMBER 11
Mario Bonino, *Union de Trabajadores de Prensa*, Killed
Bonino, a press officer for the *Union de Trabajadores de Prensa (UTPBA)*, Buenos Aires's largest media workers' union, disappeared on November 11 after he left his house to attend a union meeting. His body was found floating in a river in Buenos Aires on November 15. A coroner's investigation ruled out alcohol and drowning as the cause of death. Union spokesmen said it is not known if his disappearance and death had political motives. But one day before Bonino's body was found, the union's headquarters were broken into and a watchman was severely beaten. Calls made to the union warned against lodging protests against the government for press attacks. Bonino's death follows a wave of violence against journalists by thugs allegedly connected to the ruling Peronist party. Bonino was a former reporter for the Argentinean daily, *Diario Popular*.

NOVEMBER 14
Union de Trabajadores de Prensa, Attacked
Miguel Gavilan, Union de Trabajadores de Prensa, Attacked
Three men broke into the headquarters of the Union de Trabajadores de Prensa, the press workers' union in Buenos Aires, and proceeded to beat the union's watchman with an iron rod. Later, the office received a telephone threat warning them of more reprisals if they contin-

ued their campaign urging an investigation of recent attacks against journalists. The latest attack came three days after the disappearance of UTPBA press spokesman Mario Bonino.

Bolivia

Relations between newly elected president Gonzalo Sánchez de Lozada and the Bolivian press hit a low point this year. In November, the press refused to cover the president's visit to the state of Potosi during a massive labor strike and did not allow him to broadcast a radio message. The president called the action a violation of his freedom of expression. In retaliation, his government has tried to introduce antipress legislation. Journalists have attacked the president's economic austerity plans and massive layoffs in government agencies. Journalists reporting on drug-related corruption in the private and public sectors were targeted.

JANUARY
Cayetano Llobet, *Channel 6*, Threatened
An incendiary bomb was placed near the home of Llobet. The incident occurred during a period when the station was broadcasting reports on alleged corruption in the public and private sectors.

SEPTEMBER 1
All Media, Legal Action
The National Electoral Court introduced a bill prohibiting the publishing of analyses, trends, and projections of early results in national or municipal elections until two hours after the polling booths closed, to avoid having an influence on the electorate.

Brazil

The Brazilian media continued to play a strong, vigorous role in shaping this country's democracy. In 1992, the press displayed a new style of investigative journalism, contributing to the impeachment of President Fernando Collor de Mello. The only violent act against the press documented by CPJ in 1993 was a break-in at the home of a *Jornal do Brasil* correspondent in the state of Alagoas. But journalists have been harassed legally through the use of libel laws intended to silence the press.

JANUARY 8
Noticias Populares, Censored, Legal Action
Roberto Carlos, a well-known Brazilian singer, procured an order from the Court of São Paulo to prohibit *Noticias* from further publishing a series of articles about his childhood. Roberto Carlos claimed the articles violated his privacy.

FEBRUARY 1
All News Media, Censored
Brazilian President Itamar Franco prohibited government ministers from making statements to the press or talking with journalists. He later retracted and said he only wanted ministers to limit their comments to their areas of expertise.

APRIL 8
Reinaldo Cabral, *Jornal do Brasil*, Threatened, Harassed
Two unidentified armed men broke into Cabral's home and set fire to his car. Cabral, the Alagoas correspondent for the daily *Jornal do Brasil*, had been threatened by the commander of the state military police after he wrote an article on military violence on March 22.

Canada

Canadian courts imposed restrictions on the press to protect the right to a fair trial. Canadian law is strictly aligned with British common law.

The most celebrated restriction last year was when an Ontario judge banned reporting on a trial involving a couple accused of two grisly murders. The wife pleaded guilty in an earlier trial. But her husband's trial is expected to take place sometime in 1994. Thus, the judge limited reporting on her case to protect her husband's right to a fair trial.

The judge's ruling was being challenged by *The Star, The Toronto Sun, The Globe and Mail, The Canadian Broadcasting Corporation,* and other news organizations. No decision had been reached by the date of publication of this report.

In 1982, Canada introduced a Charter of Rights and Freedoms, which protects "freedom of thought, belief, opinion and expression, including freedom of the press." These rights, however, are limited when reporting information on events in criminal court.

This year, the government also introduced further press limits on coverage of national elections. For example, one law allows only registered political parties to publish paid political advertisements during elections. Canadian common law is based on the British system.

JULY 6
All Media, Legal Action
An Ontario Court judge imposed a gag order on media coverage of a much publicized murder trial. The case involves a Canadian couple's involvement in the sex-and-torture killings of two Canadian schoolgirls in 1991. The wife, Karla Teale, was sentenced to 12 years in prison in July 1993. The ban was issued because the judge felt the husband, Paul Teale, would not get a fair trial if the media was allowed to widely report the case. His trial is expected to start sometime this year. U.S. publications with news on the trial were banned. U.S. television news shows were censored and U.S. magazines and newspapers were seized at the U.S.-Canada border. U.S. publications sold in Canada had news on the trial excised.

SEPTEMBER 21
David Baines, *The Vancouver Sun,* Harassed
Clayton G. Schultz, executive vice president of the Vancouver Stock Exchange, said in a letter to the business editor of *The Vancouver Sun,* that the Exchange would refuse interviews with Baines. It warned the daily that Baines's activities and his articles were being monitored and scrutinized. On September 30, after adverse protests and publicity, the Exchange lifted the ban.

Chile

Press freedom returned to Chile when General Augusto Pinochet turned the government over to the democratically elected Patricio Aylwin in March 1990. Issues sensitive to the military, including cases of human rights abuses during the 17-year Pinochet dictatorship, are widely covered. Censorship charges were raised on several occasions. In March the navy seized and prohibited circulation of a publication by a retired navy captain. A Santiago court of appeals prohibited the sale or distribution of a book entitled *Diplomatic Impunity.* In August, President Aylwin requested that the national television station delay the broadcast of an interview detailing the 1976 Washington car-bombing that took the life of Orlando Letelier, diplomat and cabinet minister under Salvador Allende. The judiciary is controlled by right-wing justices appointed during Pinochet's rule.

JANUARY 28

Juan Andres Lagos, *El Siglo,* Imprisoned, Legal Action

Francisco Herrero, *El Siglo,* Imprisoned, Legal Action

Lagos and Herrero were detained and charged with defamation for an article they published in 1992 attacking the Supreme Court for transferring investigations on the 1974 disappearance of guerrilla leader Alfonso Chanfreau Oyarce to a military court. Chanfreau is believed to have been killed by the military. They were sentenced to 300 days in jail.

FEBRUARY 11

Juan Andres Lagos, *El Siglo,* Attacked

Police agents raided Lagos's house while he was detained for defamation of high government officials for an article he wrote on the Alfonso Chanfreau case.

JULY 8

All Media, Legal Action

On July 8, the government introduced a bill that would regulate freedom of expression. The bill came after a two-year study by a commission composed of media representatives and government officials. Some positive elements are in the law, such as giving civil courts exclusivity over media cases instead of military tribunals. But certain elements could restrict freedom of the press, for example, requiring news organizations to buy insurance against possible press violations that may be committed by their journalists.

Colombia

Colombia, the oldest democracy in Latin America, continues to be the deadliest for journalists. Four journalists were killed in 1993 for work-related reasons. Only the murder of Eustorgio Colmenares, editor of Cucuta's daily *La Opinion,* was solved after guerrillas of the National Liberation Army (ELN) one of two guerrilla groups fighting the government, claimed responsibility for his death. The killers in the other murders remained unidentified. In the last two decades, an estimated 30 to 50 journalists have been killed. Yet Colombia enjoys a vigorous press. Despite the uncertainty of living in a country with one of the highest per-capita murder rates, journalists maintain an adversarial role. Even in the late '80s, during the toughest periods of the drug war, when drug lords targeted journalists who opposed proposals to ban the extradition of traffickers and when simply identifying the nature of Escobar's business could get one killed, journalists remained diligent. Today there are four major dailies in Bogotá and several regional newspapers. The state owns television frequencies, but leases both facilities and air time to several television news and production companies. There are two all-news nationwide radio channels. Two legal restrictions recently introduced have the potential to immobilize the Colombian media. In 1992 the government temporarily instituted Decree 1812, prohibiting the publication of interviews with and communiqués issued by guerrilla groups and drug traffickers. The decree was a response to the Medellin Cartel's use of the media to communicate its plans to the general population. The decree became law in 1993. Another measure is the Law of "Tutela," an unusual legislation enacted by the 1991 Constitutional Assembly, which gives citizens the right to ask a court of law to defend their reputations if a news outlet has published information they find objectionable or untrue. Courts can rule in their favor even if the information is true and the journalist has back-up documentation.

MARCH 12
Eustorgio Colmenares, *La Opinion*, Killed
Colmenares, the publisher of *La Opinion*, was shot to death in his home in Cucuta, the capital of Norte de Santander. Guerrillas of the National Liberation Army took responsibility for his murder.

APRIL 19
Carlos Lajud Catalan, *ABC Radio, Barranquilla*, Killed
Lajud, a frequent critic of drug gangs and politicians, was gunned down by two men riding a motorcycle. His killers remain unidentified.

JUNE 2
All Media, Legal Action
A bill dealing with media censorship during periods of internal commotion and war was approved by the Senate. The bill allows the government to ban any news reports because of national security and to use radio frequencies for public order announcements and restrict any news stories that could interfere with military operations.

SEPTEMBER 28
Manuel Martínez Espinoza, *Radio Super*, Killed
Espinoza, 60, a veteran reporter for *Radio Super's* satire and news program "El Yunque," was killed by unknown gunmen riding on a motorcycle. His wife, Emma, was also hurt in the attack after she rushed out from their home to help him.

SEPTEMBER 30
Bienvenido Lemos, *Caracol Radio*, Killed
A reporter with the nationwide *Caracol Radio* network, Lemos was gunned down by unidentified men in the Pacific port city of Buenaventura.

DECEMBER 2
Broadcast Centers, Attacked
Under the threat of a possible labor strike by television technicians, Colombian military police occupied the national broadcast centers used by all television networks. Television technicians grouped under the Colombian Association of Television Workers (ACOTV) warned they would stop working indefinitely. The strike was settled.

Costa Rica

Strict libel laws and political meddling affected freedom of the press in Costa Rica, one of the strongest democracies in the hemisphere. Two reporters who investigated fraudulent business deals related to President-elect José María Figueres were fired because of political pressures, although the media outlets they worked for denied this was the reason for their dismissal. The reporters' position was corroborated by respected colleagues at other publications. Two other journalists lost libel suits as strict legal restrictions gain popularity as a way of silencing the press.

JANUARY 7
Isabel Ovares, *Channel 7*, Harassed
Ovares was dismissed from her job because of pressure from the opposition National Liberation Party after she reported extensively on private sector corruption involving presi-

111

dent-elect José Mariá Figueres. The party accused the journalist of slanting her coverage against Figueres during an election year. Four others on the *Channel* 7 staff resigned in protest: Pilar Cisneros Gallo, director of the program, and Vilma Ibarra, Alexander Ramírez, Jose Mairena, and Javier Rojas. *Channel* 7 management and Figueres said the scandal was connected to labor conflicts at the station.

JANUARY 17
Efrain Sánchez, *Estrella del Sur,* Legal Action
Sánchez, editor of the daily, was convicted of libel. The case against Sánchez was brought by former deputy Alberto Esquivel Volio, who charged he was libeled by a 1990 article that reported mysterious airplane movement on Esquivel's farm.

JUNE 9
Humberto Arce, *La República,* Harassed
Arce said he left his job as editor of the daily because of alleged pressure from officials close to President-elect José Mariá Figueres. Arce had been working on several articles that linked Figueres to alleged fraudulent mining deals. Management said Arce had resigned from his job.

JUNE 16
Julio Rodríguez, *La Nación,* Legal Action
The First Criminal Court of San José convicted *La Nación* columnist Julio Rodriguez of libel. Rodríguez had criticized Isaac Sasso, the manager of the Costa Rican Soccer Federation. Rodríguez has filed an appeal with the Costa Rican Supreme Court.

Cuba

Cuban journalists work under the most extreme censorship in the entire American hemisphere. Print and broadcast media are owned by the state and are controlled by the Cuban Communist Party. Even as the totalitarian government of Fidel Castro introduced major economic changes this year, Cuban journalists experienced stricter ideological censorship from Communist party leaders. Dissatisfaction among journalists mounted, and three journalists defected to the United States. In Cuba, several dozen journalists left their jobs either disenchanted with the new ideological directives at work or pressured to earn dollars in the tourism industry. Others were removed from their jobs because of ideological incompatibility.

1993
Iria González Rodiles, *Televisión Cubana,* Censored
Tania Quintero, *Televisión Cubana,* Censored
Bernardo Márquez Ravelo, *UPEC,* Censored
Nancy Estrada, *UPEC,* Censored
Fernando Velásquez Medina, *Juventud Rebelde/Others,* Censored
Xiomara González, *Juventud Rebelde,* Censored
Valentín Rodríguez, *Telerebelde,* Censored
These journalists are not allowed to exercise their profession in Cuba. Some were suspended from their jobs prior to 1993. They now stay home, collect a paycheck, but can't work in print or broadcast journalism unless Castro grants them amnesty. Ravelo and his wife, Nancy Estrada, were granted an exit visa in 1993. They are waiting for the government to grant a similar vista to their son. Valentín Rodríguez was removed from his job after he attended receptions at the home of the U.S. Interest Section director.

1993
Yndamiro Restano, *Radio Rebelde,* Legal Action
Restano is serving the 10-year sentence he received on May 20, 1992. He was a reporter

with *Radio Rebelde* until he was fired in 1985 for talking with a foreign journalist. He was arrested on December 20, 1991, for his political activism with the pro-democracy Harmony movement.

APRIL 4

Mauricio Saenz, *Semana,* Imprisoned
Saenz, foreign editor of the Colombian magazine *Semana,* was detained for one day and charged with being involved in drug trafficking. He was in Cuba with a group of other Colombian journalists. He was released after the intervention of Columbian writer Gabriel García Márquez. Cuban authorities later apologized for the incident.

SEPTEMBER 13

Eliseo Garcia, *Prensa Latina,* Left Country
Garcia, operations director for *Prensa Latina,* the Cuban official agency, sought asylum in Miami, after he fled from Mexico where he had been sent on assignment. He is one of the highest *Prensa Latina* officials to defect in history

OCTOBER 13

Maria C. Padron Martinez, *Radio Rebelde,* Left Country
Padron Martinez, general administrator of the stations *Radio Rebelde* and *Radio Taino,* said she was seeking asylum in the United States. In an interview with the Miami-based anti-Castro *Radio Mambi* she said journalists are unhappy with current censorship.

OCTOBER 19

Manuel Portuando, Left Country
Portuando asked for asylum in Honduras during the Seventh University Games of Central America and the Caribbean. He had travelled with the delegation.

OCTOBER 20

Mary Specks, *The Miami Herald,* Expelled
Cuban immigration authorities expelled Mary Specks for working as a journalist without a proper visa. Cuban authorities confiscated all her notes and film. *The Miami Herald* has been denied all visa applications for the last two years because the Cuban government accuses the newspaper of favoring the positions of the anti-Castro Cuban exile community in Miami.

El Salvador

About 50 journalists were killed covering the Salvadoran civil war between 1980 and 1991. But political violence against the press has subsided. While a number of political murders occurred in the latter part of the year, no attacks were directed against journalists. In November, a leftist mob attacked *El Diario De Hoy,* a right-wing daily. Most of the press in El Salvador is privately owned and conservative. Since peace accords were signed in 1992, two news agencies linked to former guerrillas of the Farabundo Martí National Liberation Front began operating in the country, and three radio stations were opened.

JANUARY

Francisco Parada, Killed
Parada, a well-known radio owner and fledgling television owner, was killed in front of his house in San Salvador. It is believed his death is connected to disagreements over ownership of one of his radio and television stations.

NOVEMBER 1

Diario de Hoy, Attacked
A mob attacked the building of the *Diario de Hoy* with rocks and homemade bombs. The attack caused few material damages and came after the former guerrilla commander Joaquín Villalobos denounced the newspaper and its owner, Enrique Altamirano, of being connected to death squad groups.

DECEMBER 27
All News Media, Censored
The Legislative Assembly passed a new electoral law that regulates campaign advertising and includes a ban on offensive political advertising by rival parties. Under the new law, the assembly has warned the news media that it will issue fines to any outlet that carries offending cartoons and caricatures.

Guatemala

Guatemalan journalists were in the forefront of a civilian resistance that forced President Jorge Serrano to resign after he attempted to seize dictatorial power in May. It was the first time that the press led the entire country in a civic action that ended in victory. Serrano instituted censorship, but newspapers bravely continued to print entire editions and distribute them surreptitiously. After Serrano was forced to resign, the country selected President Ramiro de León Carpio, the former human rights ombudsman, to finish off Serrano's term. For journalists who have faced exile, intimidation, and death during decades of civil war and military regimes, the victory was exhilarating. But press freedoms in Guatemala remain limited. Opposition journalists who criticize the armed forces and investigate human rights violations are still under threat. In a meeting with CPJ in June, President Carpio said his government could not yet guarantee the safe return of several journalists forced to leave the country in the past decade. A few days later, the president's cousin, Jorge Carpio Nicolle, the publisher of El Gráfico newspaper and a former presidential candidate, was killed in an ambush.

His journalistic connection is not considered to have been a motive in his death. In recent months, Tinamit, a left-wing opposition newsweekly, has been targeted. Notwithstanding the uncertainty for the press that remains in Guatemala, the effect of independent journalism during Serrano's "self-coup" must be recognized as one of the high points in the hemisphere during 1993. Such young publications as Siglo XXI, and Cronica, joined more established dailies like La Hora in their attacks against Serrano's coup.

JANUARY 1
Tinamit, Attacked, Harassed
A group of armed men broke into the magazine's printing house, poured gasoline over equipment and set it on fire. A military unit raided the offices on March 9.

JANUARY 7
Siglo XXI, Harassed
On the morning of January 7, armed men in private cars attacked seven distribution points of the daily *Siglo XXI*. They set fire to 6,000 copies of the paper, as well as issues of *Prensa Libre* and *Gráfico* that were next to them on the newsstand. On the day of the attack, *Siglo XXI* ran a front page story that detailed the human rights ombudsman's report on an attack on *Siglo XXI* journalist Omar Cano in December 1992. The report incriminated members of the Guatemalan military.

FEBRUARY 10
Omar Cano, *Siglo XXI,* Harassed, Threatened, Expelled
Cano, reporter for the daily *Siglo XXI*, and his family fled Guatemala after a wave of death threats against them. The threats began after the Guatemalan Human Rights Procurator released a public report that implicated the Guatemalan army in an attack against Cano in December 1992. Cano was the first to receive

released a public report that implicated the Guatemalan army in an attack against Cano in December 1992. Cano was the first to receive threats; however, days before their departure, both his wife and his 10-year-old son were threatened anonymously over the telephone.

FEBRUARY 12
Marta Altolaguirre Larroando, *Crónica,* Harassed
The father of Altolaguirre was intercepted in his car by two other vehicles while he was driving in Guatemala City. Men in one vehicle opened fire, destroying the back and side windows in the father's car. Altolaguirre is a contributor to *Crónica* magazine and the newspaper *Siglo XXI.* She is president of the Guatemalan Journalists Association (CAMARA).

MARCH 9
Tinamit, Attacked
The offices of *Tinamit* were raided by the military. The magazine is a harsh critic of the government. The Human Rights procurator, Jorge Mario García Laguardia, asked the government to ensure that journalists are able to work free of harassment and specifically mentioned the *Tinamit* case.

MARCH 13
Hugo Arce, *Tinamit,* Harassed
Two police patrolmen approached Arce while he was parking his car in front of his home and requested that he show them his identification papers, apparently in connection with charges of possession of explosives and cocaine that had been brought against him in 1991. At the time, he served nearly one month in prison and was released for lack of evidence. The police left after Arce requested their names. Arce is a political commentator with *Tinamit* magazine.

LATE MARCH
Otto Moran, *Tinamit,* Threatened
Carlos Rafael Soto, *Diario Gráfico,* Threatened
Byron Barrera, ACEN-SIAG, Threatened

Haroldo Sánchez, *Siglo XXI,* Threatened
Mario Roberto Morales, *Prensa Libre,* Threatened
At the end of March, a death list circulated around Guatemala City. Moran, the Editor of *Tinamit;* Soto, a reporter for *Diario Gráfico;* Barrera, the Editor of ACEN-SIAG's magazine *Pulso;* Sánchez, a reporter for the daily *Siglo XXI;* and Morales, a reporter for *Prensa Libre,* were listed among social activists and religious workers who were all threatened with death for their supposed involvement in guerilla activities. Though executions were to start on March 31, no one was killed.

MAY 25-JUNE 7
Eco, Censored
CNN, Censored
Univision, Censored
ACAN-EFE, Censored
Notimex, Censored
The government of President Jorge Serrano imposed a virtual ban on foreign news as the political situation in the country worsened, and he instituted domestic censorship, following his power grab. Television screens went blank or crackled with static whenever foreign news programs came in. The Mexican news agency *Notimex* and the Central American news agency *ACAN-EFE* were also prohibited from filing reports from Guatemala.

MAY 25
Channel 11, Censored
Channel 13, Censored
Both channels were shut down after they transmitted an interview with Ramiro de León Carpio, who then was the human rights procurator. In it Carpio called President Jorge Serrano a "dictator." Carpio managed to escape, although police surrounded his home that same night. He later was appointed president to finish off the term of former President Serrano, who was forced to resign after the self-coup.

MAY 26
Siglo XXI, Censored
Prensa Libre, Censored
La Hora, Censored
Most of *Siglo XXI's* edition for May 26 was not distributed in Guatemala City after 200 elite policemen threatened and harassed distributors. Units of national and treasury police surrounded the offices of the newspapers. The government threatened drastic measures if the newspapers did not allow censors to enter their offices. *Siglo XXI* suspended publications for a few days. *Prensa Libre* and *La Hora* published under censorship.

MAY 26
José Zamora, *Siglo XXI*, Threatened
Mario Antonio Sandoval, *Prensa Libre*, Threatened
Francisco Pérez de Anton, *Crónica*, Threatened
Oscar Clemente Marroquin, *Diario La Hora*, Threatened
Marta Altolaguirre, Threatened
Pedro Salinas, *Teleprensa*, Threatened
Ramiro Macdonald Blanco, *Guatemala Flash*, Threatened
President Jorge Serrano issued arrest warrants against these prominent journalists when he carried out a self-coup in late May. The warrants were never enforced.

MAY 31
Eco, Attacked
The offices of *Eco*, a Mexican television network in Guatemala City, were shot at from a passing vehicle. No damages were reported.

MAY 31
Mario Castro, *Prensa Libre*, Threatened
Raul Neono, *Prensa Libre*, Threatened
Castro and Neono asked for temporary asylum at the U.S. Embassy after they were persecuted by armed men who were watching the newspaper's offices during the coup. The U.S. Embassy offered temporary asylum to the journalists.

But a day later, President Antonio Serrano Elias told *Prensa Libre* that it was false he had issued arrest orders against Castro and Neono.

MAY 31
George Rodríguez, *IPS*, Threatened
Rodriguez, correspondent for the *Inter-Press Services* news agency, said he was followed and threatened by security forces all day after he tried to interview some soldiers.

MAY 31
SigloXXI, Censored
Prensa Libre, Censored
El Gráfico, Censored
After four days of censorship, *SigloXXI* again circulated on May 31 with black-and-white pages where the government censored stories. It renamed itself *Siglo IV—"Fourteenth Century."* *El Gráfico* only ran the editorial page blank and *Prensa Libre* deleted censored articles.

JUNE 1
Crónica, Attacked
Tinamit, Attacked
A small bomb exploded near both magazines, causing damage but no injuries. Offices for both magazines are in the downtown commercial area. Both magazines are in opposition.

AUGUST 1
Siglo XXI, Attacked
Unidentified men in a red car opened fire on the offices of *Siglo XXI* in Guatemala City. Windows were shattered and no one was injured. The shooting appears to have been directed at the office of Jóse Rubén Zamora, the newspaper's editor.

AUGUST 3
Jan Karel Beeck Loisa, Attacked
Loisa, a freelance Belgian journalist, was wounded during an attack by members of the Civil Self-Defense Patrols (PAC) against a crowd of peaceful demonstrators in the village of El Naranjal, Colotenango. The demonstra-

tors were calling for the dissolution of the PAC and an end to forced military recruitment. One person was killed and several were injured. The PAC have been a source of discontent in Indian villages since they were introduced in the early 1980s.

AUGUST 4
Tinamit, Harassed, Attacked
National police detained a distribution truck owned by the magazine *Tinamit* and accused the driver of transporting subversive material. The same day, army troops raided the offices of the magazine.

AUGUST 10
Juan Castillo, *Siglo XXI*, Threatened
Marco Tulio Trejo, *Siglo XXI*, Threatened
Three uniformed members of the national police stopped and threatened *Castillo* and *Trejo* when they reported on the disturbances at two schools in downtown Guatemala City.

OCTOBER 5
Hugo Arce, *Siglo XXI*, Threatened
Haroldo Shetemul, Threatened
Carlos Rafael Soto, Threatened
Haroldo Sánchez, Threatened
Marina Coronado, Threatened
A statement signed by the Anticommunist Movement "Roberto Lorenzana" was delivered to several human rights organizations. The statement warns 20 individuals, including five journalists, that they have 72 hours to leave the country or else they will be considered military targets.

OCTOBER 8
Oscar Masaya, *TV Noticias*, Threatened
Masaya, the director of a television news program, was attacked by unidentified men in Guatemala City. Masaya suffered several injuries, including a fractured shoulder blade and an inflamed pelvis.

NOVEMBER 17
Crónica, Threatened
On November 15, *Crónica's* editor, Gustavo Berganza, publicly denounced an extortion campaign against the magazine. He announced that the magazine had received a letter, written on behalf of the guerilla organization "Javier Tambriz" under orders of the general command of the Unidad Revolucionaria Nacional Guatemalteca (URNG), demanding a payment of a "war tax" of $40,000 within 15 days. The letter added that if the magazine did not submit to paying the sum of money, it would be declared a "military target." Two days after the letter was made public, the URNG denied that it was the author of the letter and accused the Guatemalan army of writing the letter in its name in order to discredit it.

NOVEMBER 25
Felipe Sigal Cervantes, *Prensa Libre*, Wounded
Cervantes was shot and seriously wounded in the capital of Guatemala City, during an attempted kidnapping by a group of men who first crashed against his vehicle and then fired at him when Cervantes got out of his car to inspect the damage. *Prensa Libre* said the attack was carried out in the style of the army's G-2 intelligence section."

DECEMBER 9
Tinamit, Attacked
A delivery vehicle belonging to the opposition magazine *Tinamit* was hijacked by six heavily armed men. When they took the vehicle, they kept the driver, mistaking him for the manager of the magazine. He was released. The vehicle was never recovered.

The Americas

117

Haiti's Media Under Attack

by Kim Brice

The military coup that toppled President Jean-Bertrand Aristide on September 30, 1991 abruptly ended a flourishing period for the Haitian media. The Haitian Armed Forces and their paramilitary squads intimidated and attacked news outlets suspected of supporting former President Aristide. They neutralized the once lively and outspoken radio network.

Two years after the coup, the media continues to be a main target of army repression. For journalists, the atmosphere is one of uncertainty and fear. Radio reporters—the sole source of information for the country's poor majority—practice self-censorship to protect themselves and their families. The print media avoids writing critical stories on the military. Security forces are on the prowl for reporters they blame for Haiti's "downfall" and Aristide's rise to power. Many of Haiti's top journalists have fled the country since the coup and scores more remain in hiding. For most of them, practising their trade is simply too dangerous.

In the first half of 1993, several private radio stations attempted to widen their narrow margin of freedom by broadcasting live news reports and, on occasion, interviews with victims of the army's abuses. In June 1993, the military signed the Governors Island Accord, in New York City, agreeing to the return of Aristide's constitutional government by October 30. Fueled with hope, radio directors who had their radio stations shut down during the coup, returned to Haiti with plans to reopen. The optimism died out quickly when Aristide's new government, headed by Prime Minister Robert Malval, was unable to take office and journalists perceived to be supporting the return of Aristide were under renewed threat.

Plans to reopen three radio stations were abandoned. Even journalists who had given up their press jobs because of intimidation right after the 1991 coup, were again hunted down. Others like photojournalist Marie Yolande St. Fleure, a founder of *Agence Haitienne de*

Photo, was repeatedly terrorized by armed civilians, known as attachés, that she had to leave the country.

The toll since the coup:

- Four journalists killed; one disappeared and presumed dead.
- More than 40 reporters illegally detained and at least 23 viciously assaulted.
- Ten radio stations have been raided by paramilitary forces; five remain closed.

Radio stations were specifically attacked because after the fall of dictator Jean-Claude Duvalier in 1986, radio turned into an important political and social tool. It turned into the central instrument of Haiti's pro-democracy movement, becoming an outlet for Haiti's disenfranchised. It filled a vacuum left by political parties that had been unable to respond to popular aspirations. Journalists were more than reporters. "In Haiti, a journalist is a psychiatrist, a marriage counselor, everything," says reporter Lilianne Pierre-Paul.

Five of Haiti's most listened-to stations were forced off the air on the first day of the coup as soldiers smashed, sprayed with gunfire, or stole their equipment and terrorized their employees. At least four other radio stations were raided by Haitian soldiers in the weeks that followed. Jacques Caraibes, the owner and director of *Radio Caraibes*, was killed. Even radio stations that had not been raided during the coup — including *Radio Métropole, Radio Soleil,* and *Radio Tropic FM*— stopped broadcasting for several weeks because of anonymous threats and the December 1991 kidnapping of *Radio Galaxie* director Felix Lamy. By early 1992, these stations had resumed broadcasting, but only intermittently.

Between December 1991 and August 1992, three other journalists were killed and one disappeared. Guy Laraque, a poet and columnist with the daily *Le Nouvelliste;* Montlouis Lherisse, a cameraman with the government-run *Television Nationale d'Haiti (TNH);* and Robinson Joseph, the former director of the Protestant radio station

7. The military authorities are responsible for the murders of
Caraibe, Lherisse and Joseph, but the motives behind the killings
do not relate to their journalistic activities. In Laraque's case, the
killers remain unknown. None of the murders have been investigated
by the authorities.

Felix Lamy, the director of *Radio Galaxie*, was abducted by soldiers from the radio station in December 1991, minutes after he
broadcast a news bulletin mentioning then Canadian Prime Minister
Brian Mulroney's support for the return of Aristide. He is presumed
dead.

Just weeks after the coup, eleven journalists were threatened
with death on a clandestine radio station operated by the Tontons
Macoutes, a paramilitary group formed under Duvalier's regime.
The Macoutes called on Haitians to eliminate "those who organize
the disorder in this country.... Come now, do your work.... Crush
them, eat them, drink their blood." A version of the program was
read on the government-run *Radio Nationale* for several days. In some
cases, addresses and phone numbers of the journalists were broadcast.
"This time it was a government station condemning us. We were
exposed to the military and to those uncontrollable agents in Haiti,"
explained Jacques Sampeur, director of *Radio Antilles*, who was
among those threatened. "It was as if this was not our country,
that we were undesirables."

The wave of intimidation that followed the coup has had lasting
effects. Only four of the nine stations raided during the coup have
resumed broadcasting: *Radio Caraibes, Radio Lumiere, Radio Plus,*
and *Radio Métropole.*

Despite the still-existing dangers, and after nearly two years
of silence, *Radio Haiti Inter, Radio Antilles,* and *Radio Quiskeya* had
planned a comeback before October 30, the scheduled return of
President Aristide to Haiti. These plans were abandoned and its
directors have been in hiding or have fled the country since
September.

Two years after the coup, criticizing the government, reporting
on anti-government demonstrations or making mention of abuses
committed by the army remain risky activities, and self-censorship

is pervasive. As soon as the 1991 international oil embargo was lifted in August 1993, violence increased dramatically and journalists attempting to report on news events were threatened.

•Colson Dormé's abduction is a striking example. Dormé, an archivist with *Radio Tropic FM*, was abducted by attaches after phoning in a live report about the arrival of UN Special Envoy Dante Caputo. Dormé said that he had been taken to an unknown location where he was kept blindfolded and was badly beaten. His captors accused him of being a member of Lavalas, the political movement that supports deposed President Aristide, and collaborating with foreigners. They promised to pay him money if he would became an agent for them. Six days later, Dormé was dumped in front of *Tropic FM's* offices. He was blindfolded, his head was shaved, and his hands and legs were tied.

•On September 8, Aristide's Minister of Information Herve Denis was attacked by armed civilians in front of City Hall when gunmen opened fire on a crowd that had gathered to celebrate the reinstallation of Port-au-Prince Mayor Evans Paul. A reporter for *Radio Tropic FM* covering the event was hit by an attaché with a plank of wood. Several foreign reporters refused to leave City Hall because they were afraid they would be assaulted.

•The government-owned and operated *Radio and Télévision Nationale* was never controlled by Aristide's people. When Herve Denis laid off employees with ties to the military, they returned with armed attachés and occupied the station. The attachés and employees continued to broadcast propaganda favorable to the Haitian military

•*Radio Caraibes*, a private radio station in the capital, ceased news broadcasts for a month after armed attaches stormed the station on September 10. They complained about reports Caraibes had aired about the violence at Mayor Paul's inauguration and asked to speak with Caraibes' director, Patrick Moussingac. He was not there at the time. The attachés threatened to detonate grenades and held three employees at gunpoint.

•Immediately after Minister of Justice Guy Malary and two of his bodyguards were gunned down in Port-au-Prince on October 14, armed police threatened to shoot news photographers at the scene.

The month before, reporters covering a mass at the Sacre Coeur Church in Port-au-Prince were harassed, threatened, and roughed up when a group of more than 20 armed civilians surrounded the church and several orthers dragged prominent Aristide supporter Antoine Izmery into the street, and shot him at point blank range. Seconds before the execution, an attaché accosted *Associated Press* photographer Daniel Morel, momentarily mistaking him for Izmery. An armed civilian confiscated *Haiti-en-Marche* and *Le Rouleau* photographer Hanz Bazard's camera and press card; gunmen were said to be looking for journalists who were at the site of the assassination.

"Informing the people is not permitted," says Guy Jean, *Radio Tropic FM's* director. "We don't know what the limits are. It's a constant game of calculated risks." News radio stations receive anonymous threats regularly and are often denounced by the pro-military press for their anti-government position.

The military leadership is unwilling to guarantee the safety of journalists or to prosecute those responsible for attacks on the press. None of the attacks described in this report have been investigated by the government. Few attempts, if any, have been made to protect journalists so that they would feel safe to resume their work. Several of the station's reporters have resigned due, in part, to the lack of security measures.

NEWSPAPERS AND MAGAZINES

Print media is far less influential than radio because most Haitians cannot afford to buy publications and many Haitians cannot read. The de facto government seems to have recognized this difference: with a few exceptions, newspaper agencies and magazines have been allowed to continue their sanitized coverage nearly unperturbed.

There were about 15 newspapers in Haiti, including three dailies based in the capital: *Le Nouvelliste*, *Le Matin*, and the government-owned *l'Union.* There are several weekly and monthly newspapers and magazines, including *Haiti Observateur, Haiti en Marche*, and *Haiti Progrés*, which are published in Haitian communities in Miami and New York. *Haiti Observateur* has been supportive of the military rulers, while *Haiti en Marche* and *Haiti Progrés* have been extremely critical of it.

Libete, the only Creole-language weekly in the country and one of about three papers distributed in Haiti's provinces, is openly opposed to the military. It was closed down after the coup, but it tried to reopen in December 1992. After enduring a long intimidation campaign, it closed down permanently in October 1993. By then the staff had received countless telephone death threats and its newspaper vendors had been beaten and harassed by the army and attaches. Last summer, a phone caller, who identified himself as a member of the police Anti-Gang unit, threatened to destroy the newspaper's offices. *Libete's* address and phone number are unlisted for security reasons. That same week, soldiers confiscated issues of *Libete* from several vendors and beat them.

Many other magazines have appeared irregularly due to insufficient financing. Since the coup, periodicals have lost advertising revenue. The financial crunch is partly the effect of the trade embargos imposed by the Organization of American States and the United Nations. But some advertisers fear doing business with publications that are considered anti-government.

PROVINCES SILENCED

Before the September 1991 coup, more than two dozen radio stations broadcast from outside of Port-au-Prince. In October 1991, at least two stations, *Radio Tät Ansanm* in Jeremie and *Radio Voix du Nord* in Cap-Haitien, were raided and had their transmitting equipment destroyed.

Attacks on radio stations outside of Port-au-Prince continued in 1993. On January 26, soldiers detained Elder Ameus, the owner of the Jeremie-based *Radio Vision* in Grande Anse, and confiscated equipment from the station. Ameus was charged with disseminating "subversive" information on a program called "Truth" and held overnight. The equipment was later returned. On March 31, soldiers destroyed the transmitter and other equipment of *Radio Transdigital*, a small radio station in Hinche established in 1992. Masner Beauplan, the director of *Transdigital* who had founded the station in 1992, was arrested and detained without charge.

Lawlessness in the provinces has forced many local journalists to work underground, to stop reporting, or to flee their homes. In the first weeks after the 1991 coup, an estimated 100,000 to 300,000 people fled into hiding. An October 1993 article in the *New York Times* estimated the number of Haitians displaced in the two years since the coup at 300,000. This exodus and the fear of reprisals led most provincial radio stations to shut down shortly after the coup and few have resumed broadcasting. To our knowledge, no provincial radio stations currently are disseminating news.

Rural "section chiefs," local military authorities, and civilian militias took advantage of the anarchy and terror spawned by the coup to settle accounts with those people, including local reporters, who had denounced their corrupt practices. Many journalists have been threatened, beaten, or detained. The systematic silencing of the media in rural areas has been so successful that the only source of news in some regions of the country are foreign broadcast services such as the *Voice of America's* Creole-language service or *Radio France-Internationale.* "In the provinces, there is no local information at all," one reporter, based in Gonaãves, told CPJ. "All the radio stations have been reduced to music boxes."

Foreign journalists who have attempted to report on conditions in the Haitian countryside have met with harassment from local authorities. In one instance, a local section chiefs threatened to kill foreign reporters who were gathering information about abuses by the army in northern Haiti. In at least two other cases, local soldiers expelled foreign journalists from their districts even though the reporters had central government approval to travel.

FOREIGN MEDIA UNDER ATTACK

Immediately following the coup, Haitians relied on foreign radio and television broadcasts for information about events in their country. In remote areas of Haiti where local radio stations have been shut down, these foreign broadcasts may remain the only sources of news.

Voice of America (VOA) and *Radio Enriquillo*, a Catholic-run radio station based in the Dominican Republic, increased the frequency of their Creole-language news programs after the coup. The radio stations and their staffs were criticized or threatened; in at least one instance, people were killed merely for listening to a *VOA* broadcast.

Dominique Levanti, bureau chief for *Agence France-Presse*, received intimidating anonymous phone calls during and after the coup and was threatened with expulsion in May 1992.

Télé Haiti, a private television station, also came under fire because of its foreign French-language news programs and its broadcasts of *Radio France Internationale's* news reports. Several weeks after the coup, *Télé Haiti* was forced to censor all local and foreign news reports about Haiti for fear of reprisals.

Foreign correspondents have been harassed and prevented from covering anti-government demonstrations. While there have not been as many attacks against foreign journalists as Haitian journalists— probably because fewer foreign journalists do on-the-ground reporting and because those who do rarely venture to the more dangerous areas outside of Port-au-Prince—foreign reporters have been singled out in recent incidents. On September 7, 1993, Patricia Benoit, a Haitian-American journalist on assignment for *Global Vision*, was assaulted by two attachés who grabbed her video camera and confiscated her video cassette. On October 12, 1993, three Miami journalists from *WSVN-TV* were abducted by armed civilians, threatened at gunpoint, and later released unharmed.

Local journalists who work with foreign media organizations labor at great risk, and many have been threatened or detained. In May 1992, a member of CPJ's delegation received a series of threatening phone calls after *Radio Métropole* broadcast an interview about the purpose of the mission and its findings. The caller, who identified himself as a newspaper owner, complained that CPJ had been co-opted into criticizing the government and said, "It is people like you who are responsible for the destruction of this country."

Kim Brice, *CPJ's Research Associate for Haiti, is a former member of the UN's human rights mission in Haiti. She was CPJ's program coordinator for Africa until June 1993. Brice is currently enrolled in Columbia University's School of International and Public Affairs.*

SPECIAL REPORT: Haiti

Haiti

Two years after the September 1991 overthrow of President Jean-Bertrand Aristide, Haiti's military rulers continued to defy international pressures to restore democracy. After agreeing to a United Nations-brokered peace accord that would have reinstated Aristide by October 30, the military boldly resisted and displayed a total disregard for international opinion. Until it became obvious Aristide would not return in October, radio journalists kept resisting the military. Some radio stations in the capital of Port-au-Prince began broadcasting live news reports on abuse of authority and human rights. In the summer, after the peace accords, several radio directors who fled after the coup returned to Haiti from exile to reopen their stations. Prime Minister Robert Malval, who had been designated by Aristide to run the country until he returned to office, had plans to reopen the state-run radio and television network. But the military never allowed this to happen. Plans for reopening private radio stations were canceled when two staunch Aristide supporters were killed, and radio directors went into hiding or left the country. As the repression increased, the anti-military *Libete,* the only Creole-language newspaper published in Haiti, ceased publishing because of threats. The violence even had a chilling effect on *Le Nouvelliste,* a moderate daily newspaper, which by the end of the year printed mostly communiqués and unsigned articles. Reporting from the provinces was halted again. Local correspondents, who have been consistently under threat of the local military since the coup, censored their reports or went into hiding.

JANUARY

Fritzon Orius, *Radio Haiti Internationalé,* Imprisoned, Attacked

Orius, a Saint Marc correspondent with *Radio Haiti Internationalé,* and his brother were beaten by a group of civilians yielding machetes, sticks, and revolvers. Orius was probably attacked because of his association with *Radio Haiti Internationalé,,* a private station perceived to be in favor of Aristide.

JANUARY 15

Norluck Dorange, *Haiti-en-Marche,* Attacked, Harassed

Armed soldiers raided Dorange's home in Port-au-Prince in search of arms that had allegedly been supplied by exiled president Jean-Bertrand Aristide. Dorange, who writes for the Miami-based weekly newspaper *Haiti-en-Marche,* had recently returned from a journalism training program in the United States. The soldiers left after they were unable to find any arms and temporarily confiscated Dorange's passport.

JANUARY 22

Jean-Émile Estimable, *Radio Cacique,* Imprisoned, Attacked

Estimable, a former reporter for *Radio Cacique,* was detained at Pont Joux in the Artibonite following an argument with the local section chief Gele. He was subsequently accused of carrying pro-Aristide leaflets. Estimable was taken to Gele's home, where he was severely beaten. The following day, Estimable was transferred to a prison in Saint Marc, where he was held until early February when a court granted his provisional release. During his imprisonment, Estimable was beaten and forced to pay the equivalent of $16 in order to stop the abuse.

JANUARY 26

Elder Ameus, *Radio Vision,* Imprisoned
Radio Vision, Harassed
Soldiers detained Ameus, the owner of the

Jeremie-based *Radio Vision*, and confiscated equipment from the station. Ameus was charged with disseminating "subversive" information on a program called "Truth" and held overnight. The equipment was eventually returned.

JANUARY 29
Ronald Labady, *Libete*, Imprisoned
Labady, a newspaper vendor who was selling issues of *Libete*, was arrested at the entrance of a stadium in Cap-Haitien by police. He was held at Cap-Haitien's central prison and later released. *Libete* is Haiti's only Creole-language newspaper. It ceased publishing after the coup and reappeared at the end of 1992.

JANUARY 30
Clarence Renois, *Radio Métropole*, Attacked, Threatened
Jean-François Rotschild, Jr., *Radio Métropole*, Attacked, Threatened
Hans Bazar, *Le Rouleau*, Harassed
Renois and Rotschild, two reporters with *Radio Métropole*, were threatened at a rally when they intervened on behalf of a group of foreign journalists who were being intimidated by demonstrators. The demonstrators were protesting the expected arrival of UN special envoy Dante Caputo, who was traveling to Haiti to negotiate a political settlement between the deposed President Jean-Bertrand Aristide and the de facto government. Demonstrators accused *Radio Métropole* of working for President Aristide and of receiving funds from the U.S. government. Renois was hit on the back. Bazar, a photographer for *Le Rouleau* magazine, had his film confiscated after taking a photograph of the demonstrators.

FEBRUARY 1
Colson Dorme, *Radio Tropic FM*, Imprisoned, Attacked
Dorme, a reporter with *Radio Tropic FM*, was hit over the head after filing a report about a demonstration at Port-au-Prince's International Airport. He was thrown, unconscious, into a pickup truck and taken away. His whereabouts were unknown until February 7, when he was dumped in front of *Radio Tropic FM's* offices. He was blindfolded, his head was shaved, and his hands and legs were tied. After his release, Dorme stated that he had been taken to an unknown location where he was kept blindfolded throughout his detention and badly beaten. Amnesty International reports that he may have been held at Delmas 33 detention center. During his ordeal, Dorme was questioned by two men who accused him of belonging to Lavalas, the political movement that supports deposed president Jean-Bertrand Aristide, and of collaborating with foreigners. His captors promised him money if he became an agent for them.

FEBRUARY 1
Dominique Levanti, *Agence France-Presse*, Threatened
Michael Tarr, *Reuter*, Threatened
Daniel Morrel, *Associated Press*, Threatened
Michael Norton, *Associated Press*, Threatened
The four journalists were threatened at Port-au-Prince's international airport by demonstrators who opposed the arrival of UN special envoy Dante Caputo. Protesters accused the reporters of bias and of favoring the deposed President Jean-Bertrand Aristide. Later in the day, the journalists were covering a similar demonstration in front of the Hôtel Montana, where the UN delegation was staying. Demonstrators threatened to kill them. The car in which Levanti, Morrel, Norton, and Tarr were passengers was stopped by members of the crowd and jostled. They were eventually allowed to leave.

The Americas

FEBRUARY 4
Jean Lumack Charles, *Radio Cacique*, Imprisoned, Attacked
Four men in civilian clothes identified Charles in the street and struck him in the head with a gun. He received at least seven blows to his head and was kicked and bitten. Charles was placed in the trunk of a car and taken first to the antigang headquarters, which refused to accept him because of his critical physical condition. He was then driven to the Corps de Génie, where his assailants received the same response. Later he was incarcerated at the Cafétéria and formally charged with resisting arrest and jailed without receiving any medical attention. Eight days later he was transferred to a hospital, but only permitted to stay a few hours. He was eventually taken to the Tribunal de Paix. When soldiers discovered that the judge was not present, he was incarcerated at the National Penitentiary. He was released on February 15, only after his family paid a judge $375.

FEBRUARY 25
Claudy Vilme, *Le Nouvelliste*, Imprisoned, Attacked
Vilme, a former photographer with the private daily *Le Nouvelliste* and *Haiti Relais* magazine, was beaten and briefly detained by armed civilians in front of the cathedral of Port-au-Prince. He was released after interventions by members of the OAS/UN Civilian Mission.

MARCH
Johnson Legrand, *Radio Tropic FM*, Threatened
In late March, Legrand, a correspondent in Gonaives for *Radio Tropic FM*, went into hiding several days after three soldiers and an attaché went to his home searching for him. Legrand was not home at the time. According to GRALIP, a Haitian press freedom organization, authorities were seeking to punish Legrand for a radio report concerning the distribution of pro-Aristide leaflets in Gonaives.

MARCH 30
Masner Beauplan, *Radio Transdigital*, Attacked
Radio Transdigital, Harassed
Soldiers in Hinche beat and searched Beauplan, the coordinator of the Journalists Association for the Haut Plateau Central and a correspondent for *Radio Quisqeya* and *Cap-Haitien* prior to the 1991 coup that deposed President Jean-Bertrand Aristide. Documents pertaining to the repression of journalists in the Central Plateau and a letter pertaining to his request for political asylum were confiscated. He was held for two days, during which time soldiers destroyed *Radio Transdigital's* transmitter and other equipment. Beauplan has since received political asylum.

MARCH 30
Jean Lumack Charles, *Radio Cacique*, Attacked, Threatened
Charles, a former reporter for *Radio Cacique*, was apprehended and beaten by three men in civilian clothes while walking in Port-au-Prince. He received several revolver blows to his face, neck, and stomach. His assailants warned that the next time they found Charles, they would kill him. *Radio Cacique* ceased broadcasting after it was attacked by soldiers after the 1991 coup.

APRIL 1
Wilfrid Jean, Attacked
Jean Robert Guillaume, Attacked
Duval Azolin, Attacked
Libete, Harassed
Jean, Guillaume, and Azolin, newspaper vendors in Port-au-Prince, were beaten by men in civilian clothing because they were selling copies of *Libete*. Dozens of copies of the newspaper were also torn into pieces.

APRIL 10
Ernst Ocean, *Radio Tropic FM*, Imprisoned
Ocean, a correspondent for *Radio Tropic FM* in Saint Marc, was held for two days by soldiers for allegedly "distributing pamphlets in favor

of Aristide." The local army captain announced on a radio program that distributing pamphlets was illegal in Haiti.

JUNE
Libete Vendor, Attacked, Imprisoned
Michel Gaspard, *Libete*, Attacked, Harassed
Justin Charles, *Libete*, Harassed
During the first week in June, security forces confiscated issues of *Libete* from Gaspard and Charles, two newspaper vendors in Port-au-Prince. Gaspard was also beaten on the head. Another vendor, who name was not revealed to us by the newspaper's staff for his safety, was beaten with a stick and detained by a uniformed soldier. He was released the following day.

JUNE
Journalists, Threatened
A unknown group calling itself "Liberty or Death" circulated a hit list with the names of 80 Haitians, including 24 journalists.

JUNE 2
Libete, Threatened
A phone caller, who identified himself as a member of the police antigang unit, threatened to destroy the newspaper's offices. The staff was particularly concerned about the threat because *Libete's* address and phone number are not publicly listed for security reasons.

JUNE 14
Thony Belizaire, *Agence France-Presse*, Threatened, Harassed
Belizaire, a photographer for *Agence France-Presse*, was threatened by a soldier in front of the Parliament building in Port-au-Prince. Belizaire's film was confiscated.

JUNE 24
Melorme Compere, *Libete*, Imprisoned, Attacked
Luckner Madena, *Libete*, Imprisoned, Attacked
Jean Azolin, *Libete*, Imprisoned, Attacked
Justin, *Libete*, Imprisoned, Attacked

Vendors of the Creole-language newspaper *Libete* were arrested while distributing the newspaper and beaten with sticks by police from the investigation and Antigang unit.

JUNE 29
Agence Haitienne de Presse, Threatened
Associated Press, Threatened
Reuters, Threatened
Andre Calixte, the de facto government's minister of information, reprimanded the *Agence Haitienne de Presse*, *Associated Press*, and *Reuters* for their reporting of a June 27 raid of the Perpetuel Secours church by police during a mass commemorating the victims who died after the Neptune capsized.

JULY 2
Claudy Vilme, *Le Nouvelliste*, Imprisoned, Attacked
Vilme, a former photographer with the daily private newspaper *Le Nouvelliste* and *Haiti Relais* magazine, was detained for a day by five armed civilians driving a vehicle with army license plates after he took a photograph of a person at a gas station paying the police directly for gasoline. The attachés took him to Fort Dimanche where he was beaten until he lost consciousness. His film was confiscated. Vilme went into hiding and was granted political asylum in the United States in August.

AUGUST
John Smith Dominique Prien, *Radio Plus*, Threatened, Attacked, Harassed
The home of Prien, an announcer for *Radio Plus*, was attacked by police and armed civilians. In early September, Prien's brother was stopped by authorities and questioned about his brother's whereabouts. It is unclear whether Prien was being harassed in connection with his

The Americas

journalism or an ongoing feud he had with a neighbor, who is an officer at Lamentin 54, army barracks in Prien's neighborhood.

AUGUST 13

Wilfred Joseph, *Libete*, Attacked, Imprisoned
Joseph, a *Libete* vendor, was detained and beaten in Mirebalais in the Central Plateau by a soldier named Paul Renel. Joseph was released the same day.

SEPTEMBER

Radio Tropic FM, Threatened
Radio Tropic FM, a private radio station based in Port-au-Prince, received numerous phone calls from individuals warning that the station's journalists would be "massacred." The director of the station sent a written appeal to Port-au-Prince police chief Lieutenant Colonel Joseph Michel Francois asking for protection. François replied in writing that the station should hire a private security company to assure the safety of its staff.

SEPTEMBER

Directors of State Media, Harassed
The directors and news staff of the state media, who were appointed by the Aristide government on September 9, were unable to begin working due to the threat posed by armed civilians protesting at the entrance of *Télévision Nationale*, the state-run television station. Between September 29 and October 1, employees of the state-run *Radio Nationale*, who had been hired after the 1991 coup, and armed civilians invaded the premises of the radio station and briefly resumed broadcasts in favor of the de facto government.

SEPTEMBER 7

Patricia Benoit, *Global Vision*, Attacked, Harassed
Benoit, a Haitian-American journalist on assignment for *Global Vision*, was prevented from filming the exterior of City Hall in Port-au-Prince when two civilians grabbed her video camera and confiscated her video cassette. She was reporting on the reinvestiture of Port-au-Prince Mayor Evans Paul.

SEPTEMBER 8

Emmanuel Laurent, *Radio Tropic FM*, Attacked
Laurent, a reporter with the private radio station *Radio Tropic FM*, suffered severe blows to his arm and back when civilians assaulted him with a large plank of wood outside City Hall in Port-au-Prince. He was reporting on the reinvestiture of Mayor Evans Pauls..

SEPTEMBER 10

Radio Caraibes, Threatened
Patrick Moussingac, *Radio Caraibes*, Expelled
Radio Caraibes' staff were threatened by 15 armed civilians who entered the radio station and demanded to see its director, Patrick Moussingac. The gunmen held the station's secretary, Miriam Valcourt, and at least two other journalists at gunpoint. The attachés warned that they would kill the journalists and blow up the station with grenades if it continued to support President Aristide. *Radio Caraibes* stopped broadcasting news temporarily. The director fled the country the following day. The station did not resume its news broadcasts until October 6. The threat may relate to the station's live report on the outbreak of violence by soldiers and attachés at Mayor Evans Paul reinvestiture several days earlier.

SEPTEMBER 11

Daniel Morel, *Associated Press*, Threatened
Hans Bazar, *Haiti-en-Marche*, Threatened, Harassed
Morel, an *Associated Press* photographer, was grabbed during a mass at the Sacre Coeur church in Port-au-Prince by an attaché who momentarily mistook him for Antoine Izmery, a prominent Haitian businessman and Aristide supporter. Izmery was later dragged out of the church and shot at point-blank range. Bazar,

a photographer for the weekly Miami-based newspaper *Haiti-en-Marche* and *Le Rouleau* magazine, was threatened by an armed man who confiscated his camera and press card.

SEPTEMBER 11
Surin Wilson, *Radio Plus*, Imprisoned
Wilson, a freelance journalist working with *Radio Plus*, was detained by six armed civilians at the Sacre Coeur church in Port-au-Prince. He was taken to the Service d'Investigation et Antigang and held for the day. The same day, Antoine Izmery was dragged out of the church during a mass and shot dead.

OCTOBER
Libete, Threatened
Haiti's only Creole-language newspaper ceased publishing in late October after unidentified individuals came to the newspaper's offices and threatened its staff.

OCTOBER 5
State Media, Threatened
The directors of state media, appointed by Prime Minister Robert Malval, decided to shut down the state-run television and radio stations due to threats. Broadcasts have not resumed.

OCTOBER 6
François Joseph, *Radio Tropic FM*, Attacked
Heavily armed attachés disrupted a meeting at the Hôtel Christopher that was attended by Port-au-Prince Mayor Evans Paul. Attachés began beating journalists who were outside the hotel. A reporter for *Tropic FM*, François Joseph, fractured one of his legs when he jumped over a wall to escape assault.

OCTOBER 11
Radio Nationale, Attacked
Armed civilians allied with Mouvement Capois la Mort, a branch of the Duvalierist Revolutionary Front for Haitian Advancement and Progress (FRAPH), took over the state-run

radio station's premises for the day. They called for Prime Minister Robert Malval to step down and broadcast messages condemning foreign intervention.

OCTOBER 12
Shepard Smith, *WSVN-TV*, Imprisoned, Threatened, Expelled
Cesar Aldana, *WSVN-TV*, Imprisoned, Threatened, Expelled
Moreau Dugas, *WSVN-TV*, Imprisoned, Threatened, Expelled
Armed civilians detained the *WSVN-TV* crew while they were covering the arrival of the *USS Harlan County* at Port-au-Prince's port. The ship was carrying American and Canadian technicians that were part of the United Nation-brokered accord. The three journalists were held at gunpoint, interrogated for several hours, and then driven to the airport and put on a plane to Miami.

OCTOBER 22-26
Radio Provinciale, Threatened
Radio Phalanstere, Threatened
The directors of *Radio Provinciale* and *Radio Phalanstere* were warned by Gonaives's Captain Senafils to be cautious of what they report and to play less "democracy music." Both Gonaives-based radio stations have stopped broadcasting.

OCTOBER 25
Luckner Desir, *Radio Phalenstere*, Imprisoned
Radio Provinciale Receptionist, Imprisoned
Desir, a technician for *Radio Phalenstere* and a receptionist with *Radio Provinciale*, were detained for a day. Captain Castera Senafils accused the radio stations of broadcasting "democracy music." Both radio stations are based in Gonaives.

OCTOBER 30
Luc François, *Radio Tele-Express*, Threatened
Unknown gunmen fired at the home of

The Americas

François, a freelance journalist working with the private radio station *Tele-Express* in Jacmel. No injuries were reported. François went into hiding in mid-October after soldiers harassed him for allegedly criticizing Duvalierists and the army in the South-Eastern Department in articles published in *Haiti Progres*, a Miami-based Haitian weekly newspaper.

NOVEMBER 1

Marie Yolande Saint-Fleur, *Agence Haitienne de Photo,* Expelled

Saint-Fleur, a founder of the *Agence Haitienne de Photo*, was forced to leave the country after repeatedly being terrorized by army soldiers and unidentified individuals. Her home was visited several times throughout the year by armed civilians, and an unknown assailant shot at her. She was not injured during the attack. Saint-Fleur believes she is being persecuted for controversial photographs that were published in publications that openly criticize the de facto government.

Honduras

Relations between the armed forces and the press deteriorated after a group of journalists filmed a murder scene in the provincial city of San Pedro de Sula. The killers were identified as members of the armed forces. The journalists were threatened, and one had to flee the country. The incident was one of several where the armed forces accused the press of selectively attacking their institution. In April, anonymous posters appeared in Tegucigalpa accusing journalists of receiving money from human rights organizations, business groups, and the U.S. Embassy. The army's discomfort was prompted by an investigation on human rights abuses that took place this year. The press covered this event widely. In December the government's human rights monitor accused the Honduran military of the murder of 187 leftists in the 1980s. The most threatening act against the press was introduced by the Honduran Congress. In a new copyright law, the Congress ruled against "the transmission or reproduction of programs...that attack the culture, morals, family integrity and good customs."

EARLY FEBRUARY

Eduardo Coto García, *Canal* 7, Threatened, Expelled

Luis Ayala, *Canal* 7, Threatened

Ricardo Amaya, *Canal* 7, Threatened

On January 29, Coto García and Luis Ayala, both of *Canal* 7, were driving around San Predo de Sula when they heard gunshots. They immediately went to the scene of the crime and proceeded to film what that aftermath of the murder of a well-known Honduran businessman, Eduardo Pina Van Tuyl. That evening, Coto García broadcast the images on his show, *Hoy Mismo* (Today). After the broadcast, Coto García noticed he was being followed by the same car he had filmed driving away from the crime earlier that morning. He decided to go into hiding at the funeral parlor that housed the body of Pina VanTuyl. There he encountered Ricardo Amaya, a cameraman for the program "En la Mira," who said the men in the car had told him that if it was he who had shot that morning's footage, they would kill him. Later Coto García moved to the newspaper *Tiempo*, where he received protection from the journalists and local human rights organizations until February 12 when he fled the country. Ayala and Amaya remained in Honduras; however, they have taken special measures to protect themselves.

FEBRUARY 5
Yani Rosenthal, *Tiempo,* Attacked
The house of the daily *El Tiempo's* board member, Yani Rosenthal, was bombed the morning after the newspaper published articles about attacks and threats against journalist Eduardo Coto García, who caught on film the murder of businessman, Eduardo Pina Van Tuyl.

FEBRUARY 12
All Media, Threatened
Chief of Police Colonel Mario Hung Pacheco announced that all journalists are closely monitored by security organizations and that the armed forces keep files on all journalists.

APRIL 26
Carlos Grant, *El Tiempo,* Killed
Grant, 67, the local correspondent for the Tegucigalpa daily *El Tiempo* in the town of El Progreso, was shot dead by a local money lender who was upset about an article Grant wrote.

Mexico

Five journalists were reported murdered in Mexico in 1993, more than in any other country in the Western Hemisphere. However, as is commonly the case in Mexico, it was impossible to show any clear linkage between these deaths and the victims' journalistic activities. In several instances circumstantial evidence suggested strongly that the homicides were common crimes committed with no apparent political motive. In no case were the victims known for controversial or critical reporting. Yet the chilling effect on Mexican journalism is nonetheless real. There have been well-documented cases in the past of journalists killed for their

reporting with the apparent complicity or even participation of local (and in some cases national) law enforcement authorities. And with the endemic failings of the Mexican criminal justice system, those who order such killings are only rarely apprehended, tried and convicted. As in Colombia, most serious physical attacks on journalists appear to have been ordered by drug traffickers. In small provincial cities, Mexican reporters have reason to fear reprisals. In the national media, however, the suppression of independent reporting has other systemic causes.

Foreign analysts conventionally ascribe the pro-government slant of most Mexican news reportage to two factors: journalists' fear of personal (and often violent) retribution, and state control of newsprint supplies and advertising budgets. Few Mexican reporters share that analysis, however. Direct physical intimidation of journalists is less frequent than it was in the past. Privatization and deregulation has greatly reduced the government's direct control over advertising. Yet coercion continues apace: the ruling Institutional Revolutionary Party (PRI) works hard to manipulate coverage through political pressure and economic favors to pro-government news organizations. Mexico continues to have the least independendent press of any major country in the Western hemisphere.

The central problem with the Mexican press is not easily remedied: it is the sycophancy and corruption of the news media itself. There are honorable exceptions, such as the muckraking weekly *Proceso;* the conservative, highly professional *El Norte* of Monterrey and its newly launched affiliate, *Reforma* in Mexico City; *El Financiero,* the country's leading busi-

The Americas

ness daily; the increasingly independent, left-leaning *La Jornada,* and *Siglo XXI,* a feisty new Guadalajara tabloid. The success of these publications has shown that independent reporting in Mexico is not only possible, but potentially profitable.

Most publishers, however, prefer the old system of under-the-table government subsidies for their underpaid reporters and over-the-table payments for official "news" placement. President Carlos Salinas de Gortari's dissolution of the state monopoly that provided subsidized newsprint was bitterly opposed by most publishers. His announced ban on cash bribes to reporters from federal offices was received with greater equanimity, since there are multiple alternative mechanisms for such payments.

Independent broadcast reporting is rare. Radio call-in and interview shows have begun to offer opposition viewpoints, but official complaints have in some cases led the radio companies to cancel the offending programs. Television news—condemned as "Stalinist" and "an embarrassment" by novelist Carlos Fuentes—hews rigidly to the government line. *Televisa,* owned by PRI fundraiser (and by Forbes' reckoning Latin America's wealthiest man) Emilio Azcarraga, has near-monopoly control of television news programming, and unapologetically uses that power to advance the interests of the ruling party. Opposition parties have regularly held street protests against *Televisa.* When Chiapas Indian rebels took arms against the government on Jan. 1, 1994, one of their principal complaints addressed *Televisa's* "biased" news reporting. In subsequent negotiations the government agreed to press for fairer television coverage of opposition views and candidates during the 1994 election campaign.

JANUARY 5

Sixto Bolanos, *Respuesta,* Legal Action, Imprisoned

Bolanos, a special correspondent for the Tabasco daily *Respuesta,* in the city of Macuspana, department of Tabasco, was jailed, tried, and convicted of defamation after he wrote a story on Xicontencatl Romero León, a local councilman accused of stealing public funds. Bolanos had documents supporting his article. He was jailed on June 2 and released a day later on bail. He was liable because he wrote the story without first taking it before a judge who could rule if the documents were valid or not. The councilman sued for clear intent to dishonor his reputation. Bolanos appealed but lost. He is awaiting sentence, which is expected to be about three years in jail. He lost his job after the trial. His paper accused him of sloppy journalism.

MARCH 8

Richard Seid, *Mexico City News,* Harassed

Seid was fired from his job as opinion page editor of Mexico's only English-language daily, after he wrote an opinion article on the lack of press freedoms for the *Christian Science Monitor.* Another *News* reporter, Zachary Margulis, was dismissed in December of last year, after he wrote an article on censorship at the *News* for the *New York Times.* Also in December, half a dozen other reporters at the *News* quit the paper after editors imposed a two-month ban on reporting on opposition political parties.

MARCH 24

Esmelin Suárez López, *Asi Es Esto,* Imprisoned, Legal Action

Suarez published an article tying members of the powerful Cattlemen's Association to a swindle where large landowners sold their sick cattle to small farmers who used government credits to purchase the animals. The article said the worst offender in the corruption was Tabasco's

Senator Arcadio León Estrada, who was a former president of the Cattlemen's Association. Suárez had documents from veterinarians showing the cattle were sick with brucellosis and testimony that showed the animals were knowingly sold in that condition. Suárez was indicted on charges of defamation and is currently free on bail. He is expected to be tried and sentenced this year.

APRIL 10
Presente, Attacked
The offices of the daily *Presente*, published in Villa Hermosa, Tabasco's provincial capital, were raided by unidentified persons. Photos and documents were removed from the newspaper.

JULY 29
Ramón Sánchez Gómez, *Presente*, Attacked
Gómez was summoned to the offices of Saul Jímenez Méndez, municipal president for the town of Jonuta, in the department of Tabasco, and proceeded to verbally insult him for an article the correspondent wrote stating that the president had failed to pay a number of debts he had with local merchants. Méndez slapped the correspondent on the face, after Méndez's private secretary shut the door to the office, and did not allow the reporter to leave.

SEPTEMBER 22
Daniel Castro, *Tabasco Al Dia*, Harassed
Manuel Ruiz Márquez, *La Tarde*, Harassed
Veronica Danell, *6:20*, Harassed
Castro, Ruiz Marquez and Danell were fired from their jobs following their participation in a meeting between journalists of the newly formed Committee for the Defense of Freedom of Expression and Tabasco's governor Manuel Gurría Ordónez. The group formed after Sixto Bolanos, a reporter for the daily *Respuesta*, was charged with defamation. The journalists asked the governor to amend the state's defamation law.

NOVEMBER 9
José F. Gallardo Rodríguez, *Forum*, Imprisoned, Legal Action
Eduardo Ibarra Aguirre, *Forum*, Threatened
Gallardo, a general in the Mexican army, was arrested after *Forum*, a periodical published by the National Autonomous University of Mexico (UNAM), ran sections of his master's thesis in which he called for the creation of a military ombudsman. In the article the general, who remains on active duty but was denied an assignment because of a festering battle with his superiors, charges that the army "violates rights with impunity" and in some cases has been involved in killings, torture, and drug deals. He is charged with defamation. A military judge warned the editor of the *Forum* that he would also be charged with defamation if he didn't cooperate with Mexican authorities.

Nicaragua

Although there has been a boom in the number of radio stations—the country's most important medium—and print media outlets, Nicaragua's news media remain partisan in their reporting. The press represents either the National Opposition Union (UNO) a coalition party that controls the executive branch, or the former ruling party, the leftist Sandinista National Liberation Front (FSLN), which holds important positions in the national assembly and the judicial branch. This year news stations supporting either the Sandinista party or UNO were harassed. A group of journalists were kidnapped and then released during the short hostage situation where former armed Contra soldiers kidnapped government officials and Sandinista supporters kidnapped UNO politicians. The three major newspapers in

the country are run by members of the Chamorro family, but they are aligned with opposing political parties. *La Prensa,* owned by President Violeta Chamorro and her late husband's family, defended her government policies. *El Nuevo Diario* and *Barricada,* which were founded in 1979 during Sandinista leadership, are run by one of the president's sons and a brother-in-law. Both continue to endorse FSLN policies.

AUGUST 20
Radio Corporación, Attacked
A group of armed men raided the studios of anti-Sandinista *Radio Corporación* and opened fire, damaging valuable office equipment and causing the station to shut down for about a week. The station is critical of the government of Violeta Chamorro.

AUGUST 22
Omar García, *Radio Ya,* Kidnapped
Fredy Potoy, *Barricada,* Kidnapped
Adolfo Montano, *Barricada,* Kidnapped
José Ángel Vivas, *Washington Post,* Kidnapped
Miguel Mora, *Extravision-TV,* Kidnapped
Juan Mairena, *Extravision-TV,* Kidnapped
Bayardo Fajardo, *Radio Ya,* Kidnapped
Mario Zelaya, *Radio Sandino,* Kidnapped
Sergio Miranda, *Radio Sandino,* Kidnapped
Nine Nicaraguan journalists working for local outlets and one working as a stringer for the *Washington Post* were kidnapped by leftist gunmen supporting the Sandinista party. The gunmen erupted into the headquarters of the opposition party National Opposition Union and kidnapped Nicaraguan Vice President Virgilio Godoy and other members of the party in retaliation for the kidnapping by Contras of government officials, including top Sandinista party officials. Most of the kidnapped journalists work for news outlets that support the Sandinista party. The journalists were released with other hostages on August 25.

SEPTEMBER 20
Radio Corporación, Attacked
Unknown assailants attacked the studios of *Radio Corporación* for the second time in a month. The nature of the attack is unclear, but apparently the assailants bound the hands and feet of a security guard before destroying the station's transmitter with explosives. The station is known to criticize the government of Violeta Chamorro.

DECEMBER 23
La Prensa, Legal Action
General Humberto Ortega, commander in chief of the Sandinista People's Army, announced at a news conference that the army will bring libel charges against *La Prensa* and its director Pablo Antonio Cuadra. The charges stemmed from a story the daily published accusing the army of bombing a 40-family hamlet. A picture from another incident accompanied the story. Cuadra said his newspaper was only reprinting stories that were published by other media. The army retracted on December 28, after Cardinal Miguel Obando y Bravo interceded.

Panama

The press situation in Panama has improved since the overthrow of General Manuel Noriega in 1989. However, laws restricting press freedoms used during his dictatorship still provide a potential weapon to be used against journalists. In 1993, dozens of journalists faced long and complicated libel lawsuits filed by government officials. In two cases, journalists were physically attacked by government officials because of a press report.

JANUARY 25
Empowerment Project, Censored
The Panama Deception, an American documentary film critical of the U.S. invasion of Panama, was banned in Panama. Showing of the film was permitted after March 18.

JUNE 9
Luis DeJanon, *La Estrella de Panama*, Attacked
DeJanon, a columnist for the opposition daily *La Estrella de Panama* was assaulted by George Weeden, a special adviser to President Guillermo Endara, and a member of the Arnulfista party. George's brother, Alvyn Weeden, a consultant to the Panamanian Customs Department, also participated in the beating. The writer had published a number of columns that implicated the Weeden brothers in money laundering investigations in Miami in the 1980s.

JUNE 12
James Aparicio, *Agence France-Press*,
Legal Action
Manuel Álvarez, *Agence France-Press*,
Legal Action
Both Aparicio and Álvarez were sued in court by Omaira Correa, the former mayor of Panama City, for the amount of $2.5 million in damages, for articles they wrote while she was in office. Aparicio is the secretary general of the Union of Persecuted Journalists. After two years, the journalists won the case. *AFP* paid $40,000 in legal fees; Correa has placed 33 other charges against Aparicio.

JUNE 20
José Luis Aranda, *Channel 13*, Attacked
A police officer assaulted José Luis Aranda of *Channel 13*, after the cameraman attempted to film the officer as he arrested a group of men. The attack left Aranda disabled. He is presently out of work. His camera was broken during the attack. Aranda is suing the police force for damages.

JULY 30
Nícolas Psomas, *Diario La Prensa*, Attacked
Hector Ramírez, *RPC*, Attacked
Psomas and Ramírez were assaulted by two Panamanian policemen while they covered the trial of men accused of killing Panamanian political dissident Hugo Spadafora. The police officers attempted to confiscate Psomas's tape recorder and Ramírez's video camera. The journalists were violating a court ban against filming of the court procedures.

SEPTEMBER 2
Honarina Rodríguez, *Hoy*, Attacked
Rodríguez, a photographer with the daily *Hoy*, was roughed up by an agent of the United States Drug Enforcement Agency after she began taking his photo as he entered the Panamanian anti-narcotics unit. The U.S. Embassy and the agent apologized but said if his picture appeared in the newspaper it would make his job difficult. Panamanian journalists said he should not have been in a public place if he did not want his picture taken.

SEPTEMBER 13
Justino González, *Diario Crítica*, Attacked
Antonio Díaz, *Diario Crítica*, Attacked
Gonzáles wrote a story implicating a member of the presidential police in the murder of a man in the provincial city of Capira. A few days later, both journalists were attacked by Carlos Bares, commander of the presidential police. Bares has apologized for the attack.

Paraguay

Five years after the ouster of longtime dictator General Alfredo Stroessner, Paraguay enjoys greater press freedom than at any other time in its history, notwithstanding several disturbing developments. On May 9, Juan Carlos Wasmosy became the first freely elected civilian president in Paraguay's history. On the morning of the elections, unidentified assailants fired at and damaged the electric transformer at Asunción's *Channel 13* and threw a hand grenade at its transmission tower. The damage delayed broadcasts and also affected *Channel 13's* radio station, *Radio Cardinal*. Both had been critical of the government policies during the campaign. By the end of the year, little had been done to investigate the attack. In addition to electoral politics, official corruption, drug trafficking, and money laundering are subjects that pose special difficulties for journalists, particularly journalists outside of the capital. Because of the Stroessner dictatorship's dismal human rights record, journalists in Paraguay are concerned about proposed legislation to reform the criminal code. The proposed legislation would create ambiguous crimes "against the peace" and "against honor." It also contains anti whistleblowing provisions, which have serious implications for the press. There is also a proposal that would exempt officials from prosecution for human rights violations if they could show "due obedience," in effect, establish an amnesty law, impeding the investigation and bringing to justice the perpetrators of violations during the Stroessner dictatorship.

MAY
Radio Cardinal, Attacked
Channel 13, Attacked
On May 9, unidentified assailants fired at the offices of *Channel 13* and *Radio Cardinal*, both owned by the Private Communications Group, RPC. The stations were critical of government policies.

SEPTEMBER 1
Emilio Ortiz, *Última Hora*, Threatened
Ortiz, correspondent for the daily, received death threats over the phone after he reported on corruption at the state telephone company.

NOVEMBER 1
Juan Pelayo, *Radio Mburucuya*, Threatened
Blanca Mino, *Radio Mburucuya*, Threatened
Heriberto Arguello, *Radio Mburucuya*, Threatened
Francisco Servia, *Radio Mburucuya*, Threatened
Four *Radio Mburucuya* reporters received numerous threatening phone calls after several programs on drug trafficking were aired. President Juan Carlos Wasmosy met with members of the Journalists' Union on November 19 and promised to give necessary attention to these cases and offered police protection for the reporters.

Peru

When President Alberto Fujimori suspended the constitution in April 1992, he ended 12 years of democratic government. Arguing that the old political system was incapable of fighting an encroaching terrorist movement and government corruption, Fujimori won the support of the military and much of the Peruvian public. He has since made great inroads in curtailing the power of Shining

Path, the Maoist guerrilla group that terrorized Peru for over 10 years. But he also created a presidential dictatorship that continues to violate basic rights, including press freedoms. The opposition press strongly criticized Fujimori's self-coup, and they paid a price. Several journalists were jailed, and newsrooms were occupied by troops. At least two journalists who were threatened by the military during the coup remain in exile. Three newsweeklies—*Oiga, Sí,* and *Caretas*—continued publishing investigations of the military's abuse of human rights. Their reports won them the government's wrath, and they were the focus of several legal actions and other threats. Military and civilian officials warned reporters that those who "vilify" the integrity of the armed forces and the government will be prosecuted. Journalists who attempted to cover the guerrilla war in the countryside were harassed and threatened by both the military and the guerrillas. Special antiterrorist measures and new laws against "subversive information" are being used to muzzle the press. Some journalists have been sued for defamation; others have been convicted of crimes against national security. Another potential weapon against journalists is a vague law that makes being an "apologist for terrorism" a crime. It is up to the courts to decide what constitutes an "apologist for terrorism." The legal system itself poses additional threats to journalists since it was redesigned by President Fujimori. By presidential decree, pretrial detention is mandatory; there is no bail. The police and the army have unlimited power to hold suspects incommunicado for extended periods of time. The new congress elected in 1992 enacted into law the antiterrorist measures

Fujimori introduced during the coup. As a result of the 1993 referendum calling for a new constitution, there is no longer prohibition against a second presidential term. Fourteen journalists who worked for *El Diario* and *Cambio,* publications allegedly linked to Shining Path and Revolutionary Movement Tupac Amaru (MRTA), respectively, remain in jail. CPJ did not include them in the report because they were not jailed for their work alone, but we are following their cases. Four other journalists accused of similar crimes were released in 1993. They are: Danilo Quijano Silva, a columnist for the opposition daily *La República;* Gisella Gutarra, a reporter for the daily *Onda,* Ricardo Gadea Acosta, of the magazine *Testual;* and Rosa Neyra, a former journalist who once worked for *Cambio.* The four were accused of having ties to the MRTA.

JANUARY
Enrique Zileri Gibson, *Caretas,* Legal Action
The Fourth Penal Superior Court banned Zileri from publishing any articles on the former presidential adviser, Vladimiro Montesinos Torres, for the next 16 months. Zileri edits the opposition magazine *Caretas.* Montesinos is also an official of the National Intelligence Service.

JANUARY 1
Francisco Igartua, *Oiga,* Harassed
Igartua, head of the opposition *Oiga* magazine, said personnel from the tax agency called Sunat were constantly monitoring the magazine's advertising activities.

JANUARY
José Antonio Álvarez Pachas, *Cambio,* Imprisoned
Pachas was detained in June 1992 for working with the leftist daily *Cambio,* which has alleged ties to the rebel group Revolutionary Movement Tupac Amaru, MRTA. He has

appealed his sentence with the support of the National Association of Journalists.

JANUARY 5
Ricardo Uceda, *Sí,* Legal Action
The Minister of Defense, Victor Malca, initiated a case against editor Ricardo Uceda for falsifying information. Through the public prosecutor, the general accused Uceda of lying about the involvement of senior military personnel in the massacre of 15 people in 1991. Uceda published the charges in an article he wrote for the magazine *Sí,* which he also edits. Authorities wanted Uceda to reveal his sources for the story. Uceda refused, and a provincial criminal prosecutor closed the case, saying the magazine acted within its rights to exercise free expression.

JANUARY 8
Jeremy Bigwood, *Gamma-Liaison,* Imprisoned, Expelled
Bigwood, a freelance photographer working for *Gamma-Liaison Agency* in New York, was detained in Moyobamba, the department of San Martín, during an attack by leftist guerillas of the Revolutionary Movement Tupac Amaru. Bigwood was charged with "acts of terrorism" because he took photographs and filmed the guerilla incursion. Bigwood was transferred to a prison in Lima where he was held for less then a week until the charges were dropped and he left the country.

JANUARY 8
Enrique Zileri, *Caretas,* Legal Action
In another act of harassment against the opposition weekly *Caretas,* on January 8, a private citizen, Santiago Sanguinetti, sued Zileri and four other Caretas journalists on behalf of President Alberto Fujimori and Attorney General Blanca Nelida Colan. Sanguinetti used a procedure known as "popular action," whereby citizens can initiate criminal complaints. Sanguinetti said he was insulted by a recent article published by *Caretas,* that questioned a Fujimori biography. The case is being heard by the 32nd District Court, headed by judge Enrique Díaz. Sanguinetti himself has a pending charge of fraud.

JANUARY 16
Press in General, Harassed
President Alberto Fujimori announced to the national press that the National Intelligence Service "will evaluate all journalistic reports which do not coincide with government versions and threaten national security." Fujimori made the announcement after reports said a coup attempt was brewing because of discontent in the security forces over low pay. Two days later, the Interior Minister, General Juan Briones, said some journalists can be compared with members of the Shining Path. "They are terrorist reporters," Briones said.

JANUARY 16
National Association of Journalists, Threatened, Harassed
An armed group of men placed a simulated explosive device wrapped in red cloth at the main entrance of the National Association of Journalists office in Lima. The association, that has defended press freedoms and protected journalists persecuted for their writings, has received continuous telephone threats.

JANUARY 17
Foreign Press, Harassed
Officers of the National Intelligence Service summoned accredited foreign correspondents and warned them that the agency was monitoring their reports.

JANUARY 29
Gisella Gutarra, *Onda,* Imprisoned, Legal Action
In June 1992, Peruvian journalist Gisella Gutarra was released after having been imprisoned for five months on suspicion of terrorism. She was accused of working as a journalist for

publications linked to leftist terrorists. She was never tried for the charges. She was detained on January 29, on her way to vote during the municipal elections.

FEBRUARY 3
Magno Sosa, *La República*, Legal Action, Expelled
Sosa was freed five months after he was detained for allegedly sympathizing with the Maoist Shining Path guerrilla group. Sosa, a correspondent for *La República* newspaper in the southeastern city of Ayacucho, left the high-security Canto Grande prison a week after a judge had ordered his release due to lack of proof against him. After his release, the journalist asked for police protection, saying his life was in danger. Later, he decided to leave Peru and now he is living in Caracas, Venezuela.

FEBRUARY 27
Cecilia Valenzuela, *Caretas*, Threatened
Valenzuela, a reporter for the opposition weekly magazine *Caretas*, received a package that contained a picture of her smeared with blood attached to the head of a dead chicken. The package arrived shortly after she had written an article on the trial of army officers accused of an attempted coup in November 1992.

EARLY MARCH
Cecilia Valenzuela, *Caretas*, Legal Action
Valenzuela, a reporter for *Caretas* magazine, received a one-year suspended jail sentence for statements she made on an interview in a local television program. She accused a senior army officer of witnessing the torture of suspected terrorists in Ayacucho.

MARCH 3
Cesar Hildebrant, *América Televisión*, Legal Action
An arrest warrant was issued against Cesar Hildebrant, former director of the television

program "En Persona." He is being charged with contempt of court, after he failed to appear in court in a lawsuit brought by Retired General Clemente Noel, former commander in the Ayacucho military emergency area. Hildebrant, an outspoken critic of the Fujimori government, interviewed witnesses who accused the general of torturing terrorist suspects in Ayacucho. Hildebrant is exiled in Spain. He would be jailed if he returned to Peru.

MARCH 11
Carlos Basombrio, *Ideele*, Legal Action
Ernesto de la Jara, *Ideele*, Legal Action
Basombrio, editor of *Ideele* magazine, a publication of the Legal Defense Institute, a lawyers' human rights group, and de la Jara, director of the institute, were sued in court by private citizen Santiago Sanguinetti, who charged the journalists with libel against President Fujimori. But Fujimori issued a public announcement in rejecting the charges. The case was closed.

APRIL 5
Danilo Quijano Silva, *La República*, Imprisoned, Legal Action
On May 13, 1992, Quijano, a columnist for *La República*, was imprisoned on charges of belonging to the terrorist group Revolutionary Movement Tupac Amaru (MRTA). The charges were based on former business ties with MRTA members. On April 5 he was found guilty and sentenced, by a faceless judge, to five years imprisonment. Although he was found guilty by the court, there was no clear proof against him. On May 26 he was exonerated and released.

APRIL 23
Cecilia Valenzuela, *Caretas*, Threatened
Valenzuela, a reporter for *Caretas* magazine, received a death threat on her cellular phone— a number known only by her close friends and family. On May 1, Valenzuela's birthday, she received a dozen pink roses and a birthday card

with a death threat as she prepared for her birthday party at a friend's house.

JUNE 2
Juan Guerra, *Radio Vecinal,* Imprisoned, Legal Action, Harassed
On June 2, Juan Guerra was detained for two weeks by police officers. Guerra is a radiojournalist based in the city of Piura, capital of Piura department in the north of Peru. Guerra is a known critic of police brutality in his radio program. He has also reported on alliances between Peruvian police officers and known drug traffickers in the area. During his two-week arrest, his family received numerous anonymous telephone threats, as well as written death threats. On June 15, the provincial attorney in Piura ordered his release.

JUNE 10
La República Harassed
In a communiqué dated June 10, the Peruvian Armed Forces accused the newspaper *La República* of deliberately vilifying the institution by publishing allegedly false information and by criticizing the military's counterinsurgency strategy. The Armed Forces communiqué obliquely referred to the media as "enemies of Peru" and, indirectly, as allies of the armed opposition. The President of the Special Investigative Commission said that freedom of expression is not only a right but a responsibility to be exercised with dignity, without having to resort to the tactic of smearing institutions."

JUNE 15
Victor Camasca Zapata, *Labor,* Imprisoned
Camasca Zapata, editor of the magazine *Labor,* in the city of Pisco was released from prison on December 12, after nearly six months in detention. He was accused of having links to the rebel group Revolutionary Movement Tupac Amaru, MRTA. A special military tribunal freed him.

JULY 10
Ricardo Uceda, *Sí,* Harassed
Uceda, editor of *Sí* magazine, was accused of obstruction of justice by Congresswoman Martha Chávez. She said Uceda was being criminal for writing a story that identified a clandestine grave where the bodies of nine university students and their professor are buried. Obstruction of justice is a crime punishable with prison in Peru.

JULY 15
Ricardo Uceda, *Sí,* Harassed
The Attorney General Blanca Nelida Colan told members of the Human Rights Committee of Congress that *Sí* magazine had committed an offence against the administration of justice in the way they denounced the existence of common graves in a district of Lima called Cieneguilla.

AUGUST 2
Walter Pérez, *El Día/Panamericana Televisión,* Imprisoned
Will La Torre, *Panamericana Televisión,* Imprisoned
On August 2, journalists Walter Pérez and Will La Torre were detained in Pucalpa, Peru. Pérez is the director of the daily newspaper *Al Dia* in Pucalpa and is a correspondent for the news program "24 Horas" for *Panamericana Televisión,* the most important television network in Peru. La Torre is a camera operator. Both journalists were detained in the region of Ucayali, at a military checkpoint staffed by marines from the antiterrorist base called Von Humbolt nearby. They were accused of being terrorists. They were released five days later.

SEPTEMBER 6
Caretas, Legal Action
On September 6, the Supreme Court issued a public notice that authorized the public prosecutor to proceed with legal action against the opposition magazine *Caretas.* The magazine

incurred the wrath of the court after it published an article on accusations made against the Supreme Court by the company Promatco, which accused the court of soliciting bribes in exchange for favorable legal rulings on the company's behalf.

SEPTEMBER 10
Miguel Calderón, *Colegio de Periodistas,* Attacked
Juan Carlos Hernández Caycho, National Association of Journalists, Imprisoned
Carlos Ramos Nique, Photographers' Association, Imprisoned
Calderón was beaten as he tried to talk to policemen who broke off a street march organized by the *Colegio* in downtown Lima, two blocks from the presidential palace. The marchers were also attacked by police with tear gas pellets. Caycho and Nique were also detained at the march and held until the night of the day of the march. Calderón suffered second degree burns from the tear gas pellets. He has sued the minister of the interior, General E. P. Juan Briones, for damages.

SEPTEMBER 14
Radio Sinfonia, Censored
Radio Super Stereo, Censored
Radio Estudio 99, Censored
Radio Ritmo, Censored
The four stations based in Puerto Maldonado, in the province of Madre Díos, were closed down by the government for operating without a license. The stations had applied for a license, but the decision has been held by the local government for about a year. Before the closure, the radio stations were conducting an educational campaign on the October 31 referendum, informing listeners on the new political constitution. Local officials have warned radio directors that if they reopen the stations, they must limit their programming to music, sports, and cultural themes.

SEPTEMBER 14
Radio Stereo Villa, Censored
Channel 45, Censored
Mayor Salvador Vásquez Torres shut down and canceled the licenses of the two grass-roots media outfits, which operate Villa El Salvador in a working-class neighborhood that has won several international prizes for community organization. The decision was handed down in a municipal decree that came in retaliation for the wave of criticism lodged against Torres's administration by the residents of Villa El Salvador.

SEPTEMBER
Francisco Reyes, *La República,* Imprisoned, Attacked
Francisco Reyes, a reporter for the Lima daily *La República,* was physically assaulted and detained by air force officers at the Yurimaguas airport in Peru. He was released on September 21, but was accused of attempts against national security and espionage. He received several telephone threats following his release. Reyes had gone to Yurimaguas to cover the withdrawal of U.S. Drug Enforcement Agency officers who had come to Peru to help the Peruvian government fight drug trafficking. Reyes was accused of having taken pictures of the airport. In the past Reyes had written articles based on his investigations linking top-ranking officials of the Peruvian army and drug lords.

DECEMBER 8
Ricardo Gadea Acosta, *Testual,* Imprisoned
Gadea was detained on August 17 by order of a naval judge. He was accused of having links with the Revolutionary Movement Tupac Amaru. At the time of his arrest he worked for the magazine *Testual,* and other alternative press in Peru. He spent four months in detention awaiting trial.

DECEMBER 10

María Carlín Fernández, *RTPN,* Killed

Fernández, former anchorwoman for the local channel of *Peruvian Radio and Television Network*, was shot dead in a restaurant in Chimbote in the northern coast of Peru. She had received threats after she began investigating the death of a cousin who was killed in a barroom brawl that involved an army intelligence officer. The police have claimed that Fernández was the victim of a botched robbery, but the fact she was shot in the back 11 times belies this explanation.

DECEMBER 10

Alvaro Villavicencio Whittembury, *La República,* Imprisoned

Villavicencio Whittembury was absolved on December 10 by a special anonymous tribunal of having links with terrorist groups. He had been held in jail almost a year, awaiting trial. He wrote articles on education for the newspaper *La República*, and worked as an editor and proofreader for international news agencies. He was detained when his name appeared on a list of contacts found in the possession of a terrorist suspect.

United States

The Haitian community in Miami was shocked by another murder of a prominent Haitian broadcaster. Dona St. Plite was the third journalist killed in the last three years. His murder continues a disturbing trend where reporters working for foreign language media get silenced by fellow countrymen. This was documented by CPJ in a report entitled "Silence by Death." The 1991 murder of another foreign language newspaper reporter, Manuel de Díos de Unanue, was finally solved. Police arrested three Colombians involved in plotting the murder of the Cuban-born journalist because of his reporting on drug trafficking. An 18-year-old Colombian hitman was arrested and charged with the actual murder. But the Drug Enforcement Agency contends that Unanue's murder was ordered by José Santa Cruz Londono of the Cali Colombian cocaine cartel. In another well-known case, in Arizona, a mob-connected building contractor was sentenced to life in prison for the 1976 carbomb slaying of Arizona Republican Don Bolles. The murder of Bolles was investigated by a team of reporters from around the country and led to the establishment of the Investigative Reporters and Editors, which promotes investigative journalism.

MAY 14

Richard Scarce, Legal Action

Scarce, an author, freelance writer, and doctoral candidate in sociology at Washington State University, was cited for contempt of court and jailed for 159 days because he refused to tell a federal grand jury about a confidential conversation he had had with an animal rights activist who was suspected of taking part in a break-in at a WSU animal research laboratory. Scarce said he promised the activist confidentiality in order to gain information for publication, including his doctoral research. Scarce's standing as a journalist was controversial, but the Ninth Circuit Court of Appeals considered him a reporter for the purpose of legal analysis and ruled that journalists could not protect confidential sources in such circumstances.

SEPTEMBER 28

All Media, Harassed

The U.S. Treasury Department released a 220-page investigation report criticizing the media coverage of the raid against Branch

(continued on page 149)

Journalists Killed in the United States 1976-1993

by Greg Victor

SPECIAL REPORT: United States

When Manuel de Dios Unanue, a crusading reporter and editor in Queens, New York, was murdered in cold blood in 1991 because of his anti-drug reporting, Americans were stunned. Only two U.S. journalists have been killed in this country because of their reporting. In 1984, Alan Berg, a popular Denver-talk show host was shot down by members of a white supremacist group. And in 1976, Don Bolles, an Arizona Republic investigative journalist, was killed by a mob-connected businessman.

Yet, the De Dios murder brought to light a growing trend in the United States that had gone unnoticed by the mainstream media: the murder of journalists working for ethnic community newspapers.

•14 journalists were killed between 1976-1993, including Bolles and Berg.

•10 were foreign born and worked for non-English publications. They were specifically targeted and killed by fellow countrymen because of their political views or because they exposed corruption.

HISPANIC

Manuel de Dios Unanue, New York, 1992. Exposed drug dealers connected with the Cali cocaine cartel.

Born in Cuba, De Dios wrote extensively for the Spanish-language press about the drug trade. As a reporter, columnist, and editor-in-chief in his 12 years at El Diario-La Prensa (1977-1989), de Dios frequently identified and denounced drug dealers and money launderers. At the time of his death he was publishing two magazines, El Crimen and Cambio XXI, which specialized in crime news.

De Dios was shot twice in the head at point-blank range as he ate in a favorite restaurant in Elmhurst, Queens. On October 26, 1993, three Colombians pleaded guilty and admitted their roles in the killings. A fourth man, Wilson Alejandro Mejia Velez, has been charged with the actual shooting. The trial for the other three suspects started February, 1994.

HAITIANS (3)

Dona St. Plite, Miami, 1993
Fritz Dor, Miami, 1991
Jean-Claude Olivier, Miami, 1991.

Hosts of Creole-language radio talk shows. Supporters of deposed President Jean-Bertrand Aristide. They used the radio waves to promote their political views. St. Plite worked for *WKAT;* Dor worked for *WLQY;* Olivier worked for *WLQY.* Dor and Olivier were killed with the same gun. St. Plite was killed outside the school where a benefit in honor of Dor's family was taking place. Three accomplices in the three murders are in jail in Miami. Two have been tried, a third is awaiting trial. The triggermen remain at large.

VIETNAMESE (5)

Triet Le, Virginia, 1990
Nhan Trong Do, Virginia, 1989
Tap Van Pham, California, 1987
Nguyen Dam Phong, Texas, 1982
Doung Trong Lam, California, 1981

These cases remain unsolved. In two cases—Lam and Pham—anti-communist Vietnamese groups claimed credit. All of these killings appear to have been politically motivated and they remain unsolved.

CHINESE (1)

Henry Liu, San Francisco, 1984.

Killed by agents of the ruling Nationalist Party in Taiwan, apparently in retaliation for exposing corruption in the party and opposing its policies. Case is solved. Several conspirators were tried and convicted in Taiwan. Only one member of the conspiracy was tried in the United States.

U.S. BORN (4)

Danny Casolaro, West Virginia, 1991.

Possibly killed for investigating corruption involving U.S. government officials. Authorities have ruled his death a suicide.

lan Berg, Denver, 1984.
Controversial radio talk show host, killed by white supremacists.
Solved.

Maurice Williams, Washington, D.C. 1977
Killed on the job as he tried to cover the takeover of buildings by
militant Muslims. Killed in crossfire.

Don Bolles, Arizona, 1976
Killed for investigating mob-connected corruption in Arizona.
Solved.

•While the FBI was able to investigate, prosecute and convict
the killers of Berg and Bolles, they have not been able to prosecute
the triggermen in the 10 Haitians and Vietnamese cases.

•The Vietnamese and Haitian murders received substantial local
media coverage, but there were fewer reports by the national press
than in the killings of journalists working for mainstream English
media. The Manuel de Dios Unanue case was highly publicized
because New York Police and the Drug Enforcement Agency focused
their resources when they learned that the Colombian Cali drug
cartel was involved in its planning.

The United States remains one of the safest places for mainstream journalists to write and speak freely. Physical attacks and
threats are much more common in other places. But for immigrant
journalists, who work for ethnic news media, the dangers they left
behind in their homelands often find them here.

The non-English media are a vital part of immigrant communities. Hundreds of publications, cable television shows and radio programs inform the newly arrived. Many of these outlets are highly
partisan, but most provide valuable information on this country for
newly arrived immigrants, and on the motherland, for those who
remain homesick.

But political and criminal factions use violence to silence those
who endorse different points of view. Journalists in the Vietnamese,
Haitian and Chinese communities have also suffered bomb attacks,
death threats and other violence. Among the Vietnamese, agressive
anti-communist groups have chilled free expression in communities

throughout the country. Among the Haitians, three murders in Miami have frightened an already terrorized population.

In the Vietnamese community, the National United Front for the Liberation of Vietnam and the Vietnamese Party to Exterminate the Communists have also claimed responsibility for numerous threats, arson attacks, beatings and killings of Vietnamese who oppose their views. In the Haitian community, supporters of the army officers who deposed democratically elected President Jean-Bertrand Aristide, have taken to brazenly circulating death lists in Haitian communities in the United States.

"It's a kind of unofficial censorship stronger than any kind of government censorship that I know," a Vietnamese-American lawyer said.

FEDERAL INVESTIGATIONS ARE NOT FRUITFUL
Progress in all the investigations involving ethnic journalists is slow. The impact the unsolved crimes have on the communities is immeasureable.

Greg Victor, *CPJ Publications Director, was formerly a Freedom Forum Fellow in Asian Studies.*

Davidian leader David Koresh, in Waco, Texas, on February 29. Treasury was especially critical of the role played by the *Waco Tribune-Herald*, which published a series on the Davidians entitled "Sinful Messiah," against the objections of Treasury. The report also said Jim Peeler, a cameraman for *KWTX* in Texas, tipped off a cult member to the impending raid against the Davidians. Peeler, the report charges, mistook a cult member driving a vehicle with "U.S. Mail" painted on the door for a postman and warned him about the raid. *KWTX* has denied the charges. A report by the Society of Professional Journalists said journalists acted responsibly and that there was no evidence that the media tipped off the cult to the raid.

OCTOBER 24
Dona St. Plite, *WKAT, Miami,* Killed
St. Plite, a Haitian-born reporter and commentator for radio station *WKAT* in Miami, was murdered at a benefit for the family of Fritz Dor, a colleague killed two years earlier. His name had appeared on a hit list of supporters of ousted Haitian president Jean-Bertrand Aristide. He was the third Haitian-born journalist killed in Miami in the last three years. The murder is still under investigation.

Venezuela

Venezuela's traditionally free press was put to the test for the second year in a row by truly momentous events in the nation's history. In May 1993 the Supreme Court took the unprecedented action of suspending President Carlos Andres Pérez under charges of corruption. His dismissal came on the heels of two unsuccessful military coup attempts in February and November of 1992. In 1993, the press was hampered in its efforts to follow up on the coup stories as well as in its coverage of the Pérez trial. Physical attempts against journalists had escalated before and in the aftermath of the coup attempts. Following the president's departure, there were rumors of still another coup attempt, and security forces continued to refuse journalists access to military installations.

JANUARY 3
Gustavo Frisneda, *Últimas Noticias,* Harassed
Frisneda, a photographer who covers military affairs, was detained on January 1 for taking pictures in the military headquarters of San Carlos in Caracas. Two days later he was chased by military officers as he ran to his office, located a few blocks from San Carlos, when the head of Venezuela's chiefs of staff complained after Frisneda took his picture. Frisneda continued to have problems with his coverage. He was again detained temporarily by the National Guard on August 28.

JANUARY 12
Raquel García, *Televen,* Attacked
Freddy Henríquez, *Diario De Caracas,* Attacked
García and Henríquez were hurt during a demonstration that was broken up by the police with tear gas. Henríquez was hit on the knee by shrapnel. The demonstration was called by the social democratic Movement toward Socialism. The case was denounced in court but there was no judicial action.

JANUARY 15
María Verónica Tessari, *CMI,* Killed
Tessari was wounded in the head by shrapnel from a tear gas canister fired by military police last March 1992. She was hurt while covering an antigovernment march. She never recuperated from the head wound and died of complications. Her case was brought before the courts, but no one was ever charged in her death.

The Americas

149

JANUARY 26

Orlando Ugueto, *Diario de Caracas*, Legal Action
Alcides Castillo, *El Nacional*, Legal Action
Both reporters were summoned by a military tribunal that demanded they reveal the whereabouts of members of a guerrilla group they had interviewed in late 1992. After the journalists presented themselves in front of the tribunal with legal counsel, all pressures ended.

FEBRUARY 1

All Media, Threatened
Army Commander General Pedro Rangel Rojas threatened all media that he would initiate defamation and libel lawsuits against all journalists because recent press coverage was destabilizing the country. The National Journalists Association filed a protest with the government.

FEBRUARY 17

Diógenes Carrillo, *El Nacional*, Imprisoned
Castillo was sentenced to a five-day jail term by the president of the Supreme Court, who was enraged after Carrillo wrote a critical story about him. Carrillo was released after three days in jail, when the National College of Journalists intervened on his behalf.

FEBRUARY 18

Ali Gómez, *El Nacional*, Harassed, Attacked
Gómez was roughed up by military police when he traveled to a prison in the area of San Francisco of Yare, where a group of military officers who led one of two coups in 1992 is being held. He initially entered the prison grounds with members of the national legislature, but was intercepted by police when he tried to leave before the rest of the group.

FEBRUARY 20

William Ojeda, *Última Noticias*, Harassed, Threatened
Ojeda is the author of a book on the failed military coup that was carried out by military officers on November 27, 1992. His book was

confiscated from bookstores. Later, he was warned in a telephone threat against writing about that event.

MARCH 1

Elias Santana, *VTV*, Censored
Santana's television program on the state-owned television network was censored and canceled after he produced a number of programs that criticized partywide elections where voters selected the entire platform presented by each party, rather than individual candidates.

MARCH 18

José Cohen, *El Nacional*, Harassed
Cohen was roughed up when he attempted to take pictures of an antigovernment demonstration in the town of Guarenas, department of Miranda.

MARCH 31

Jenny Silva, *VTV*, Harassed
Silva was fired from her job as director of the news program for *Veteve* after he refused to write an editorial condemning the military officers who staged one of two coups against President Carlos Andres Pérez in 1992.

APRIL 1

Judith Martorelli, *El Globo*, Threatened
Martorelli received several telephone threats because of her involvement with the human rights committee run by the National Association of Journalists.

APRIL 1

Rod Towlinson, *Reuters*, Attacked
Towlinson was beaten by state police in Anzoategui state.

APRIL 3

Vanessa Davies, *El Nacional*, Threatened
Davies, a reporter for *El Nacional* who covers human rights and social conflicts, was the victim of a defamation campaign in March.

On April 3 she received an anonymous death threat from a male voice that said she would die for being a communist.

APRIL 18

Sandra Suárez, *El Nacional*, Harassed
Suárez is the military reporter for *El Nacional* in Maracay state. She was banned from military installations in the area.

APRIL 20

José Antonio Cedeno, *La Ciudad*, Attacked
Cedeno was assaulted by military police when he was covering a street demonstration before Congress in Caracas. The demonstration turned violent when police arrived.

APRIL 21

Radio Caracas Televisión, Censored
Venevisión, Censored
Two satirical television programs run by the television networks were banned by the government. The programs were *Radio Rochela* which aired on *Channel 8*, *Radio Caracas Televisión*, and *Cheverísimo*, which was broadcast on *Channel 4*, *Venevisión*.

APRIL 22

Jurate Rosales, *Zeta*, Attacked
A hand grenade was lobbed from the street against the home of Rosales, causing considerable damage. Rosales is the editor of the political magazine, *Zeta*. Rosales's son was the only person in the house at the time of the explosion. No one has been charged.

APRIL 26

Hindu Anderi, *El Globo*, Attacked
A bomb damaged the apartment of Anderi, who covers street events for the daily *El Globo*. She also received repeated anonymous telephone threats.

MAY 1

Vadell Hermanos, Attacked, Censored
Vadell Hermanos, a publishing house, was raided by police forces in May. Police seized a series of publications on the current political situation.

MAY 18

Diario de Caracas, Censored
Police bought off a large part of the editions put out by the daily *Diario de Caracas* for the days May 18 and May 19. The daily focused both editions on the corruption trial against former president Carlos Andres Pérez.

MAY 19

María Elena Morales, *Panorama*, Attacked, Harassed
Julio Reyes, *Panorama*, Attacked, Harassed
Morales and Reyes were assaulted in a residential area of Maracaibo while they covered a demonstration that was dispersed violently by state police.

JUNE 13

Elba Romero López, *Diario de Caracas*, Legal Action
Berenice Gómez, *El Nacional*, Legal Action
Both journalists were summoned by a military tribunal to reveal information they had on the involvement of military officers in drug trafficking. The military court has not followed up on the case.

JUNE 24

José Luis Olivares, *El Nacional*, Harassed
Olivares was denied access into Fuerte Tiuna, Venezuela's "Pentagon."

JULY 1

Eddy González, Harassed
González had his camera equipment damaged by policemen dressed in civilian clothing when he and four other unidentified local reporters were waiting in front of Miraflores, the presidential house.

JULY 9

Armando Yelamo, *El Universal*, Attacked
Alexander Berriós, *Radio Caracas*, Threatened
Yelamo, a reporter for *El Universal*, was
wounded by members of the National Guard
when he and other journalists were attacked and
harassed for covering a murder trial involving
two National Guardsmen. Berriós was roughed
up and verbally threatened.

AUGUST 1

Marciel Granier, *Diario de Caracas, Radio Caracas*,
Attacked
Assailants fired shots at the home of Granier,
director of the publishing company that runs
the opposition newspaper *Diario de Caracas* and
Radio Caracas. The assailants remained unidentified, but they were believed to be connected
to progovernment groups. The attack comes
after the newspaper published a series of stories
on freedom of the press and recent attacks
against journalists.

AUGUST 1

Alenis Bracho Vizcaya, *El Nacional*, Imprisoned
Bracho was detained by police on orders of the
governor of Guarico state. The governor was
upset at a column Bracho wrote in his newspaper. Prior to Bracho's detention, the governor
ordered police to surround the installations of
the daily for 24 hours.

AUGUST 12

Ben Ami Fihman, *Exceso*, Threatened
Fihman, an editor of *Exceso*, denounced telephone threats he received at his home. The
caller identified himself as a member of an
unknown anti-Semitic phalangist group and
ordered Fihman to leave the country.

AUGUST 18

Luis Aguilera, *El Nacional*, Threatened
State police raided the offices of the daily *El
Nacional* on orders of the governor of the State
of Nueva Esparta. An order of detention was

also issued against Aguilera, who is the newspaper's correspondent in the area. Aguilera presented a formal charge before the state court,
but no action was taken.

AUGUST 20-24

Radio Rumbos, Threatened
Radio Caracas, Threatened
Diario Reporte, Threatened
Radio Popular, Threatened
Televen, Threatened
Radio Sur, Threatened
TV Guayana, Threatened
Radio Pentagrama, Threatened
Between August 20 and August 24, the above
mentioned news organizations received false
bomb threats by telephone. *Radio Rumbos, Radio
Caracas, Diario Reporte*, and *Televen* are located
in the capital of Caracas. *Radio Popular*, which
received two false bomb threats, is located in
Maracaibo, in the state of Zulia. *TV Guayana*,
Radio Sur, and *Radio Pentagrama*, are located
in Ciudad Guayaná, in the State of Bolívar.

AUGUST 28

José Luis Olivares, *Últimas Noticias*, Imprisoned
Gustavo Frisneda, *Últimas Noticias*, Imprisoned
Jorge Cuello, *Últimas Noticias*, Imprisoned
Olivares and Frisneda, both journalists for the
daily *Últimas Noticias*, and Cuello, their driver,
were briefly detained by the National Guard.
The journalists were investigating the arrest
of a group of persons, who were detained at a
guard precinct for attempting to visit the military officer who led the February 1992 coup
attempt against President Carlos Andres Perez.

SEPTEMBER 1

Eduardo Molina, *La Frontera*, Attacked
Molina attended an event in the governor's
residence in the state of Mérida. There he
objected to the manner in which journalists
were being searched by state police and com-

plained. Police reacted harshly. Other journalists present at the residence intervened and were hurt. Molina suffered a heart attack.

SEPTEMBER 30
Margarita Oropeza, *Venevisión*, Harassed
Adela Leal, *El Nacional*, Harassed
Armando Pernia, *Diario de Caracas*, Harassed
Oropeza, Leal, and Pernia were harassed and roughed up by members of the presidential guard as they attempted to interview President Ramon J. Velásquez, who took office after former president Carlos Andres Pérez was forced to resign.

OCTOBER 25
José Vicente Rangel, *Televen/Diario de Caracas*, Legal Action
Rangel was summoned by the Second Military Court after he made statements in his television news program, "José Vicente Today," that Vice Admiral Radames Munōz, the Venezuelan defense minister, knew the names of four generals who were planning a coup attempt. Rangel said he did not know the names, but urged the minister to reveal them. Coup rumors are extremely explosive in Venezuela following two coup attempts in 1992 against then President Carlos Andres Pérez.

NOVEMBER 25
Rodolfo Benítez, *Diario de Caracas*, Attacked
Benitez was beaten by members of the Military Police who tried to confiscate rolls of pictures he had taken during a student demonstration in Caracas.

DECEMBER 5
Juan Ramón Tovar, *Regional Paper*, Harassed
Tovar was harassed by military officers in the town of Maracay, located about 70 miles west of Caracas.

DECEMBER 23
William Ojeda, *Últimas Noticias*, Legal Action
Ojeda was summoned by the Division of Military Intelligence after he conducted an interview with the officers who led the February 4, 1992, coup against former President Carlos Andres Pérez.

The Americas

Asia

BANGLADESH

AFGHANISTAN

CHINA

SOUTH KOREA

PAKISTAN NEPAL

INDIA

MYANMAR

HONG KONG

THAILAND VIETNAM

PHILIPPINES

SRI LANKA

SINGAPORE

PAPUA NEW GUINEA

SOLOMON ISLANDS

WESTERN SAMOA

INDONESIA

FIJI TONGA

AUSTRALIA

Asia

by Vikram Parekh

Ethnic and religious conflicts continued to impede press freedom in South Asia, while journalists in some of the more autocratic East Asian states were frequently jailed for violating state secrecy laws. Together with the ongoing suppression of dissident voices in China and Vietnam, these developments were emblematic of regional press freedom violations during the year.

If East Asian countries, with the exceptions of Myanmar (Burma) and Indonesia, saw comparatively little in the way of ethnic strife, they had their own share of hazards as far as journalists were concerned. Chief among these was the frequent detention of journalists for breach of state secrecy laws. In China and Singapore, financial information emerged as conspicuous areas of government sensitivity, with Xi Yang's arrest for reporting the gold exchange plans of the People's Bank of China, and the trial of two *Business Times* editors for publishing Singapore's estimated quarterly growth rate before the official figures had been released. Xi's case, in particular, was alarming to many of his fellow Hong Kong journalists in its implicit admission that investigative reporting such as they had been accustomed to would not be countenanced following China's takeover of Hong Kong in 1997. Other notable state secrecy cases

included China's detention of Gao Yu, another correspondent for Hong Kong newspapers, for providing as yet unspecified information to foreigners, and the two year sentence imposed by a Korean Court on Japanese defense writer Masato Shinohara for showing classified military documents to Japanese embassy personnel in Seoul.

While the year saw the release of China's most prominent dissident, Wei Jingsheng, a caveat attached kept him from having his articles published in either the domestic or foreign press. In Vietnam, on the other hand, well-known dissident Doan Viet Hoat received his second lengthy prison sentence—this time for publishing a newsletter, *Freedom Forum*, that advocated democratization and respect for human rights. Stiff prison terms were also handed down to seven other *Freedom Forum* contributors. Hanoi's suppression of press freedom and other civil liberties was little discussed in the debate that preceded the lifting of United States trade restrictions with Vietnam. Proponents of the argument that free trade leads inevitably to a free press need only have looked at the example provided by China to find ample evidence suggesting otherwise.

With the exception of Afghanistan, where a deadly civil war has prevented the press from rebuilding itself, the countries of South Asia share a vibrant and diversified press as a common denominator. Unfortunately, they also share violent separatist movements and a rising tide of religious zealotry and chauvinism, resulting in attacks on journalists by all parties concerned.

The major insurgencies in India —those in Kashmir, Punjab, and Assam—have seen their fortunes ebb and flow over the years, and the position of journalists covering them has varied accordingly. In Kashmir, the press has continually faced attempts at intimidation by the Indian Border Security Forces and the various separatist groups jockeying for leadership of the movement. And in all three regions state security laws, particularly the Terrorist and Disruptive Activities Act (TADA) and the National Security Act (NSA), have often been as effective at silencing journalists as firearms.

Sri Lanka's civil war between the Sinhalese-dominated army and the Tamils of the island's north and east shows no sign of abating. Far from it, in fact, as a recent pair of military victories left Tamil guerillas enough captured weaponry to prosecute their war for a long while to come. These losses, predictably, have been a sore spot with the army, and an astonishingly blunt intimidation campaign was waged against the journalist who took the lead in covering them. However, a multitude of such episodes in recent years has had a collateral effect that the army and government probably never anticipated—the growth of a local press freedom movement that is unparalleled in South Asia.

The attacks on journalists by Hindu extremists during and after the destruction of the Babri Masjid mosque in December, 1992, alerted many Indian journalists to the need for a similar press freedom group of their own. The electoral support enjoyed by the Hindu right, and sometimes sympathy for its agenda, led in far too many cases to government inaction in the face of right-wing attacks on the press. Despite repeated appeals by *Business India* correspondent Ruchira Gupta, who faced a year-long campaign of harassment by Hindu extremists, government officials took no action to investigate the threats made against her, or to prevent their recurrence. A comparable situation occurred in Bangladesh, where columnist Taslima Nasreen had to obtain a court order to get police protection from Islamic fundamentalists who had openly "sentenced" her to death for allegedly blasphemous writings.

Vikram Parekh *is CPJ's Asia Program Coordinator. He holds a J.D. from Rutgers Law School and a B.A. in Politics from the University of California, Santa Cruz. He is a former Ford Foundation Fellow at New York's International Center for Law in Development, and has worked for the International Human Rights Law Group in Washington, DC and the International Institute of New Jersey.*

Former CPJ Associates Allison Liu Jernow *and* Andrew Robinson *contributed to this report, as did* Kim Brice, Suzanne Hopkins, *and* Mark Johnson.

Asia

Asia

Afghanistan

Like Afghanistan's other institutions, the press was devastated by a 13-year war against the Soviet-backed regime. Now the country is mired in strife between the various factions that toppled the communists. Kabul, the capital, is chaotic, and the three main papers, all of which support the current government of President Burhanuddin Rabbani, publish only intermittently—not surprising given the destruction of the major printing press, a crippled communications infrastructure, and chronic ink, paper, and typewriter shortages. Despite this state of affairs, Rabbani saw fit to approve a press law in mid-December that endorsed press freedom while simultaneously mandating a press "based on Islamic culture," in which "no one's prestige or honour shall be attacked." By month's end, the press law appeared immaterial as provincial warlord General Abdul Rashid Dostam defected to the side of Rabbani's main rival, Prime Minister Gulbuddin Hekmatyar, imperiling Rabbani's already limited authority. Hekmatyar, based east of Kabul, maintains his own radio station, as does Dostam. As the conflict between the warring parties escalated, foreign correspondents evacuated the country en masse.

NOVEMBER 8
John Jennings, *Associated Press*, Imprisoned, Attacked, Harassed
Terrence White, *Agence France-Presse*, Imprisoned, Attacked, Harassed
Jennings, an *Associated Press* correspondent, and White, a New Zealand reporter working for *Agence France-Presse*, were captured while covering a battle outside Kabul between Prime Minister Gulbuddin Hekmatyar's Hezb-i-Islami group and forces loyal to President Burhannudin Rabbani. Suspecting that they were military advisers to Rabbani, the Hezb-i-Islami fighters who captured the reporters initially kicked and shoved them, stole $700, and seized their cameras, binoculars, and glasses. After being identified as journalists, however, Jennings and White say their captors treated them well and regularly changed the dressing on a foot wound that Jennings had sustained during the battle. The two, released on November 15, remain in Afghanistan—among the last foreign correspondents to do so.

Australia

In three separate cases during the year, journalists were held in contempt of court for refusing to divulge their sources. One of the reporters, Christopher Nicholls, was given a four-month sentence, the longest ever handed down in Australia for protecting a source. Australia's Media, Entertainment, and Arts Alliance (MEAA) protested Nicholls's sentence and called for a statute that would override common law and "protect journalists who are under an ethical obligation not to reveal confidential sources." Nicholls's actions were in keeping with a code of ethics promulgated by the MEAA.

APRIL 19
Christopher Nicholls, *Australian Broadcasting Corporation*, Legal Action
The Adelaide District Court acquitted Nicholls on charges of false pretense, forgery, and

impersonation that stemmed from a case of official corruption he was investigating. However, when Nicholls refused to divulge a source that he said had provided him with bank documents, he was found guilty of contempt of court and sentenced to four months in jail.

MAY 14

David Hellaby, *Adelaide Advertiser,* Legal Action
In relation to articles published in July 1992, the State Bank of South Australia filed a libel suit against Hellaby. The articles alleged criminal activity within the bank. During the trial, Hellaby refused to identify a source. On May 14, the Supreme Court found Hellaby guilty of contempt of court and fined him approximately $3,500.

SEPTEMBER 8

Deborah Cornwall, *Sydney Morning Herald,*
Legal Action
The New South Wales Supreme Court sentenced Cornwall to two months in prison for contempt of an administrative tribunal. Cornwall had refused to reveal the sources of an article she wrote about police corruption to the Independent Commission Against Corruption. The Supreme Court later reduced Cornwall's sentence to 90 hours of community service.

Bangladesh

Although Bangladesh's three-year-old democratic government avoided blatant intimidation of the press, it wielded the power of the pocketbook, using its estimated 75 percent share of all newspaper advertising to reward and punish papers for their coverage. The main threat to press freedom, however, was posed not by the government but by Islamic fundamentalist organizations. In a case that drew international attention, a group calling itself the Soldiers of Islam issued a death warrant for well-known columnist Taslima Nasreen after finding her recent novel *Lajja* blasphemous. Nasreen was provided no armed security until she obtained a court order for the government to do so, three weeks after the death threat was issued. A larger fundamentalist group, the Jamiat-e-Islami, was suspected of bombing a newspaper office in retaliation for an article about the group's arms training program at a local college.

SEPTEMBER 17
Ajker Kagoj, Attacked
Three journalists were injured when 20 homemade bombs were hurled at the Dhaka offices of *Ajker Kagoj,* a Bengali-language daily. Staff members said the attackers also fired pistol shots into the office. The paper held the fundamentalist Jamiat-e-Islami responsible for the bombing, which followed the publication of an article stating that fundamentalists were secretly instructing students in the use of arms at a Bangladeshi college campus. The Jamiat-e-Islami, however, denied responsibility for the attack.

SEPTEMBER 23
Taslima Nasreen, Threatened
At a public meeting in the northeastern town of Sylhet, a previously unknown group called the Council of the Soldiers of Islam offered $1,250 for the death of Nasreen, a well-known novelist, poet, and newspaper columnist. Characterizing Nasreen's latest novel, *Lajja* (Shame), as blasphemous, the group further demanded that the government arrest and punish Nasreen by October 7 and seize all of her writings. On

Asia

October 8, the council led a six-hour general strike in Sylhet to press its demands. Nasreen, however, only received armed security on October 14, after a court granted her request for police protection. The government itself banned *Lajja* in July, saying it contained "substance prejudicial to the state" and posed a threat to communal harmony. *Lajja* depicted Muslim attacks on a Bangladeshi Hindu family following the destruction of India's Babri Masjid mosque in December 1992.

SEPTEMBER 25
Mujibur Rahman Badal, Attacked
At least 25 people, including Badal and several other journalists, were injured when a police jeep rammed into a rally held against the bomb attack on Ajker Kagoj a week earlier. The rally took place in Narayanganj, near Dhaka. Several of the police involved were suspended following the incident.

Asia

China, People's Republic of

With more journalists in prison than any other country, China easily maintained its abysmal press freedom record. An alarming trend that emerged was extension of state secrecy laws to mainland-born journalists writing for Hong Kong newspapers. The most celebrated of these cases was that of *Ming Pao* reporter Xi Yang, who faced a closed trial for obtaining confidential information from a People's Bank of China contact. Less publicized was the case of Gao Yu, a Hong Kong newspaper correspondent detained on the eve of her departure for the Columbia University School of Journalism, reportedly for having shared state secrets with foreigners. In both cases the reporters were gathering and disseminating information in a manner routine in the Hong Kong press, but apparently anathema to Beijing. These developments provided an ominous sign to Hong Kong-based journalists of conditions likely to prevail following the territory's reunification with China in 1997. Contacts whom foreign correspondents relied upon in China also ran afoul of the state secrecy law, with a Foreign Ministry alumnus sentenced to 10 years' imprisonment and a *Xinhua News Agency* editor sentenced to a life term, after each provided allegedly classified documents to foreign press members. The September releases of prominent dissident journalists Wei Jingsheng and Wu Xuecan were widely seen as a ploy to shore up China's bid to host the 1996 Olympics. The releases, moreover, constituted something of an empty gesture, as both Wei and Wu had served all but a few months of their sentences. Wei, who soon published a series of letters written in prison to Chinese leader Deng Xiao Ping and an op-ed piece for the *New York Times,* was subsequently warned by the Chinese Public Security Bureau to cease writing articles for publication. Wu, a former *People's Daily* editor who supported the 1989 democracy movement, was reportedly impoverished and unable to find work.

JANUARY
Culture News, Censored
China's Cultural Ministry ordered the temporary closure of *Culture Weekend,* the weekend edition of the government-run newspaper

(continued on page 164)

China's Press Trade

by Allison Liu Jernow

When I was in Beijing in April, identical red posters covered every available foot of wall space and were pasted to the rear windows of all the taxi cabs. In English and Chinese they read, "An Open China Awaits the Olympics." But just how open is China now? Ask Qin Yongmin, a man from Wuhan who was arrested last spring for the "crime" of writing letters to the government and foreign newspapers opposing Beijing's Olympics bid.

With the Clinton administration's June renewal of most-favored-nation (MFN) trading status, China had access to its largest export market guaranteed for another year. And until late September, when the International Olympic Committee named Sydney the site of the 2000 Summer Olympics, China was a serious contender to host the games. Almost five years after the Army invaded Tiananmen Square and massacred unarmed civilians, the country seems to have shed its pariah image. Unfortunately, the distance between appearance and reality is still wide.

Beijing's sales pitch depended on projecting a sanitized image to the International Olympic Committee (IOC) and the rest of the world. But the red banners proclaiming openness that blanketed the capital had little to do with the truth. I asked every cab driver I met whether he wanted to hang the Olympic slogan in his car. The uniform response: "Of course not. I had no choice."

By Beijing's accounting, more than 3,000 "counterrevolutionaries" are in prison, including 22 journalists. Just as disturbing as the imprisonment of these journalists is China's willingness to use them as bargaining chips in international trade negotiations.

On May 26, after spending more than 12 years in jail, mostly in solitary confinement, activist and editor Xu Wenli was released by Chinese authorities. A leader in the Democracy Wall movement of the late 1970s, Xu had founded an influential underground journal called *April Fifth Forum*. He was arrested in April 1981 and sentenced

SPECIAL REPORT: People's Republic of China

to 15 years in prison on charges of being a counterrevolutionary. His parole on the eve of President Clinton's decision on MFN may well have tipped the balance in China's favor.

Equally transparent were the releases of two long-term prisoners in September, just as the IOC neared its decision on the 2000 Summer Games. Wei Jingsheng, an editor of the dissident journal *Tansuo* ("Explorations") and veteran of the Democracy Wall movement, was released on September 14, after serving all but six months of a 15-year prison term. Wu Xuecan, a *Renmin Ribao* ("People's Daily") editor who had published an unauthorized "extra" edition during the 1989 Tiananmen Square demonstrations, was released two days after Wei, and just three months prior to the completion of his four-year sentence. Both of these releases demonstrated Beijing's desire to gain maximum political leverage out of minimal concessions; Wei and Wu were due to be released shortly anyway, and their paroles were accompanied by a "deprivation period" of their already limited political rights. Neither was able to resume his work as a journalist.

Fortunately, the IOC didn't buy the ploy. But the scenario is likely to be repeated before Congress' next annual review of China's MFN status in June, 1994.

Historically, freedom of speech has been one of the best indicators of the pace of liberalization in China. The ebb-and-flow cycle began with the 1957 Hundred Flowers campaign, when Chairman Mao Zedong first invited people to criticize government policy and then promptly locked up those who did. In the reform-minded late 1980s, semi-independent publications like the *World Economic Herald, New Observer,* and *Economics Weekly* flourished. These three, and many others, were closed in the post-June 4 Tiananmen crackdown. Their writers and editors, many in jail or exile, remain silenced. I visited one woman whose newspaper had been banned and who had spent a year in prison. When I left I saw the two men who stood watch over her apartment. A well-known and respected journalist, she is prevented from publishing within China.

More recently, the long arm of Beijing stretched all the way to the United Nations in New York. When the Chinese Mission learned that student dissident Shen Tong had been invited to speak by the

UN Correspondents Association, it lodged a vehement protest. Bowing to pressure from the mission, Secretary-General Boutros Boutros-Ghali canceled Shen's press conference—the first time such a step had ever been taken by a Secretary-General—and then denied the dissident access to UN grounds. Shen eventually held his conference in front of a crowd of journalists gathered outside. It was a vivid replay of last September's incident in Beijing when Chinese authorities arrested Shen and expelled his foreign colleagues in order to prevent them from holding a press conference.

Although the political atmosphere has improved greatly since the dark months following the June 1989 crackdown, a propaganda campaign launched last spring targets what the government terms "chaotic" media development. Through new regulations, harsh criticism, and forced closure, authorities are strengthening their control over writers of unauthorized biographies and popular entertainment weeklies and the owners of private newsstands and bookstores.

Despite pretended indifference to criticism on human rights, the regime is acutely sensitive to world opinion, particularly when it imperils economic advances. Tough rhetoric from Clinton during the campaign and more recently by Assistant Secretary of State for East Asia Winston Lord no doubt prompted Beijing's latest paroles. Rather than accept China's statements at face value, the international community must continue to measure the distance between what the government would have us believe and what we discover to be the truth. It is important, too, that those in China know that the rest of the world can tell the difference.

If pressure on human rights issues eases, China is unlikely to reform on its own. Typically, the government has dealt with internal critics by either ignoring or imprisoning them. This is where outspoken allies abroad can help. One private businessman I spoke to said simply, "The leaders are on top, the people on the bottom. We have to listen to whatever they say, but they never hear what we say."

Allison Liu Jernow, *CPJ's Asia Associate until June 1993, is presently a student at the Columbia University School of International and Public Affairs. Earlier versions of this article appeared in the* **Christian Science Monitor** *and the* **San Francisco Chronicle.***

SPECIAL REPORT: People's Republic of China

China Cultural News. The ministry ordered the ban after foreign news reports brought attention to an interview it published with well-known actress Liu Xiaoqing in which she discussed the prospects of nudity and sex in domestic feature films. The paper also printed several nude photographs of women.

JANUARY 11
Wang Biao, *People's Daily*, Censored
Biao was suspended from his reporting and editing duties at the Communist Party's official newspaper for leaking news of a landmark libel suit against the paper. Two local newspapers published exposés about the suit. Even though the case had already gone to court, the *People's Daily* had yet to publish any news about the suit. It was the first time since the Communist Revolution in 1949 that a lawsuit against the newspaper had gone to trial.

FEBRUARY 22
Lena Sun, *Washington Post*, Threatened
Andrew Higgins, *The Independent*, Threatened
The February 22 issue of *Outlook Weekly* magazine claimed that foreign reporters were stealing state secrets and called for urgent measures to be taken. The report singled out *Washington Post* reporter Lena Sun and Andrew Higgins, a reporter for the London-based *Independent* newspaper, accusing them of "appearing as reporters" to steal intelligence about China's politics, economy, military affairs, and technology. The article contradicted the State Security and Foreign Ministries' previous statement that surveillance of foreign reporters would ease, which was widely interpreted by the Western media as a way of improving China's image as it sought to win the bid to hold the Olympic Games in Beijing.

MARCH 1
Sun Lin, *Shanghai Television*, Imprisoned
Sun, a former cameraman for *Shanghai Television*, was arrested and taken to Shanghai Detention Centre Number One. Sun had not been allowed to work since June 1989, apparently in retaliation for taking photographs of the demonstrations at Tiananmen Square. He was "exempted from prosecution" and allowed to go home in July.

MAY 20
Lena Sun, *Washington Post*, Attacked
The Beijing Intermediate People's Court gave Bai Weiji, a former Foreign Ministry employee, a 10-year prison sentence for providing "secret" documents to the *Washington Post's* Lena Sun. Bai's wife, Zhao Lei, was sentenced to six years for the same crime. Ms. Sun was a good friend of the Bai family. Three others, including a newspaper reporter, an assistant to a cabinet minister, and Wang Jun, a journalist at *People's Daily*, were also convicted and given prison sentences.

JUNE 26-27
Fu Shenqi, *Legal Action*
Alison Moore, *Australian Broadcasting*, Imprisoned
Fu Shenqi was detained while Australian Prime Minister Paul Keating was visiting Shanghai. The move was apparently meant to prevent Fu from talking to the numerous foreign correspondents who had gathered in Shanghai. Fu was subsequently sentenced without trial to three years in "education through labor" camps for inciting trouble and speaking to foreign journalists. At least two other dissidents in Shanghai, Yang Zhou and Wang Fu Chen, were detained on June 27 for several hours after agreeing to meet with Australian journalist Alison Moore. Public security officers also detained Moore for over three hours on the same day when she visited Yang's house for a scheduled interview.

JULY
Zhang Fenqying, Harassed
Ren Xiaoyuan, Harassed
Zhang Fenqying and Ren Xiaoyuan, the wife and teenage daughter of Ren Wanding, a former *Democracy Wall* journalist who has been imprisoned since June 1989, were detained by police for six days. Police accused Fenqying of violating public order rules by inviting four foreign journalists to wait for her outside a police station while she sought a meeting with a high-level police official.

AUGUST
Wu Shishen, *Xinhua News Agency,* Legal Action
Ma Tao, *China Health Education News,* Legal Action
Editor Wu Shishen was sentenced to life in prison for allegedly selling a "state-classified" document to Hong Kong reporter Leung Wai-man of Hong Kong's Chinese-language daily *Express* for 50,000 yuan. The controversial document was a copy of Communist party chief Jiang Zemin's address to the Chinese Communist Party's Congress in October, 1992. *The Express* published the speech several days before it was delivered. Editor Ma Tao of *China Health Education News* received a six-year prison term for assisting Wu in the incident. According to the *Associated Press*, Ma is believed to be Wu's wife.

AUGUST 14
All media, Legal Action
The government announced regulations requiring all news conferences to be registered. The order prohibits the local media from reporting on unregistered news conferences and sponsors of news conferences from leaking party and national secrets.

SEPTEMBER 27
Xi Yang, *Ming Pao,* Legal Action
State security officials arrested Beijing correspondent Xi Yang on charges of "stealing and espionage of state secrets." These secrets, according to the official *Xinhua News Agency,* were unpublished savings and loan interest rate changes for the People's Bank of China, as well as information on the bank's plans for international gold transactions, provided to Mr. Xi in both cases by Tian Ye, a bank official. On December 22, the Beijing Municipal Intermediate People's Court told *Ming Pao* that Xi would be tried in secret, and that he "did not want a lawyer." Since detaining Xi, security officials have denied him all contact with Ming Pao and granted him only one visit by a family member—a half-hour meeting with his father in which discussion of his case was prohibited.

OCTOBER 1
Xu Keren, *Xinmin Evening News,* Harassed
Airport officials prevented Xu, a senior editor, from boarding a plane bound for Tokyo and confiscated his passport and other documents. According to reports, Xu had recently written an article exposing alleged police collusion in a Shanghai bar owner's scheme to defraud customers. A Shanghai court has accepted a suit filed by the city's public security bureau charging Xu with defaming the bureau and with violating regulations requiring advance permission for any reports on actions of the police, the procuracy, or the courts. The case is set to go to trial.

OCTOBER 2
Gao Yu, Imprisoned
Gao Yu, a well-known dissident journalist who writes for Hong Kong newspapers, was taken from her home by local security officials. She was due to depart the following week for the United States to take up a one-year research fellowship at the Columbia University School of Journalism. Though formal charges had not been filed as of late November, Gao was reportedly accused of providing state secrets to persons across the border.

Asia

DECEMBER 5
Wei Jingsheng, Threatened
Wei Jingsheng, the former co-editor of the prodemocracy journal *Tansuo* (Explorations), was released on September 14, after serving 14-and-a-half years of a 15-year prison sentence. On November 18, the *New York Times* published an opinion piece written by Wei in which he criticized China's positions on democracy and human rights. In early December, the Public Security Bureau warned Wei that the essay's publication constituted a violation of his parole terms and ordered him to cease submitting articles for publication, whether to the Chinese or foreign press.

Fiji

In its second year of civilian rule since the 1987 military coups, Fiji saw a perceptible increase in press freedom. The government lifted visa restrictions on foreign journalists in early February, and the region-wide Pacific Islands News Association (PINA) held its first convention in Fiji in six years. However, tension between ethnic Indians and indigenous Fijians continued to shape press laws, with the government unveiling new guidelines on coverage of culturally and racially sensitive material.

JULY 29
All Media, Censored
The Fijian government announced media restrictions on coverage of racially inflammatory speeches or culturally sensitive information as well as parliamentary speeches deemed libelous. The government also said television coverage must give priority to important ministerial statements. The government had stopped coverage of Parliament the previous month until guidelines were created.

AUGUST 1
Daily Post, Censored
The government-owned Fiji Post and Telecommunications Company banned advertising in the *Daily Post* because it said reports on the appointment of a new company chief general manager contained inaccurate information. The reports forced the government to investigate company operations.

Hong Kong

With China set to assume control over Hong Kong in 1997, the British territory has seen an increase in self-censorship on the part of cautious editors and reporters. Their fears seem to be justified. In early 1993, the *South China Morning Post* published a list of newspapers that it said the mainland government had blacklisted as unfriendly. And Tao Siju, China's public security minister, has conceded that the Hong Kong branch of the official *Xinhua News Agency* is monitoring the territory's media and keeping tabs on reporters and editors filing unfavorable stories. The Hong Kong Journalists' Association has tried to address these developments by monitoring the media's performance, documenting cases of censorship, and publishing its findings in a new journal. The association, which has also been at the forefront in calling for greater democratization, hopes 17 laws will be revised or repealed before 1997, including a broadcasting ordinance that gives Hong Kong's governor the power to review or limit news in an ill-defined emergency—a nebulous loophole that Beijing could easily use to quash press freedom.

NOVEMBER

Daisy Li Yuet Wah, *Ming Pao*, Censored
Organizers of a late November symposium on
journalism in Hong Kong, Taiwan, and the
People's Republic of China censored an article
by Li, Deputy Assignment Editor of *Ming Pao*
and Chair of the Hong Kong Journalists
Association. The article, intended for the wel-
coming brochure of the symposium, reviewed
a "freedom index" poll that surveyed the opinions of Hong Kong residents about the degree
of freedom they have. Regarding freedom of
speech and press freedom, the poll showed
that 70 percent of respondents expected less
freedom after 1997. The News Executives
Association of Hong Kong had invited Li
to write the article, but then said it was too
"sensitive" for publication.

India

Ethnic and religious tension remained a
major threat to press freedom. The year
began under the rubble of the Ayodhya
mosque demolition, and that cataclysmic
event—in which many journalists were
assaulted—set the tone for attacks on
the press over the ensuing 12 months.
Nowhere were the repercussions of
Ayodhya felt more strongly than in
Bombay, where in January the Shiv Sena,
a Maharashtrian Hindu political party,
encouraged a pogrom on the city's
Muslims, destroying businesses, forcing
thousands from their homes, and killing
several hundred. Journalists, too, were
targeted—regardless of faith. In Baroda,
a journalist who had earlier been threatened by a Shiv Sena leader was brutally
murdered as he entered his office. And in
Bombay, Shiv Sainiks attacked a journalists' convention, singling out journalist
Nikhil Wagle for especially severe abuse.
Why these assaults on journalists? Shiv
Sena leader Bal Thackeray has proclaimed
Singaporan-style authoritarianism as the
form of government he would like to establish, and negative press coverage has little place under such a regime. Personal
grudges may factor in as well. When
questioned about the Bombay convention
attendees, Thackeray told CPJ, "They are
not accepting my daily *[Samna]* as a
newspaper, so I do not accept those journalists as journalists." Separatist movements provided another arena for
violations of press freedom, in which the
government and military were often
directly culpable. In the northeastern
state of Assam, the army has frequently
used the loosely defined National Security
Act (NSA) and Terrorist and Disruptive
Activities Act (TADA) to crack down on
local press coverage of a secessionist
movement. Persons charged with violating
these acts lose many civil rights that the
Indian Constitution otherwise guarantees.
In Kashmir, journalists remained subject
to the exigencies imposed upon them by
the increasingly lawless Border Security
Forces (BSF), which at least twice "retaliated" against militant actions with whole-
sale attacks on civilian homes and
businesses. Reporter Yusuf Jameel, trying
to cover one such attack, was threatened
with death by a BSF trooper. At the same
time, journalists continued to be caught
in the proverbial crossfire between rival
separatist movements, some seeking an
independent state and others, union with
Pakistan. Punjab, by contrast, saw a
marked decline in attacks on journalists.
The sole casualty was Bhola Nath
Masoom, president of the Punjab and

Asia

167

Chandigarh Journalists Association, shot dead by suspected Punjabi separatists on January 31. However, the undercurrent to Punjab's surface calm was a relentless police campaign against the separatists, in which torture and disappearances reportedly are routine.

JANUARY - DECEMBER

Ruchira Gupta, *Business India,* Harassed, Threatened

Business India reporter Gupta was physically attacked by Hindu fundamentalists while covering the demolition of Ayodhya's Babri Masjid mosque on December 6, 1992. During the second week of January, a month after appearing in a widely telecast press conference with other journalists who were assaulted at Ayodhya, Gupta received a videotape in the mail depicting the gang rape of a Muslim woman. A note attached to it warned, in Hindi, "This can happen to you, too." In July, following the worldwide telecast of a *BBC* documentary on Ayodhya that she had helped produce, the Hindu nationalist group Rashtriya Swayamsevak Sangh (RSS) ran a front-page story in its party organ, *The Organiser,* denouncing Gupta as "anti-national" and "crypto-Communist." The night of its publication, copies of Gupta's articles on Ayodhya were affixed to her car with obscenities scrawled over them in Hindi. Over the next four weeks, her car was vandalized two more times, with her tires slashed on one occasion and the Hindi word *mardunga* ("will kill") painted across it on another. On December 6, a letter was mailed to the Indian Home Ministry listing the names of persons who were "against the cause." Among the half-dozen names were Gupta's own and that of Lal Das, a Hindu priest at Ayodhya who died recently under mysterious circumstances. Despite Gupta's repeated complaints, no action has been taken by either the Delhi police or the home ministry.

JANUARY 31

Bhola Nath Masoom, *Hind Samachar,* Killed

Masoom, a stringer for *Hind Samachar* and president of the Punjab and Chandigarh Journalists Association, was shot by two suspected militants near his home in the town of Rajpura. He died the same day.

FEBRUARY

Parag Kumar Das, *Boodhbar,* Imprisoned

Atanu Bhuyan, *Ajir Batori,* Imprisoned

Krishna Kanta Barua, *Boodhbar,* Imprisoned

Nripendra Sarma, *Boodhbar,* Imprisoned

Das, the editor of *Boodhbar,* and Atanu Bhuyan, a reporter for *Ajir Baroti,* were arrested under the Terrorist and Disruptive Activities (Prevention) Act. According to the South Asian Human Rights Documentation Center, both were arrested in connection with articles published about the United Liberation Front of Assam. Krishna Kanta Barua and Nripendra Sarma, respectively the publisher and printer of *Boodhbar,* were also reportedly arrested.

FEBRUARY 20

Arupa Barua, *Mukti Dhoot,* Attacked

Bhogeshwar Dutta, *Sapthahik Jonomat,* Attacked

Arupa Barua, editor of *Mukti Dhoot,* and Bhogeshwar Dutta, editor of *Sapthahik Jonomat,* were hospitalized after police attacked them and several other journalists who were protesting the arrests of Parag Das and Atanu Bhuyan

APRIL

Ananda Bazar Partrika, Legal Action

Bengal Chief Minister Jyoti Basu filed a defamation suit against Ananda Bazar Patrika, after the paper ran an article suggesting that he had links with Rashid Khan, a Calcutta underworld figure. Khan was charged in June with involvement in a bomb blast that killed at least 65 people in a Calcutta slum.

APRIL 10
Yusuf Jameel, Harassed
Jameel, a correspondent for *Reuters* and the *BBC*, was threatened at gunpoint by a Border Security Forces (BSF) trooper as he attempted to enter a square in downtown Srinagar where that morning several dozen people had torched a building used by the BSF and where the BSF had retaliated by setting fire to a number of houses and shops.

MAY 22
Dinesh Pathak, *Sandesh*, Killed
Pathak, a resident editor of *Sandesh* newspaper in Baroda, was stabbed to death by a group of assailants while entering the newspaper's office. About six months earlier, during the November Navratri festival in Gujarat, Shiv Sena Chief Raju Risaldar publicly threatened to kill Pathak, who had written articles critical of the Hindu nationalist party.

AUGUST 5
Izhar Wani, *Agence France-Press*, Attacked
Imdad Saqi, *DPA (German Press Agency)*, Attacked
Gulzar Ahmed, *Srinagar News*, Attacked
While covering a lawyers' procession at Lal Chowk in Srinagar, Wani, Saqi and Ahmed were threatened and then physically assaulted by members of India's Border Security Forces (BSF). The procession was held to protest the recent killing of a family by the BSF. The security forces struck the journalists with batons and rifle butts.

AUGUST 7
Shanmugasundaram, *Nakkheeran*, Attacked
On August 7, a group of armed men severely beat Shanmugasundaram as he was boarding a bus in Shivagangai, in the state of Tamil Nadu. Shanmugasundaram was hospitalized for his wounds, which included deep cuts on his left hand and injuries to his head and right arm. Shanmugasundaram said the attackers were

associated with Kannappan, the Tamil Nadu Public Works Department minister. According to a writ petition submitted by *Nakkheeran's* editor to the Madras High Court, one of the attackers had shouted that the fingers "which write against our minister" should be cut off. In a *Nakkheeran* issue released for sale on August 5, Shanmugasundaram had written that Kanappan was involved in corrupt activities.

AUGUST 17-18
Kapil Patil, *Aaj Dinank*, Threatened
Amit Joshi, *Aaj Dinank*, Attacked
Nikhil Wagle, *Mahanagar*, Attacked
On August 17, Patil received a threatening phone call from Dattaji Salvi, chief of the Union Trade Wing of the Hindu-oriented party, Shiv Sena. Salvi was angered by an article in that day's issue of *Aaj Dinank*, one of Bombay's Marathi-language evening papers, which claimed that Shiv Sena leader Bal Thackeray wanted to dismiss him. The next morning, several Shiv Sena members entered *Aaj Dinank's* offices, broke several chairs, beat up senior reporter Joshi, and assaulted two other employees, including one pregnant woman. Later that day, dozens of Shiv Sena activists disrupted a journalists' conference at the Indian Merchant's Chamber. As they chanted slogans and broke equipment, several of the activists attacked Wagle, dealing him a series of blows.

SEPTEMBER 10
Aftab, Threatened
Aftab, an Urdu-language daily in Kashmir, announced that it was suspending publication on September 10, after the pro-Pakistan fundamentalist group Jamiat-ul-Mujahideen threatened it for refusing to print a statement that criticized the Jammu and Kashmir Liberation Front, a secular pro-independence group. In its September 10 issue, the paper said its editor had been summoned to appear before the

Asia

Jamiat within a week. A Kashmiri editors' conference had earlier resolved not to publish statements by separatist groups that criticized any of their separatist rivals.

DECEMBER 23
Parag Kumar Das, *Boodhbar*, Censored, Attacked, Harassed
On December 23, police officers raided Das's office and seized 1,000 copies of a book he had recently published, as well as his manuscript of the book. The officers formally charged Das under the Terrorist and Disruptive Activities Act and ordered him not to leave Guwahati, the capital of Assam state. Two days later, the police raided the offices of *Boodhbar*, the Assamese-language newspaper for which Das is an editor, and confiscated manuscripts of articles that he had published in the paper.

Indonesia

Despite hints of a more open media during the year, Indonesia's repressive press laws remained on the books. Journalists practiced self-censorship, particularly on topics such as the President and his family, religious, racial and ethnic issues. President Suharto, entering his sixth term after 28 years in power, called for more extensive debate and greater political openness. Though a fairly commonplace gesture, the press interpreted the speech as an indication of eased restrictions. The printed press carried dissenting views and was more vocal in criticizing the government, even if low-level rather than high-level officials were the targets. Broadcasting rules for the first time allowed private television to broadcast nationally. In February, the government issued new permits to four private television networks, raising the number of private networks to five. However, Suharto's children own two of the stations, and a business associate of the president owns another. The foreign media attended the trial of East Timor resistance leader Xanana Gusmao, but foreign journalists still experienced difficulty in obtaining permission to visit the former Portuguese territory. Aceh Province, in North Sumatra, where another group of separatists is fighting the government, was off limits as well.

AUGUST 16
Lindsay Murdoch, *Melbourne Age and Sydney Morning Herald*, Imprisoned, Expelled
Government authorities barred entry to Murdoch and detained him for 12 hours at Jakarta International Airport. After confiscating his ticket and passport, immigration officials deported Murdoch to Singapore and told him he was on a blacklist. Indonesian officials have accused Murdoch of writing "tendentious" articles in the past.

Nepal

Nepal's two largest circulation dailies continued to be government organs, and the state remained the only radio and television station owner. Still, scores of independent publications provided Nepalese with diverse points of view. Existing press regulations provide a litany of restrictions on Nepalese journalists, but the transgressions most often enforced were those that appeared to defame the royal family. One incident involved a journalist's quote from a book that implicated the king's brother in a drug smuggling operation. The journalist was charged with offending the royal family and was released pending trial.

APRIL 11
Mathbar Singh Basnet, *Punarjagaran,*
Imprisoned
Sharad Chandra Wasti, *Punarjagaran,*
Imprisoned
Basnet and Wasti, respectively the publisher
and editor of the weekly *Punarjagaran,* were
detained and charged under the State Offences
Act. They were held for three days. The
charges relate to the publication of a photo-
graph of a member of the Nepalese royal
family with an Indian movie star.

APRIL 11
Shambhu Shrestha, *Drishti,* Imprisoned
Shrestha, the publisher of the weekly *Drishti,*
was arrested and charged under the State
Offenses Act. The charge stemmed from
the publication of an article about Prince
Gyanendra, based on a book entitled *Shopping
for Buddhas,* that suggested he was involved
in drug trafficking. Shrestha was released
on April 14.

Pakistan

With the exception of its cautious coverage of the army, the Pakistani print media
operates in a climate of considerable
press freedom. But in a year that saw
three prime ministers in office, it was perhaps inevitable that the media would suffer from the prevailing political tumult. The
dismissal of Prime Minister Nawaz Sharif's
government in April and its short-lived
reinstatement the following month were
marked in each case by attacks on media
organizations that the main opposition
party saw as mouthpieces for Sharif. The
sentencing of a noted journalist to 16
years' imprisonment in late September
brought attention to a little-known region

of Pakistan near the Afghan border.
Operating under the Frontier Crimes
Regulation, a holdover from the British
colonial era, the Federally Administered
Tribal Areas lie outside the Pakistani court
system's jurisdiction, and tribal councils,
or jirgas, conduct all trials in accordance
with Islamic law, tribal custom, and often
the dictates of the civil service's local
political agent. Needless to say, there
is no right to counsel.

APRIL 24
News Network International, Legal Action
On April 24, Federal Information Minister
Maulana Kausar Niazi ordered a probe of a
recently established news agency, *News Network
International (NNI),* to determine whether it had
received assistance from the previous government of Nawaz Sharif. Before charges had been
filed against the agency, however, the Press
Information Department canceled the Senate
passes of several of its reporters and the accredi-
tation card of its Editor-in-Chief, Hafiz Abdul
Khaliq, prompting a walkout by the parliamentary opposition on May 5.

MAY 30
Pakistan Television (Lahore), Attacked
A procession of workers from Benazir Bhutto's
Pakistan People's Party attacked the Lahore
station of *Pakistan Television (PTV)* on May 30,
throwing stones at the building, smashing
nearly all of the window panes, and damaging
the telephone exchange. Thirty vehicles were
also damaged in the attack, and the recording
of several programs was hindered. The demonstrators apparently singled out *PTV* because
of its close identification with Nawaz Sharif,
whom the Supreme Court had recently restored
as prime minister. According to reports, the
Lahore police took no steps to protect the
station until after the attack had ended.

SEPTEMBER 24
Sailab Mahsud, *Daily Jang, The News,*
Imprisoned

Mahsud, a correspondent for the *Daily Jang* and *The News*, was arrested in the Federally Administered Tribal Area (FATA) of South Waziristan on September 24 and charged with conspiracy to commit war against Pakistan, harboring offenders, and resistance to lawful apprehension. The charges apparently stemmed from an interview he had conducted with Amanullah Kundi, a convicted drug trafficker who had recently escaped from police custody in South Waziristan. The arresting officers seized Mahsud's taped interview with Kundi and held him incommunicado until his trial by a tribal jirga (council), which sentenced him to 16 years in prison on October 13. Though jirga decisions are unappealable under the law governing FATAs, demonstrations by Pakistani journalists and widespread press coverage prompted the jirga's reconvening and Mahsud's acquittal about a month later.

Philippines

Press freedom in the Philippines varied widely by locality. While Manila reporters operated in an environment largely free from government interference, those in outlying areas were sometimes subjected to serious abuses, particularly when reporting government corruption.

Zambales newspaper publisher Romeo Lagaspi, who disappeared in January after writing a column about police corruption, is still missing. Another journalist, Clovis Nazareno wrote about illegal logging and corruption in Bohol Province and was hospitalized for several days after a businessman assaulted him. A major problem for
independent reporting outside Manila stems from the fact that politicians and powerful families own most of the provincial papers and use them as vehicles for self-promotion.

JANUARY 6
Elmer Umacob, *People's Daily Forum,* Attacked

Umacob, city editor of the *People's Daily Forum*, was slapped and manhandled by a police officer inside the city hall of General Santos City, apparently because the officer objected to news columns linking him to a series of kidnappings there.

JANUARY 11
Romeo Lagaspi, *Voice of Zambales,* Disappeared, State Involvement Suspected

Lagaspi, publisher of *Voice of Zambales*, was last seen by his family on January 11, 1993. After being charged with criminal libel for a column he wrote on police corruption, he filed a countersuit which was still pending when he disappeared. Police showed Lagaspi's family photographs of a charred corpse, which they hinted was that of the journalist.

JUNE 14
Clovis Nazareno, Attacked

Nazareno was attacked by a businessman in the presence of a police officer in Poblacion, Bohol Province. The officer and municipal chief of the Philippines National Police, arrested Nazareno and detained him for two hours. Nazareno had been threatened in the past and accused by the military of involvement in the New People's Army, the armed wing of the Communist Party. He has frequently written columns critical of the government, including ones exposing abuses in Bohol Province and illegal logging linked to government officials. Nazareno was hospitalized for several days following the assault.

Singapore

Although Prime Minister Lee Kwan Yew formally stepped down in 1990, his belief that press freedom must take a back seat to economic growth remains official policy. The city-state's major newspapers adhere to the government line on domestic issues, and foreign publications are subject to strict caps on their circulation. Last August, the government restricted *The Economist* **to 7500 copies per issue, after the British magazine refused to grant the government a right of reply. And in an ongoing matter, two** *Business Times* **editors ran afoul of national secrecy laws, when they published unreleased estimates of Singapore's economic growth rate.**

OCTOBER 21
Patrick Daniel, *Business Times,* Legal Action
Kenneth James, *Business Times,* Legal Action
Daniels and James were charged in December 1992 with breaching Singapore's Official Secrets Act by obtaining and publishing unofficial estimates of Singapore's second quarter growth rate, before the figures were officially released to the press. Their joint trial, along with two economists implicated in the affair and Tharman Shanmugaratnam, Singapore's Monetary Authority director, began on October 21. Although Senior District Court Judge Richard Magnus ruled on December 4 that the prosecution had failed to establish the first link in the chain of communication—the case against Shanmugaratnam—he denied the defense's motion that the charges against the other defendants be therefore dismissed. Instead, Magnus amended the charge against Shanmugaratnam from communicating classified information to acting in a manner endangering the secrecy of classified information. On December 9, Magnus ruled that the prosecu-

tion had made out a case on the amended charge and ordered the defense to answer in a four-week hearing scheduled to begin on February 21.

Solomon Islands

Press freedom in the Solomon Islands suffered fallout from an ongoing civil war in neighboring Papua New Guinea. Prime Minister Solomon Mamaloni's banning of news about Papua New Guinea's Bougainville crisis apparently related to a major arms purchase aimed at shoring up the Solomon Islands border forces. Although Papua New Gunea charged that the weapons were to be used in support of the Bougainville rebels, the Solomon Islands' government claimed they were intended to protect the Islands' citizens from raids by Papuan security forces.

APRIL 21
Solomon Islands Broadcasting Corporation (SIBC), Censored
Prime Minister Solomon Mamaloni banned the *SIBC* from broadcasting any news about a war in Bougainville, Papua New Guina, on the grounds that it was "likely to contravene the principles of the Public Security and Official Secrets Acts." Secessionist forces in Bougainville are waging war against the central government of Papua New Guinea.

Asia

South Korea

Though South Korea came under elected civilian rule in February for the first time in nearly 30 years, security concerns continued to infringe on media freedom. The National Security Law (NSL), for example, still limited access to North Korean media, as well as media said to have a pro-Communist slant. Edited North Korean news broadcasts were, however, regularly shown on South Korean television. And security concerns were invoked when a Seoul court sentenced a Japanese defense correspondent to two years' imprisonment for obtaining classified military documents and showing them to military attachés at the Japanese Embassy.

JUNE 11

Chong Jae-hon, *Joon-ang Ilbo*, Imprisoned
On June 11, the Seoul daily *Joon-ang Ilbo* reported that Defense Minister Kwon Hae-young had been barred from leaving the country in connection with an investigation into corruption in the country's arms procurement program. The article, written by Chong, was apparently based on an unconfirmed list of persons who were not allowed to leave the country. Following a phone call from Kwon, the editors pulled Chong's article from the second edition and subsequently published a retraction and apology. Kwon nevertheless filed defamation charges against Chong, and the reporter was taken into custody for questioning. On June 20, however, Kwon withdrew the case, and Chong was released.

DECEMBER 22

Masato Shinohara, *Fuji Television*, Legal Action
Shinohara, Seoul bureau chief of Japan's *Fuji Television* network, was sentenced by the Seoul District Criminal Court on December 22 to two years in prison for illegally obtaining classified military documents and handing copies thereof to military attachés at the Japanese Embassy. Korean officials had detained Shinohara on June 26 and had arrested him on July 13 on charges of violating the country's military secrets law. Shinohara, who contributed to Japanese defense periodicals on a freelance basis, insisted throughout that he had collected the information for his own research purposes. He filed an appeal with the Seoul High Court on December 23.

Sri Lanka

The Sri Lankan government continued to use the country's protracted ethnic civil war as a pretext to infringe on press freedom through emergency regulations, bureaucratic machinery, and extra-legal devices. Despite these onerous conditions, Sri Lanka retains a vibrant independent press and a strong local media freedom group to support it. The back to back assassinations of opposition leader Lalith Athulathmudali and President Ranasinghe Premadasa rocked Sri Lanka in the spring. For much of the Sri Lankan press, an end to the old acrimonies seemed at hand with the assumption of the presidency by the more cautious Dingiri Banda Wijetunga and the premiership by Ranil Wickremasinghe, the scion of a newspaper-owning family. Subsequent developments tempered these expectations. Critical coverage of a major army offensive on the Jaffna peninsula brought a protracted campaign of harassment against respected defense correspondent Iqbal Athas, while papers that supported the beleaguered journalist were them-

selves threatened. The threats subsided when Sri Lanka's relatively young Free Media Movement mobilized support for Athas in Sri Lanka and abroad. The December resignation of Army Commander Cecil Waidyaratne, at least in part an outcome of Athas's reporting, served as a reminder of the power that press freedom can bring to bear. The latter was equally apparent at year's end, when the president's attempt to reintroduce a sedition law that could potentially embrace almost any political reporting was thwarted by the Free Media Movement and other vocal press representatives. Judgments were issued during the year on two cases brought under the Parliamentary Powers and Privileges Act, a rarely invoked statute that bans criticism of members of Parliament. In one case, a paper was ordered to print an apology to the aggrieved party, while in another, a paper was barred from Parliament for one week. But the most far reaching consequence of these decisions was a requirement by the Parliamentary Privileges Committee that all coverage of parliamentary affairs be based on the Hansard—the official record, which is subject to excision by members of Parliament and which is often published weeks after a given debate has taken place.

FEBRUARY
Lankadipa, Harassed, Legal Action
The Parliamentary Privileges Committee recommended in late July that the newspaper *Lankadipa* be barred from the Parliament for a one-week period. The decision came in response to a December 16, 1991, article in *Lankadipa*, which reported the use of derogatory words in a parliamentary debate. The committee followed this move by issuing a new set of guidelines requiring that all coverage of par-

liamentary proceedings be based on the official record thereof, known as the Hansard.

FEBRUARY 1
Yukthiya, Harassed
Lakdiva, Harassed
Aththa, Harassed
Ravaya, Harassed
Former President Ranasinghe Premadasa criticized "anti-government newspapers" and suggested that they were receiving foreign aid after the Free Media Movement held a freedom of expression rally in Nugegoda on January 26. One week later, officers from the Inland Revenue Department visited the offices of *Yukthiya, Lakdiva, Aththa*, and *Ravaya* to check on payment of taxes, sales revenue, and sources of income. On the same day, the Colombo Municipal Council, the Labour Department, and the utility boards visited *Ravaya*. Officials from the electricity and water boards also visited Lalitha Kala, the commercial press that prints the paper, and ordered that the water service be turned off.

FEBRUARY 3
Wijeya Publications, Attacked
Two officials from the Employees Trust Fund visited the offices of Wijeya Publications, which publishes the *Sunday Times* and *Lankadipa*, and removed some records for investigation.

FEBRUARY 5
Lakdiva, Harassed
On the evening of February 5, members of the Colombo Municipal Council sealed *Lakdiva's* offices.

APRIL 30-MAY 3
The Island, Threatened
Yukthiya, Threatened
Lankadipa, Threatened
Shortly after the assassination of Lalith Athulathmudali, leader of the Democratic National Front Party, an unidentified caller

Asia

warned *The Island* newspaper that its offices would be attacked on May 1. Many believe that the warning was in response to *The Island's* report that the government may have been involved in Athulathmudali's assassination. Several other newspapers, including *Yukthiya* and *Lankadipa*, also received telephone threats.

MAY
Asiaweek, Censored

Sri Lanka's Customs Department held up distribution of the May 12 issue of *Asiaweek* until May 23, when the attorney general cleared it for release. The issue contained a cover story about the recently assassinated Sri Lankan President Ranasinghe Premadasa, which stated that many Sri Lankans held Premadasa's men responsible for the murder of opposition leader Lalith Athulathmudali, and that Premadasa was informed of a plan to "pick up" journalist Richard de Zoysa on February 18, 1990—the night before de Zoysa's tortured body was found near a Colombo beach.

JUNE 6
Ravaya, Legal Action

On June 16, *Ravaya* was informed that it had breached parliamentary privilege by reporting on March 17, 1991, that a member of Parliament had failed to pay a substantial bill incurred at a guest house on the south coast. The Parliamentary Privileges Committee reached this decision without ever having given *Ravaya* an opportunity to be heard. *Ravaya* was asked to publish a correction and apology, and it did so after a two-week deadline was set in a letter dated July 9, 1993. However, in the same issue the paper also published a letter of protest written by its editor, Victor Ivan.

OCTOBER 10
Iqbal Athas, *Sunday Times (Colombo)*, Harassed, Threatened
Yukthiya, Threatened
Sama Samaja, Threatened

Athas, defense correspondent for the *Sunday Times* of Colombo, published an article on October 10 exposing the Sri Lankan military's losses in a recent offensive against the secessionist Liberation Tigers of Tamil Eelam. Shortly thereafter, Athas received a series of phone calls threatening him with death and the kidnapping of his child. On November 6, a funeral wreath was delivered to his house; the wreath was addressed to his wife and bore the names of two Sri Lankan army units that had participated in the operation. In an off-the- record remark, Army Commander Cecil Waidyaratne reportedly told the *Sunday Times* publisher that "Eelamists" [Tamil separatists] on his staff should be "burned on tires." Athas's harassment sparked protests by Sri Lanka's Free Media Movement and drew coverage from other local papers. Two of these papers, *Yukthiya* and *Sama Samaja*, were themselves subjected to threats, and a prominent contributor to *Sama Samaja*, Bernard Soysa, was told that "he would be finished by the end of the month." Following a second military setback, however, Waidyaratne resigned his command—reportedly under government pressure to do so.

DECEMBER 20
All Media, Legal Action

On December 20, President D. B. Wijetunga issued a series of emergency laws on sedition and incitement. The laws, which carried penalties of up to 20 years' imprisonment, made it a crime for any person to write material seeking to bring the president, government, constitution, or administration of justice into hatred or contempt, to raise or create discontent or disaffection among any of the country's inhabitants, or to promote or foster communal hatred or hostility. Widespread criticism of the laws from opposition groups and the media prompted the government to rescind these provisions on January 6, but it retained another section criminalizing handbills or posters prejudicial to "public security [or] public order."

Thailand

Since returning to democratic rule in late 1992, Thailand has seen a gradual relaxation of government control over the media. Military-produced commentary, formerly mandatory on national newscasts, was rejected by two university stations during the year without reprisal. And although self-censorship continues with regard to the royal family and the Buddhist clergy, government officials frequently face harsh media criticism. On one such occasion in May, the Prime Minister retaliated against a column that had labeled him a dictator by filing a libel suit against both the columnist and the paper.

MAY 13
Thai Rath, Legal Action
Prime Minister Chuan Leekpai filed a libel suit against *Thai Rath*, the country's largest daily, following the publication of a column that he said had damaged his reputation. In the May 11 piece, columnist Santi Viriyarangsarit, writing under the pen name "Typhoon," condemned the brutal suppression of a farmer's protest by police in northern Thailand a few days earlier and described Chuan as being "no different from a military dictator." In his lawsuit, Chuan demanded an apology from *Thai Rath*, to be published in six widely read Thai newspapers for 15 consecutive days. If successful, the suit also carries penalties of a two-year jail term and a fine of about 200,000 baht. Chuan is the first prime minister of Thailand to sue a newspaper while holding office.

Tonga

'Akilisi Pohiva, editor and publisher of *Kele'a* and member of Parliament, continued to fight government gags and libel suits which, over the years, have totaled nearly $40,000 in damages. Pohiva has championed press freedom and other democratic reforms in Tonga for at least a decade.

JANUARY 4
'Akilisi Pohiva, *Kele'a*, Legal Action
Tonga's solicitor-general filed a writ against Pohiva ordering him to stop publishing information that was subject to the Official Secrets Act—in short, classified and confidential government information. When Pohiva did not comply by the January 4 deadline, the government sought a Supreme Court permanent injunction, an appeal it lost on February 10. The court ruled that a full trial was necessary; it took place in April. Pohiva won the case with costs.

MARCH 30
'Akilisi Pohiva, *Kele'a*, Legal Action
Pohiva lost a civil defamation suit brought by the Speaker of the Legislative Assembly for an article in April 1990 alleging that the Speaker won his seat in Parliament by betraying a fellow noble. The article also suggested that if the Speaker could betray a noble, he could do as much to ordinary people. The judge ordered Pohiva to pay damages to the Speaker.

JUNE 30
'Akilisi Pohiva, *Kele'a*, Legal Action
Pohiva lost an appeal on a Supreme Court injunction and an order to reveal sources in connection with the Tonga Development Bank and its alleged mismanagement of loans. The bank had sued *Kele'a* for defamation and breach

(continued on page 181)

Asia

No Forum for Debate

by Vikram Parekh

For the second time in his life, Doan Viet Hoat is serving out a prison sentence of over ten years. His crime? Publishing an informal newsletter called *Freedom Forum* that presented a variety of non-governmental viewpoints on domestic and international issues. However low-key this venture may have been, the Vietnamese government found it sufficiently alarming to convict Hoat and seven of his colleagues of conspiring to "overthrow the administration"—this during a year in which Hanoi ostensibly sought to leave a favorable impression on Capitol Hill.

Unfortunately for Hoat, the state of press freedom in his country never materialized in the Congressional debate over lifting trade restrictions on Vietnam, and his own severe sentence—20 years, reduced on appeal to 15—rarely drew notice. Had recognition of press freedom been made an issue, Congress might have learned why Hoat's publication was so significant to Hanoi: in a country where all media is tightly controlled by the state, *Freedom Forum* was one of the lone vehicles for dissent.

Hoat himself had acted with great courage in editing and publishing *Freedom Forum*, for the newsletter's first issue appeared within months of his February 1988 release from twelve years' detention without charge. A professor at Saigon's Van Hanh University until 1975, Hoat was originally arrested during a crackdown on Vietnamese intellectuals. Despite the advice of friends who urged him to join his two sons and brother in the United States, Hoat elected to remain in Vietnam and pursue his ideals through peaceful avenues such as *Freedom Forum*.

Over the next two years, Hoat edited and published at least four issues of the newsletter. Though *Freedom Forum* was passed hand-to-hand by readers, witnesses say there was no secrecy surrounding it. On November 17, 1990, Hoat was seized by police at his home in Ho Chih Minh City, and held incommunicado for six months before his family was allowed to visit him. Seven other contributors to the newsletter were also detained without charge.

Hoat and his colleagues were never afforded the opportunity of a fair trial. On May 6, 1992, before any charges had been filed, the state newspaper *Saigon Giai Phong* informed the public that a "reactionary group" led by Hoat had employed the *Freedom Forum* newsletter "as a most important means of rallying forces to oppose and sabotage our country." The invective that the paper launched against the *Freedom Forum* writers was a significant portent of things to come, for political trials in Vietnam are often preceeded by media condemnation of defendants.

The eight detained writers were finally tried on March 29 and 30 of 1993, and found guilty of subversion. Hoat had been forced to represent himself, as the California-based attorneys whom his wife had approached to take up his case were denied visas by Hanoi. The sentences themselves shocked even seasoned observers of the Vietnamese political scene, with Hoat receiving a twenty-year term, and his colleagues anywhere from eight months—reportedly in the case of a defendant who "confessed" —to sixteen years.

Hoat was also denied representation by the counsel of his choice at his June 3 appeal hearing, where his sentence was reduced by five years. The other *Freedom Forum* defendants also received slight reductions in their prison terms, reductions that the *Vietnamese News Agency* attributed to the fact "that their plot had been nipped in the bud before causing any serious damage."

Undeterred, Hoat continued to write in the prison and labor camps at which he was held over the next six months. Through contacts in the camps, he managed to smuggle out a few essays in which he discussed, among other topics, the relevance of international human rights to Vietnam. Hoat's limited contact with the outside world soon proved to be too much for his jailers. In a move that was widely seen as a bid to silence Hoat, Vietnamese authorities transferred him on December 16 from Chi Hoa prison, located near Ho Chih Minh City, to Camp A20 Xuan Phuoc, situated some 650 kilometers to the north. Two other *Freedom Forum* writers, Pham Duc Kham and Le Duc Vuong were also relocated to Xuan Phuoc.

Long notorious as one of Vietnam's most brutal labor camps, Xuan Phuoc posed an arduous three-day journey for Hoat's wife, who until now had been the sole provider of the medicine Hoat needed for his kidney stones. This condition, which developed during Hoat's previous incarceration, also stood to be exacerbated by the hard labor assignments given prisoners at Xuan Phuoc.

Hoat's son, Long Doan, who accepted CPJ's press freedom award on his father's behalf in November, remarked recently that the lifting of trade restrictions had removed the United States' principal bargaining chip for the release of the *Freedom Forum* writers. There are, in fact, other avenues to pursue, such as an impending human rights dialogue between the State Department and Le Bang, Vietnam's Ambassador to the United Nations. And the work of securing the release of Hoat and his colleagues should now also be undertaken by members of the business community who claim, with regard to Vietnam as well as China, that free expression will flow from free trade.

Vikram Parekh *is CPJ's Asia Program Coordinator. CPJ has tracked the* ***Freedom Forum*** *case since Hoat's detention in 1990.*

of client confidentiality after a series of articles in early 1992. The Supreme Court dismissed the defamation charges in December 1992, but then filed the injunction.

Vietnam

While its conciliatory stance on American MIAs paved the way for lifting of U.S. trade restrictions, Vietnam continued to uphold a repressive media policy. The sentencing of longtime dissident Doan Viet Hoat and seven other *Freedom Forum* writers in March dealt a severe blow to the country's only independent print media— newsletters similar to the trailblazing *samizdat* publications of the former Soviet Union. At year's end, Hoat's already poor health was further imperiled by his relocation to a hard labor camp in the north. In July, a new law called on state-owned press and publishing houses to bolster the Party's economic reform program and fight hostile forces threatening the "socialist motherland." Vietnam thus appeared to be adopting China's approach under Deng Xiao Ping, in which economic liberalization coexists with political repression. An optimistic note, however, was struck in the south, where newspapers published more articles exposing government corruption.

LATE MARCH

Doan Viet Hoat, *Freedom Forum,* Legal Action
Pham Duc Kham, *Freedom Forum,* Legal Action
Nguyen Xuan Dong, *Freedom Forum,*
Legal Action
Le Duc Vuong, *Freedom Forum,* Legal Action
Pham Thai Thuy, *Freedom Forum,* Legal Action
Hoang Cao Nha, *Freedom Forum,* Legal Action
Nguyen Van Thuan, *Freedom Forum,* Legal Action

In late March, Hoat and seven other writers were found guilty of attempting to overthrow the government, a charge stemming from their involvement with a pro-democracy newsletter, *Freedom Forum.* Hoat, the editor and publisher of *Freedom Forum,* was sentenced to 20 years of hard labor and five years of political rights deprivation upon his release. At both his March trial and an appeal hearing in early July, where his sentence was reduced to 15 years, Hoat was denied representation by the lawyer of his choice. On December 16, Hoat, Kham, and Vuong were moved from Chi Hoa prison, near Ho Chih Minh City, to Camp A20 Xuan Phuoc—650 kilometers from the former South Vietnamese capital and notorious for its brutality. Although no reasons were given for the transfer, the move came shortly after the overseas press published statements on human rights that Hoat had made from prison. Hoat suffers from kidney stones, a disorder that he developed during an earlier twelve-year incarceration for alleged anti-government activities. Without proper medication, which the Vietnamese government does not provide him, he has severe back pains and difficulty standing for prolonged periods of time. Hoat received one of CPJ's five annual press freedom awards in November 1993.

Western Samoa

In Western Samoa, the government introduced new legislation requiring disclosure of sources in defamation cases. The Pacific Islands News Association (PINA) protested the law as a form of censorship and expressed concern that the bill was never opened to public debate.

Asia

FEBRUARY
All Media, Legal Action
The Newspapers and Printers Act passed by
Parliament in early February would require
defendants to produce correspondence and
written material and name sources of information in the event of a libel suit. The penalty for
breaching the proposed law is U.S. $1,400 or a
prison sentence not longer than three months.
A new Defamation Act was also passed later in
the month that would ban publishing defamatory statements made in court about a third
party.

Eastern Europe

(including the republics of the former Soviet Union)

OVERVIEW
OF
Eastern Europe (including the republics of the former Soviet Union)

by Leonid Zagalsky

The newly emerged democratic governments of the former Soviet Union and Eastern Europe have started to push hard to gain control of the media—often relying on discredited and almost abandoned communist-style orders. Many governments directly interfere with the functioning of television and printed media. By law, the press is free in every country in these regions. Even Albania has adopted a new press law that allows media independence. But in reality, these laws give the state the right to close down news outlets for relatively vague reasons. Sometimes they shut down print and broadcast media without any explanation. These laws are being used by the authorities in Russia, former Yugoslavia, Tajikistan, Georgia and Albania.

Many restrictions on access to public government documents still exist in newly independent states of the former Soviet Union and Eastern Europe. The very idea of state secrets and what should be open to the public is still alien to many governments. Therefore, journalists often do not have a chance to provide the audience with truthful and objective information on political and economic developments. Because salaries for reporters are low, many journalists are paid on the side by government and private entities, in exchange for favorable coverage. Russian journalists are well aware of the meaning of the term writing "according to the purchaser's order."

Perhaps the most significant challenge to the press in these regions is the media's dependence on state support. In Russia specifically, very few print organizations and almost no broadcast media can survive without state subsidies. The criteria for determining which mass media is eligible for receiving government funding are very vague. This gives authorities free reign to use "the power of the purse" and restrain publications which are in opposition. Editors of the media organizations are not yet familiar with the idea of impartial coverage. One editor in Russia publicly declared that his newspaper "respected Yeltsin and was going to support his government even if he was wrong."

Europe and the former Soviet Union are still among the most lethal regions for journalists. Central Asia and Yugoslavia are facing ethnic fights and civil wars. In the former Yugoslavia, the death toll for journalists continued to climb and reached 34 since the beginning of the war in 1991. The tough political situation in the former Yugoslavia gives very little hope that it will stop being one of the most dangerous places for journalists.

In Georgia the civil war has pitted Georgians who support President Eduard Shevardnadze against Georgians who back the forces of former President Zviad Gamsakhurdia (he committed suicide under mysterious circumstances). This war is complicated by the fact that in Abkhasia, a small minority is fighting both groups for independence. Three journalists were killed in Abkhasia while they were in the line of duty.

Tadjiks have brought back old communist values and Moscow now is stuffed with Tajik intellectuals who have fled from the reactionary communist government that took power last year. Tajik journalists are among those in greatest danger. They are persecuted by the National Front, a paramilitary group linked to the Communist government which seized power in 1993. The deaths of four journalists were fully documented, but CPJ continues its investigation of the murder of eleven reporters who died under suspicious circumstances. Russian troops, while guarding Tadjik frontiers, are fighting against Afghans.

Kirgizstan is trying hard to break through to the modern world. Meanwhile the Kirgizian government has excepted the law which eliminates any opportunity for journalists to write independently. This new law requires mass media to receive permission to publish "not secret materials."

Freedom of the press in Albania recalls the darkest communist years when people were not even allowed to dissent in their thoughts. Journalists who challenge the government are harassed and often imprisoned.

The failure of the October 1993 coup in Russia in which seven journalists were killed and 13 wounded could have become an important lesson for the Russian government, but it did not happen. President Yeltsin shut down 15 opposition print and broadcast news outlets, using administrative measures after the Moscow October 1993 standoff. In its letter of protest, The Committee to Protect Journalists stated that "We understand that some might find the content of the... media to be offensive. Yet if a 'state based on law' is going to be established in Russia, the media must be allowed the greatest latitude in which to operate. An atmosphere in which all points of view may be openly debated is essential for true democracy to come to Russia."

All these regions are so different. It hardly seems possible that such nations were ever part of a single communist environment. For their own reasons, these states have chosen freedom. The only thing that unites them now is the high price they are paying for that choice. This complicated transition from totalitarianism to democracy has not proved yet a total blossom of press freedom.

Leonid Zagalsky *is Program Coordinator for Eastern Europe (including the republics of the former Soviet Union). Zagalsky was a recipient of the John S. Knight Fellowship for professional journalists at Stanford University. He has written widely on political and economic affairs and is a contributing editor for* **The Bulletin of the Atomic Scientists,** *a Chicago-based magazine.*

Andrew Yurkovsky, *former CPJ researcher,* **Dimitry Danilyuk** *and* **Yalman Onaran** *contributed to this report.*

Albania

Although Albania now has a democratically elected government, journalists complain that little has changed for the working press. New publications have emerged since 1991, but they are ruled by the same iron hand that oppressed writers under the Communist regime. Journalists are routinely arrested and prosecuted and subjected to constant harassment by a police force that operates with impunity. A new press law signed by President Sali Berisha in October 1993 allows prosecutors to confiscate publications without a court order. The law, which also puts limits on the coverage of political issues and court proceedings, establishes fines of $8,000 for each violation. In a country where the average monthly wage is approximately $30, a financial penalty of that size would drive many small publications into bankruptcy. It is the opposition press—any publication not associated with the ruling party—that faces all the legal and extra-legal harassment. That means newspapers, magazines, and, most recently, books. All radio and television programming is owned and controlled by the government.

JANUARY-DECEMBER
Shyqyri Meka, *Zeri i Popullit,* Imprisoned
Thoma Gallci, *Zeri i Popullit,* Imprisoned
Panajot Zoto, *Zeri i Popullit,* Imprisoned
Koco Danaj, *Zeri i Popullit,* Imprisoned
Fredi Dalipi, *Zeri i Popullit,* Imprisoned
Bashkim Koci, *Zeri i Popullit,* Imprisoned
Zeri i Popullit, the main opposition newspaper in Albania, is under constant pressure from the government. Its editor-in-chief, Thoma Gallci,

was detained for a day on July 30 by the police, who accused him of taking part in an illegal demonstration. Gallci was covering a rally organized by the Socialist Party. During the same rally the photographer for *Zeri i Popullit,* Fredi Dalipi, was beaten by the police. One of the newspaper's reporters, Panajot Zoto, was sentenced to one month in prison for an article he wrote regarding allegations of corruption at the finance ministry. He was released in December after serving his sentence. Bashkim Koci, one of the editors, was put under house arrest for one month for insulting the president in one of his articles. Shyqyri Meka, the deputy editor, was arrested on December 26 by the police for an interview with a former member of the opposition party published in the newspaper. He is still in custody. Koco Danaj, another *ZP* correspondent, fled the country for fear of his life after being threatened by the president. The staff of *Zeri i Popullit* says that the pro-government newspaper *Rilindje Demokratike* has recently started calling in its editorials for the closure of *Zeri i Popullit.* *Zeri i Popullit* is closely linked with the opposition political party.

JANUARY-DECEMBER
Nikolle Lesi, *Koha Jone,* Legal Action
Frrok Cupi, *Koha Jone,* Exit denied
Koha Jone, Censored
The biggest independent newspaper in Albania has been under constant harassment from the government. Lesi, *Koha Jone's* director, has been under investigation for over a year by the government prosecutor for articles published in the newspaper. He was taken to court but acquitted for one of these cases. Cupi, one of *Koha Jone's* reporters, has been forbidden to leave the country for a year. Cupi was formerly the editor of the *Rilindje Demokratike,* the ruling party's

newspaper. *Koha Jone* claims that the government has given it a hard time because Cupi refused to let his former newspaper become a puppet of the government before he was removed from his position. In addition to all the harassment its journalists have faced, the newspaper was also censored by the ministry of state control 28 times in 1993, according to the paper's officials.

JANUARY-DECEMBER
Abdurrahim Ashiku, *Zeri i Popullit,* Attacked
Zeri i Popullit, Attacked
The Peshkopia (in northern Albania) correspondent of *Zeri i Popullit* Abdurrahim Ashiku was beaten by unknown persons in his office. The newspaper contends that the authorities have been indifferent to the incident and have not even investigated it. Readers and distributors of the newspaper also face harassment. *Zeri i Popullit* readers complain that they have lost jobs just for reading the newspaper. A distributor in the village of Lusbnja was beaten and fined by the police for selling *Zeri i Popullit,* say the newspaper officials.

APRIL
Aleksander Frangaj, *Koha Jone,* Imprisoned
The editor-in-chief of the Albanian newspaper *Koha Jone* was arrested and charged with treason after his newspaper published an article about tank movements in northern Albania. He was acquitted in the trial. If found guilty, he could have been sentenced to five years in prison. Frangaj spent 25 days in custody before he was released.

AUGUST 24
Ricardo Orizio, *Corriera della Sera,* Imprisoned, Attacked
Orizio, a reporter with the Italian daily *Corriera della Sera,* was taken into custody and spent a night in a Tirana prison cell after his interview with the widow of the deposed Albanian leader Nexhmije Hoxha appeared in his newspaper. Orizio says he was beaten up "lightly" and interrogated three times during the night about his news sources. After the Italian embassy's intervention, he was taken to the airport and put on the next plane to Italy, although he was not formally expelled. Orizio says part of the deal struck with the Albanian government was that he would obey an unwritten, unofficial order to not enter Albania "in the near future." Local journalists are treated even worse than he was, Orizio says. "Anytime a newspaper criticizes the government, they close it down for a day or two. During the communist regime, you would never hear of journalists being harassed or newspapers being shut down because in those days being an Albanian journalist meant being progovernment. Now that it is possible to have an opposition press, it has also become possible to shut it down or treat it badly."

OCTOBER 24
Reporteri, Harassed
When the first issue of the *Reporteri,* a newspaper published by journalism students at the University of Tirana, carried an article and a cartoon criticizing the press law about to be passed, the president of Albania was not happy. Four days after the newspaper came out, the three Americans who were working with the students in publishing the newspaper found their office with all the computer equipment locked. It took them two months to restart the publication of the student newspaper and then only after they severed their ties with the University of Tirana. Now they rely completely on their own resources from American foundations, and Albanian journalism students continue to publish an independent newspaper.

189

The official version of the "lock-out" story given by the government was that it was the lack of coordination between the three Americans in charge of the project and journalism faculty at the University of Tirana. *Reporteri* was launched as an independent newspaper in Albania with the hope that it would lead the way to other independent media ventures. Currently, most news organizations in Albania rely on some political party for financing. Financed by two American foundations, *Reporteri* hopes to pioneer in breaking that strong link.

OCTOBER 25

All Print Media, Legal Action

Albanian President Sali Berisha signed the press law passed by the parliament. The new law puts many restrictions on the Albanian press and was assailed by all news organizations including the governing party's newspaper. The law puts limits on coverage of political issues and court proceedings, gives powers of confiscation to the prosecutor without a court order, and levies a fine of $8,000 (an incredibly high amount for Albania where the average monthly wage is $30) for illegal acts not laid out in the law. While the law was under consideration in the parliament, most newspapers joined a protest campaign in which several pages would come out blank with headlines declaring "If the press law is passed, Albania newspapers will look like this." Despite all the protests and the fact that all opposition parties opposed the proposal, the governing party passed it with the majority of votes it holds in the parliament. The president is also from the governing party.

Bosnia-Herzegovina

Nearly two years after the civil war broke out, local as well as foreign reporters in Bosnia-Herzegovina are daily targets of snipers and regional military groups on all three sides, Serb, Muslim, and Croat. It is suspected that snipers deliberately target journalists in order to bring more attention to the war, while local military groups routinely confiscate reporters' money and equipment to make their job as difficult as possible. Not unlike the citizens of Sarajevo and other besieged cities of Bosnia, journalists have to do their duty under constant shelling. In less than three years, at least 36 journalists have been killed in former Yugoslavia. It is really a problem for a journalists to survive and still get the story in this region. The breakup of Yugoslavia, coming shortly after the collapse of the Soviet Union, has brought back ethnic conflicts to Bosnia-Herzegovina. More likely, it is a territorial conflict with clever politicians using ethnic differences as an issue. When Bosnian Serbs and Croats decided to carve up Bosnia, a civil war was unavoidable. Today, the name of the game is who can grab the most land before a peace agreement is signed. With the civil war in its second year, the United Nations has failed to bring the conflict to an end. Air strikes on Bosnian Serbs have so far proven to be empty threats, and several seize-fires have been broken as the leaders of the three factions are unable to agree on the new map of Bosnia. Pressure to stop the conflict continues to mount on the UN, mostly from the Middle East. Arming the Bosnian Muslims has been suggested, but that may further

escalate the conflict. Apparently, former Yugoslavia will remain one of the most dangerous places in the world and journalists should be very careful on their assignments.

JANUARY 10

Karmela Sojanovic, *Oslobodjenje*, Killed

Sojanovic, who worked for the daily *Oslobodjenje*, was killed by a sharpshooter at her home in Sarajevo. Two of her colleagues at the paper were killed in 1992, while two others disappeared and are presumed dead.

FEBRUARY 9

Antonine Gyori, *Sygma*, Attacked

Gyori, of France, was working for the *Sygma* photo agency when he was shot in the neck by a sniper as his clearly marked car headed down Sarajevo's airport road. Gyori was reportedly in stable condition.

MARCH 8-9

Walter Skerk, *Italian Television RAI*, Imprisoned
Luciano Masi, *Italian Television RAI*, Imprisoned
Italian Television RAI, Harassed

Skerk, a driver, and Masi, a cameraman, working for *Italian Television RAI*, were held for two days in Ilidza police station. Their lives were frequently threatened at knifepoint. Bosnian Serb officials said that they were angered by a filmed report done by *RAI* correspondent Franco DiMare about a Muslim woman who had been raped and had given birth to a daughter. The Bosnian Serb officials demanded that DiMare, who was in Sarajevo, personally come to retrieve the television station's armored car, in which Skerk and Masi had been traveling. DiMare refused after UN officials told him they could not guarantee his safety. Skerk, and Masi were eventually released; DM 3,700 was taken from Skerk and 2 million lire ($1,500) was taken from Masi. The armored car was confiscated.

MARCH 22

Joel Brand, *The Times* (London), *Newsweek*, Imprisoned
Brian Green, *Worldwide Television News*, Imprisoned
Janine di Giovanni, *Sunday Times* (London), Imprisoned

Brand of *The Times* (London) and *Newsweek* (USA), Green of *Worldwide Television News*, and di Giovanni of the *Sunday Times* (London) were detained by Bosnian Serb police in Kobiljaca. Green had $2,000 taken. Di Giovanni was strip-searched, humiliated, and had DM 6,000 taken.

MAY 29

Guido Puletti, *Mondo Economico, Brescia Oggi*, Killed

Puletti, who freelanced for the Italian publications *Mondo Economico* and *Brescia Oggi*, and a group of four relief workers were traveling on the road between Gornji Vakuf and Novi Travnik in Central Bosnia when they were ambushed by unknown assailants on May 29. There are conflicting reports as to the nationality and affiliation of the assailants. Puletti and two of the relief workers were shot and killed. The motive for the attack may have been the food the workers were transporting.

JUNE 2

Dominique Lonneux, *Mexican Television*, Killed

Lonneux, a Belgian cameraman who was working for a *Mexican Television* news team, was wounded and later died when a United Nations Protection Force convoy was attacked in western Herzegovina.

JUNE 27

Tasar Omer, Killed

Omer, a Turkish journalist, was killed by a sniper in Sarajevo while attending the funeral of seven young people who died in shelling the day before.

191

JULY 10
Ibrahim Goskel, Killed
Goskel, a journalist carrying a British passport, was shot and killed at Sarajevo airport.

OCTOBER
Paul Marchand, *Radio France Internationale,* Attacked
Marchand, a correspondent for *Radio France Internationale* and *Radio Canada,* was seriously wounded by a sniper in a suburb of Sarajevo controlled by Serbs. His car was fired on after he was turned back at a Serb checkpoint leading out of Sarajevo.

Croatia

Though no journalists were killed in Croatia in 1993, it remains a difficult place for independent journalists to work. In January 1993 two Serbian journalists were sentenced to long prison terms for carrying out their duties. The government of Croatia under President Franjo Tudjman has been attempting to suppress the independent press by asserting greater control over the publicly-owned media. At least one newspaper, *Slobodna Dalmacija,* has been taken over by government. The government appointed a new board of directors and a new editorial board to keep the newspaper in line. The government already owns approximately half of the mainstream media outlets and has a virtual monopoly in printing and distribution. Through control of printing and distribution the government is able to influence privately-owned media. Using the country's economic difficulties, Tudjman's government imposed self-censorship on journalists through constant "restructuring" of government controlled media. Because they fear losing their jobs, journalists usually censor themselves.

JANUARY 28
Ognjen Tadic, *Serbian Television,* Imprisoned, Legal Action
Milovan Pejanovic, *Serbian Television,* Imprisoned, Legal Action
Tadic and Pejanovic, journalists with *Serbian Television* in Pale, were arrested by Croatian police on the Peruca Dam on January 28. In early April, they were sentenced to six and seven years' imprisonment, respectively. They are being held in a prison in Split, Croatia.

Georgia

In this year alone, CPJ has been able to confirm that one local and two foreign journalists have been killed while carrying out their professional duties in Georgia. Abkhazian forces are believed to be responsible in the three incidents. Perhaps the death of *Wall Street Journal* stringer Alexandra Tuttle signified the ethnic turmoil. She was on an airplane that was shot down by an Abkhazian ground-to-air missile in Sukhumi, the capitol of Abkhazia. An unconfirmed number of Georgian journalists have disappeared in Abkhazian prisons after being arrested while covering the conflict on Abkhazian territory. There is still very little information available about the number of these journalists and the charges leveled against them. Georgians have also arrested Abkhazian and Russian journalists but no one is believed to be killed. Like other countries, which also refused to join the Commonwealth of Independent States (CIS), Georgia viewed the CIS as nothing more than a refurbished empire. The idea of independence from Russian "big brother" was very attractive but going it alone led to insoluble economic and political problems. But independence from Russia was paid by human lives. Since it broke away from the Soviet Union in April of 1991, Georgia has been torn by civil war. The war has claimed over 15,000 lives and left more than 200,000 homeless. The economy was collapsing under the burden of military expenditures. Hundreds of thousands of people were at the brink of starvation.

The conflict began in South Ossetia, in northeastern Georgia, after Zviad Gamsakhurdia became the first popularly elected president of Georgia. After Gamsakhurdia was ousted in January 1992, and the former foreign minister of the Soviet Union Edward Shevardnadze was installed, two more factions were created, rebels loyal to Gamsakhurdia and a separatist faction in Abkhazia. Russian involvement in the region continues. The Abkhazian military advance in northwest Georgia in October 1993 prompted Shevardnadze to agree to join the Commonwealth of Independent States, something he was reluctant to do earlier. Abkhazian rebels were immediately driven back, many believe with Russian help. Not long afterwards, under questionable circumstances, Gamsakhurdia was reported to have committed suicide.

JULY 4
Vladimir Popov, *Krasnaya Zvezda (Red Star),* Attacked
Popov, correspondent of *Krasnaya Zvezda* (Red Star) newspaper, was wounded in the back in Gudauta (Georgia) while Georgian troops bombed the city. He had surgery in the local hospital.

SEPTEMBER 22
Alexandra Tuttle, *The Wall Street Journal,* Killed
Tuttle, a correspondent for *The Wall Street Journal,* was killed aboard a military aircraft when it was hit by an Abkhazian ground-to-air missile. The plane crashed and burned as the

pilot attempted to make an emergency landing in Sukhumi. Tuttle boarded the flight in Tbilisi and was on her way to conduct an interview with Eduard Shevardnadze.

SEPTEMBER 27
Andrei Soloviev, *ITAR-TASS,* Killed
Soloviev, a photocorrespondent for *ITAR-TASS,* was killed by a sniper as he covered the fighting in Sukhumi.

SEPTEMBER 27
Yuri Gavva, *Democraticheskaya Abkhazia,* Imprisoned, Legal Action
Gavva, editor-in-chief for *Democraticheskaya Abkhazia,* was arrested in Sukhumi by Abkhazian separatists on September 27. He was held prisoner in an Abkhazian town of Gudauta, and was released three months later.

LATE OCTOBER
David Bolkvadze, *Worldwide Television News,* Killed
Bólkvadze, a Georgian journalist who worked for the *British Worldwide Television News,* was killed in the town of Kobi as he covered the Georgian conflict. Abkhazian soldiers are suspected in the killing.

OCTOBER 4
Sergei Chernyh, *Komsomolskaya Pravda,* Imprisoned
Chernyh, 24-year old correspondent for *Komsomolskaya Pravda,* was detained by Georgian intelligence (IRS) and accused of espionage. He was released from prison where he spent 2 days and celebrated his birthday.

NOVEMBER 3
Petra Prohazkova, *Lidove Novina,* Imprisoned, Attacked
Prohazkova, correspondent of a Prague weekly, was captured by Gamsakhurdia supporters when she attempted to interview the former Georgian president. She spent three days under arrest in Gamsakhurdia's headquarters.

Eastern Europe

Lithuania

Lithuania is adjusting quickly to its independence by adapting a western-style democracy and establishing a tradition of freedom of the press. However, drastic changes after years of communism present their share of problems. Lithuania has to deal with a communist legacy of corruption among top public officials and industry leaders. It also must face new problems such as the rise of organized crime. These are problems of a young nation that lacks strong economic laws and has an underdeveloped legislative system. In the tradition of press freedom, journalists have a responsibility to keep their government and big business in-check by exposing corruption and misuse of power. This trend has already begun, as a few brave journalists, at great personal risk, attempt to uncover corruption. In October 1993, Vitas Lingis, 33, founder and publisher of the popular daily newspaper *Respublica,* was shot at point-blank range near his home. Lingis, who gained prominence for a series of articles exposing organized crime in his country, had been the target of numerous death threats. In the morning of his assassination he planned to meet one of the government officials who was supposed to give him important information. This murder was a terrible blow against the freedom and independence of the Lithuanian press.

OCTOBER 12
Vitas Lingis, *Respublica*, Killed
Lingis, 33-year-old deputy editor of *Respublica* newspaper, was killed by three shots to his head and spine as he was approaching his car. Lingis, who had written frequently about corruption, had been investigating a story about the Lithuanian criminal underworld. On the day he was shot he was supposed to meet a government official who had agreed to give him some important information.

Russia

The Russian news media, which could play an important role in promoting democratic values and economic reform remains completely disabled. The newly appointed leaders who promised reforms and change have resorted to old tactics, adeptly using the carrot and the stick or, as Russians would say, the whip and the cake, to get the media in line. They censored some newspapers and they closed others. Some news media outlets were forced to change their names on their mastheads, without any legal recourse, just because of a presidential order.

In the current atmosphere, the news media cannot provide fair news coverage. It cannot report on every twist and turn of current political events, nor accurately describe the positions of leading politicians nor report accurately on the president and his government. The breakup of the Soviet Union and an aggressive change toward a market economy has put the Russian reform movement in jeopardy. Russia is facing an economic crisis, causing some to question the pace of the reforms.

Continuing economic trouble has given rise to reform opposition in the Russian Parliament. The conflict between President Boris Yeltsin and the anti-reform members of parliament resulted in a violent confrontation. On October 3, after a 10-day standoff with the president, supporters of Rutskoi and Khasbulatov attempted to seize Ostankino Television Center. The following day,

President Yeltsin ordered the military to seize the Russian Supreme Soviet Building, where the defiant members of parliament were holding out.

During the two days of violence, seven journalists were killed and 49 were wounded or beaten by police and demonstrators, making Russia one of the deadliest countries for journalists in 1993. In the weeks following the conflict, a number of opposition publications were closed down, by presidential decree, and those that remained open were carefully censored.

The December 1993 parliamentary elections, scheduled by President Yeltsin after the old parliament was disbanded, revealed the vulnerability of the reform movement in Russia. According to Boris Yeltsin's order No. 1792 each political party was allotted an equal amount of free television and radio time for advertising and presenting its political, economic and social program. The same order practically eliminated professional journalists from pre-election coverage on television. The candidates brought their own public relations personnel to run their political shows. No candidates were asked direct questions and most of them simply read their speeches.

Ultranationalist Vladimir Zhirinovsky, leader of the right-wing Liberal Democratic Party of Russia, won the election over the pro-Yeltsin Russia's Choice party, giving President Yeltsin the prospect of facing heavy opposition from the new parliament. Zhirinovsky got the best hours on television and made the best use of it.

The partisan nature of Russian journalism and the political dependence of journalists are chronic problems. These phenomena proved especially detrimental during the parliamentarian campaign, when candidates selectively granted interviews only to organs supportive of their political positions.

The results of the parliamentary elections and disagreement about the pace of the reforms have caused a rift among reformers in Russia's Choice party. The latest blow to the reform movement was the resignation of party leader Yegor Gaidar and Finance Minister Federov.

MARCH 22
All Media, Censored
President Boris Yeltsin issued a decree on March 22 that placed radio and television under his control and put all media under the protection of the ministry of the interior. On March 28, the parliament, in turn, voted to disband the Federal Information Center and to put state television and radio under its own control. (The Federal Information Center, which oversees the *Ostankino Television Company* and the *TASS* news agency, was created in 1992 by order of President Yeltsin to promote the course of reforms in Russia.) Later, according to a report by the *United Press International*, the parliament passed a resolution to create an "oversight" council to guarantee objectivity of television and radio reporting.

APRIL 7
Will Englund, *Baltimore Sun*, Harassed
Russia's Ministry of Security summoned Will Englund, a reporter for the *Baltimore Sun*, for questioning in connection with his reporting on the Russian chemical weapons program.

APRIL 14
Dmitry Krikoryants, *Expresskhronika*, Killed
Krikoryants, a correspondent for the Moscow-based weekly *Expresskhronika* in the Chechen city of Grozny (northern Caucasus), was murdered in his apartment by unknown assailants. After opening machine gun fire on Krikoryants through the door of his apartment, the killers broke in, put several bullets through his head, and cut his throat before disappearing. His colleagues fear that he was targeted because

(continued on page 199)

Eastern Europe

195

Russia Revives a Monster

by Leonid Zagalsky

Boris Yeltsin's bloody victory in the recent standoff with the Russian Supreme Soviet resurrected the old monster of censorship from the defeated communist past.

It was not difficult. After Yeltsin gave the word, censors appeared like mushrooms after a rain and went to work. The Russian censorship bureaucracy is a durable one.

Confusion, fright, political in-fighting, and public and economic pressure all contributed to the amazingly sudden revival of the old ways. Moreover, these developments may have cancelled out any progress toward democracy that Yeltsin made by restoring order.

The popular expression that television is the mirror of life took on an ironic meaning during the night of October 4, when Nikolai Bragin, chairman of the *Ostankino TV Center,* switched off the broadcasting button and all the screens across the nation that were tuned to the national television system went blank for a few hours.

Bragin was simply frightened that the armed mob of communists and ultra-nationalists might succeed in capturing the center and would turn it over to the leaders of the rebellious Supreme Soviet. His action was unnecessary. If the anti-government forces had actually made their way to the studios and started broadcasting, the system could have been switched off from any of at least four other locations in the city. But as Russians say, fear has big eyes.

Meanwhile, Russians who wanted to know what was happening turned to *CNN*—and continued to do so throughout the crisis. *Russian Television* cameras were never sent out to cover the events taking place in the city. *Moscow TV,* which never got turned off, didn't have enough footage to show what was going on in the streets. This station got permission, as the national network did later, to broadcast Ted Turner's news throughout the country.

While television is still largely a government-run institution in Russia, the print media have supposedly become independent. One editor, Lev Gushchin of *Ogonyok* magazine, expressed his frustration, therefore, when newspapers appeared on October 6 with blank spots where censored articles would have run: "What were we fighting for by supporting Yeltsin and his team? To bring back the old times, when the real editor of any publication was the censor?"

It was a rhetorical question. Gushchin and other editors would testify to the fact that censorship really did not come on suddenly. The way was paved by economics. As publishing costs and the price of paper inflated rapidly during the past two years, a helpful government distributed financial aid to publications in distress. The price of a subsidy from the ministry of press and information was simple: loyalty to Yeltsin.

Publications opposing Yeltsin were hardly more objective. All Yeltsin's orders were "insane," "stupid" or "senseless." Members of his team were "the crowd of bastards." Their beloved parliament was beyond criticism. Needless to say, these papers did not get a single kopek from the government.

Most journalists themselves have lined up on one side or the other. Russian journalism, which was for decades simply "pro," has become divided between "pro" and "con" without gaining objectivity.

It is hard to conjure up sympathy for many of the 15 publications and television programs banned by Yeltsin's order of October 4. The common theme for many of them is "kill Jews and save Russia." Reports from behind the scenes at *Ostankino* suggest that personal interests and power struggles had much to do with which television voices were silenced. Some welcomed the ban as fuel for the next political battle.

But surely some opposition is better than none. The results of this new wave of censorship will become agonizingly clear in the months ahead, when Yeltsin begins to enjoy his freedom from criticism.

Already the press is creating a simple myth, which the public is apparently willing to buy: the great democratic president, who really cares for the nation, for democracy, and for a free market economy, had no choice except to oust the conservative communist parliament, which was blocking the road to reform.

This media myth cost the lives of seven journalists, killed in the night of October 4, and put bullets in the bodies of thirteen others.

One can now read in every published newspaper that Yeltsin had no choice. No one asks whether he might bear some responsibility for more than 360 lives lost in the uprising and its suppression, or whether he might have avoided the whole mess by calling elections a year ago, or even two.

If you believe *Russian TV*, people interviewed on the street all are calling for death to Yeltsin's opponents Rutskoi and Khasbulatov, Makashov and Anpilov. These interviews echo 1937, when people were calling for death sentences for members of Stalin's Politburo who had been branded "traitors of the nation."

Yeltsin has called for elections for the Federal Congress (no more Supreme Soviet) on December 12. Aside from the near impossibility of organizing democratic elections within two months, it is clear that without an opposition media, opposition opinion will not be heard during the short campaign.

It remains to be seen how the media will respond to all this. Yeltsin took his stand without the backing of a court decision. Without legal guarantees, journalists who dare to criticize the way democracy is being implemented risk becoming the latest "traitors to the nation" or "enemies of the people."

Censorship is one of the first acts of a dictator. Western governments did well to support Yeltsin's fight for democracy. But now that democracy has won, they should take care not to support dictatorship in the name of democracy.

Leonid Zagalsky *is Program Coordinator for Eastern Europe (including the republics of the former Soviet Union). A version of this article appeared in **The St. Petersburg Times** on December 12, 1993.*

of his reporting on alleged Chechen government corruption in oil trading.

APRIL 29
Asef Dzhafarli, *Megapolis-Kontinent*, Attacked
Asef Dzhafarli, a correspondent for the Moscow weekly *Megapolis-Kontinent*, was assaulted by three unknown persons near his home in Moscow late at night as he returned home. They blinded him with gas and beat him up. When Dzhafarli regained consciousness, both his wrists had been broken. In the week before the attack, the journalist had received threatening phone calls at home and work. The assailants threatened him with physical violence because of his articles critical of the National Front of Tajikistan.

SEPTEMBER 21
Alexey Bogomolov, *Moscovsky Komsomolets*, Attacked
Sergei Shakhidzhanyian, *Moscovsky Komsomolets*, Attacked
Correspondent Alexey Bogomolov and photocorrespondent Sergei Shakhidzhanyian were beaten up by pro-Communist demonstrators near the Russian Supreme Soviet Building.

SEPTEMBER 22
Kyle Eppler, *NBC*, Attacked
Marjorie Rouse, *NBC*, Attacked
Christopher Booth, *NBC*, Attacked
Eppler, Rouse, and Booth were beaten by police near Belorussky Railroad Station two days before the standoff between President Yeltsin and the parliament.

SEPTEMBER 22
Yuri Feklistov, *Ogonyok*, Harassed
Feklistov, a photocorrespondent for *Ogonyok* magazine, had his film confiscated by a member of the Union of Russian Officers in the Russian Supreme Soviet Building.

SEPTEMBER 23
Rossiskaya Gazeta, Censored
All Parliamentary Newspapers, Radio and Television, Censored
The government issued a decree according to which it would take control of all parliamentary newspapers and radio and television programs. The parliament's newspaper, *Rossiskaya Gazeta*, had not come out as of September 18, 1993, and authorities have since said that paper will be reregistered, with the government as publisher.

SEPTEMBER 24
Michael Johnson, *CNN*, Attacked
CNN technician Michael Johnson was beaten by police on two occasions near the Russian Supreme Soviet Building during the standoff between President Boris Yeltsin and the hardline parliament. Johnson was first beaten on September 24, when the standoff began. The second incident occurred on October 4, during President Yeltsin's assault on the Russian White House.

SEPTEMBER 25
Ostankino Television Company, Censored
Vyacheslav Bragin, the chairman of the *Ostankino Television Company*, refused to run the public affairs program "Krasny Kvadrat" on September 25, 1993. The episode, devoted to the subject of the parliament's dismissal, included appearances by Sergei Filatov, President Yeltsin's chief of staff; Valery Zorkin, chairman of the constitutional court; and Andranik Migranyan, a member of the presidential council and a regular guest on the program. The program's director reportedly described the act as "the crudest form of political censorship," while *Ostankino* issued a statement saying that the episode served as a "platform call to arms."

Eastern Europe

SEPTEMBER 28
All Journalists, Harassed
On September 28, 1993, police refused to allow journalists entry to the parliament building, limiting the public's access to information about the situation in the parliament and the views of Parliament members.

SEPTEMBER 29
Vladimir Kosenchuk, *TV-ASAHI*, Attacked
Yevgeny Yeroshenko, *TV-ASAHI*, Attacked
Videotechnician Kosenchuk, cameraman Yeroshenko, and Laskov, an interpreter, were beaten by police on Krasnopresnenskaya Street. The incident occurred on the fifth day of the standoff between President Boris Yeltsin and the hardline parliament at the Russian Supreme Soviet Building.

SEPTEMBER 29
Eddie Opp, *Commersant-Daily*, Attacked, Imprisoned
Opp, a photocorrespondent for *Commersant-Daily*, was beaten and arrested by police near the Russian Supreme Soviet Building during President Yeltsin's standoff with the parliament.

SEPTEMBER 29
Guillermo Marclin, *News Agency* (Argentina), Attacked, Harassed
Marclin, a cameraman for *News Agency* (Argentina), was beaten by police near Smolenskaya Metro Station during the stand-off between President Boris Yeltsin and the Parliament. His camera was also broken.

SEPTEMBER 30
Ruslan Linkov, *Channel 5* (St. Petersburg), Attacked
Laura Ilyina, *Commersant-Daily*, Attacked
Alexey Kudenko, *Commersant-Daily*, Attacked
Vasily Shaposhnikov, *Commersant-Daily*, Attacked
Photocorrespondents Linkov, Ilyina, Kudenko, and Shaposhnikov were beaten by police near Barikadnaya Metro Station during the standoff between President Boris Yeltsin and his rivals in parliament.

OCTOBER 1
Alexander Krasnik, *Rossiyskiye Vesti*, Attacked
Krasnik, photocorrespondent for *Rossiyskiye Vesti* newspaper, was beaten by police on two occasions during the conflict between President Boris Yeltsin and the hardline parliament. Krasnik was attacked at noon on October 1 on Krasnopresnenskaya Street, and on October 4 on Gruzinskaya Street.

OCTOBER 2
Yuri Voronin, *Vozvrascheniye*, Attacked
Voronin, correspondent for *Vozvrascheniye* magazine, was beaten by police near Moscow City Hall on October 2, and near the Russian Supreme Soviet Building on October 4.

OCTOBER 2
Maya Skurikhina, *Pravda*, Attacked
Skurikhina, photocorrespondent for *Pravda* newspaper, was beaten by police on two occasions during the confrontation between President Boris Yeltsin and the hardline parliament. She was beaten by police on Krasnopresnenskaya Street on October 2 and at *Ostankino Television Company* on October 3.

OCTOBER 3
Rory Peck, *ARD Television*, Killed
Peck, a cameraman from Germany's *ARD Television* company, was killed at *Ostankino Television Company* in Moscow during the stand-off between supporters of Yeltsin and Khasbulatov. He was filming the capture of the Ostankino Television Center until the last minute of his life.

OCTOBER 3
Yvan Scopan, *TF-1*, Killed
Scopan, cameraman for *TF-1 Television*, France, was killed during the confrontation between

President Yeltsin and the hardline parliament, when the hardliners attempted to seize the Ostankino Television Center.

OCTOBER 3
Sergei Krasilnikov, *Ostankino Television Company*, Killed
Krasilnikov was killed in a gun battle at the Ostankino Television Center, when supporters of the hardline parliament stormed the government television center.

OCTOBER 3
Igor Belozerov, *Ostankino, Channel 4*, Killed
Belozerov, member of staff at *Ostankino, Channel 4*, was killed at the Ostankino Television Center. He was caught in a crossfire when parliament supporters, attempting to seize the building, clashed with military forces loyal to President Yeltsin.

OCTOBER 3
Alexander Smirnov, *Molodezhny Kuriyer*, Killed
Smirnov, correspondent for the *Molodezhny Kuriyer* newspaper, was killed at the Russian Supreme Soviet Building. President Yeltsin ordered the military to seize the Russian White House after hardline members of parliament refused to surrender.

OCTOBER 3
Vladimir Drobyshev, *Priroda I Chelovek*, Killed
Drobyshev, correspondent for *Priroda I Chelovek* (Nature and Man) magazine, was killed at Ostankino Television Center, when forces loyal to parliament hardliners attempted to take control of the government television center.

OCTOBER 3
Otto Pohl, *The New York Times*, Attacked
Julie Brooks, *The New York Times*, Attacked
Igor Michalev, *RIA-PHOTO*, Attacked
Vladimir Sychov, *SIPA Press*, Attacked
Mark Stinebock, *Ogonyok*, Attacked
Pierre Selarier, *Le Qoutidien de Paris*, Attacked
Igor Tobolin, *Pozitsiya*, Attacked

Georgy Shabad, *Baltic News Service*, Attacked
Patrick Buourrat, *TF-1*, Attacked
Ernesto Monzani, *News Agency* (Argentina), Attacked
Photocorrespondents Pohl, Brooks, Michalev, Stinebock, and Sychov, correspondents Selarier, and Tobolin, bureau chiefs Shabad and Buourrat, and a cameraman, Monzani, were all wounded in the crossfire near Ostankino Television Center.

OCTOBER 3
Vladimir Dodonov, *Commersant-Daily*, Attacked, Harassed
Dodonov, a photocorrespondent for *Correspondent-Daily*, was beaten by police near Ostankino Television Center on the night supporters of Rutskoi and Khasbulatov attacked the complex. His cameras were also stolen.

OCTOBER 3
Danila Galperovitch, *JIJI Press Agency*, Attacked
Galperovitch, a correspondent for the Japanese *JIJI Press Agency*, was beaten up by demonstrators near the Russian Supreme Soviet Building.

OCTOBER 3
Alexander Izotov, *Moscovsky Komsomolets*, Attacked
Izotov, a correspondent for *Moscovsky Komsomolets*, was beaten up on the Krimsky Bridge by the Russian Supreme Soviet supporters.

OCTOBER 4
Sevodnya, Censored
Moskovskaya Pravda, Censored
Nezavisimaya Gazeta, Censored
Pravda, Censored
Den, Censored
Russky, Censored
Poraydok, Censored
Sovetskaya Rossiya, Censored
Rabochaya Tribuna, Censored
Glasnost, Censored

Eastern Europe

Narodnaya Gazeta, Censored
The ministry of information directly censored such mass circulation publications as *Sevodnya, Moskovskaya Pravda,* and *Nezavisimaya Gazeta,* among others. Under the state of emergency, the government decided to suspend the publication and distribution of as many as 10 anti-government newspapers, including *Pravda, Den, Russky, Poraydok, Sovetskaya Rossiya, Rabochaya Tribuna, Glasnost,* and *Narodnaya Gazeta.*

OCTOBER 4
Alexander Sidelnikov, *Lennauchfilm,* Killed
Sidelnikov, cameraman for *Lennauchfilm Studio* (St. Petersburg Documentary Film Studio), was killed at the Russian Supreme Soviet Building when President Boris Yeltsin ordered the military to seize the building.

OCTOBER 4
Larisa Solodukhina, *Postfactum,* Attacked
Maxim Khrustalyov, *Postfactum,* Attacked
Rustem Safronov, *Russian Television,* Attacked
Postfactum News Agency correspondents Solodukhina and Khrustalyov and television correspondent Safronov were wounded in the crossfire at the Russian Supreme Soviet Building.

OCTOBER 4
Yuri Mityunov, *Radio Marti & SBS-CMQ(USA),* Attacked
At about 8 p.m. on October 4, Yuri Mityunov, correspondent for *Radio Marti* and *SBS-CMQ (USA),* was attacked at his apartment by police officers. The incident occurred in the aftermath of the confrontation between President Boris Yeltsin and the hardline parliament.

OCTOBER 4
Alexander Kokotkin, *Moscow News,* Attacked
Alexander Tsiganov, *Ogonyok,* Attacked
Dmitry Pleshkov, *Federal News Service,* Attacked, Imprisoned
Correspondent Kokotkin, photocorrespondent Tsiganov, and *Federal News Service* correspondent Pleshkov were beaten by police near the Russian Supreme Soviet Building. The incident occurred as they covered the attack on the building by troops loyal to President Boris Yeltsin. Pleshkov was later arrested and spent two days in the internal Moscow police prison.

OCTOBER 4
Alexey Fomin, *Moskovsky Komsomolets,* Attacked
Fomin, a correspondent for *Moscovsky Komsomolets,* was beaten by police near the main entrance to his office.

OCTOBER 4
Michail Anosov, *Vechernaya Moskva,* Attacked, Harassed
Anosov, a correspondent for *Vechernaya Moskva,* was beaten by police on Krasnopresnenskaya Street during President Yeltsin's attack on the Russian Supreme Soviet Building. Police also took away Anosov's presscard.

OCTOBER 4
Kirill Svetitsky, *Vek,* Attacked, Imprisoned
Vladimir Vedrashko, *Vek,* Attacked, Imprisoned
Correspondents for a weekly newspaper *Vek,* Kirill Svetitsky and Vladimir Vedrashko, were beaten and arrested by police near the Russian Supreme Soviet Building during the assault on the building by President Yeltsin's troops.

OCTOBER 4
Tatyana Romamemko, *Rossiyskiye Vesti,* Attacked
Romamemko, a correspondent for *Rossiyskiye Vesti,* was beaten by police near the Russian Supreme Soviet Building during the attack on the parliament building by President Yeltsin's forces.

OCTOBER 4
Victor Ilyukhin, *Pravda,* Attacked
Ilyukhin, the deputy editor for *Pravda,* was beaten by police in the Russian Supreme Soviet Building after President Yeltsin's military seized the building.

OCTOBER 4
Michail Voytehov, *Leviy Informsentr Agency,*
Attacked
Voytehov, a correspondent for *Leviy Informsentr Agency,* was beaten by police in the Russian Supreme Soviet Building after the building was seized by President Yeltsin's forces.

OCTOBER 5
Vladimir Filatov, *Radiotelevisione Italiana,*
Attacked
At 2:00 a.m. on October 5, *Radiotelevisione Italiana* cameraman Vladimir Filatov was beaten by road police near Rizhsky Railroad Station.

OCTOBER 6
Moskovsky Komsomolets, Attacked
Itar-Tass, Attacked
Moscow Television Stations, Attacked
During the October conflict between the Russian parliament and the government of President Boris Yeltsin, proparliament protesters attacked the Moscow offices of *Moskovsky Komsomolets* and the news agency *Itar-Tass.* There were also armed raids that forced television stations off the air.

OCTOBER 22
Lev Fyodorov, *Moscow News,* Imprisoned
Vil Mirzanyanov, *Moscow News,* Imprisoned
Argumenty i Fakty, Attacked
Moscow News, Attacked
Russia's ministry of security detained scientists Lev Fyodorov and Vil Mirzanyanov on October 22 in connection with the publication of an article in *Moscow News,* which alleged that Russia was continuing development of chemical weapons in violation of international agreements. Mirzanyanov was held for eight days and charged with disclosing state secrets. At about the same time, representatives of the ministry of security reportedly searched and took materials from the home of a *Novoye Vremya* correspondent and the offices of the papers *Moscow News* and *Argumenty i Fakty.*

SEPTEMBER 30
Roman Ukolov, *Commersant-Daily,* Attacked
Ukolov, a correspondent for *Commersant Daily,* was beaten by police near Barikadnaya Metro Station during the standoff between President Yeltsin and the hardline parliament.

NOVEMBER 29
Kubanski Kurier, Attacked
In the editing room of *Kubanski Kurier* newspaper in Krasnodar, a bomb explosion killed one person and injured another. Reason for the attack remains unknown.

Tajikistan

The civil war in Tajikistan has created one of the most repressive environments against press freedom documented by CPJ. In a deliberate attempt to suppress the media, the Communist government of Tajikistan, which seized power after last year's coup, has begun a crackdown on independent journalists. The National Front, a paramilitary group loyal to the regime, is believed to be responsible for most cases of persecution. CPJ has documented the deaths of four journalists while the murders of 11 other journalists continue to be investigated. A number of journalists have been harassed, arrested, and some were forced to flee the country in fear of government reprisal. In addition, the government has censored or closed most of the independent newspapers in the country. Many cases are difficult to confirm due to the growing complexity of the political situation in the region. After the disintegration of the Soviet Union, the independence movement in Tajikistan turned into a power struggle among opposition groups which has led to a civil war. The opposition groups range from democratic reformists to Islamic fundamentalists to communists. Regional and ethnic conflicts further complicate the situation.

Eastern Europe

203

The government crackdown has primarily been applied in Dushanbe, the nation's capital. The national economy, dependent largely on cotton exports, continues to collapse due to the instability caused by the civil war. Government attempts to stabilize the region by ordering the population to surrender their weapons have thus far failed. Most people are afraid to give up their guns, while the National Front simply refused. As a valuable strategic region in Central Asia, forces outside Tajikistan's borders have been drawn into the conflict as well. Russia does not appear to be willing to give up its interests in the region, and its troops maintain a presence on the Tajik-Afghan border. At this time, however, the government of Tajikistan favors Russian involvement because of the threat of Islamic opposition groups which are supported by Muslim fundamentalists in Afghanistan, Iran and Pakistan. The territorial integrity of Tajikistan and the stability of the whole region may be in danger.

JANUARY
Saidmurod Yerov, *Farkhang*, Killed
Yerov, executive director of *Farkhang* magazine was arrested by National Front members in January 1993. His body was reportedly found in a mass grave in Dushanbe on February 2.

MARCH
Zukhuruddin Suyari, *Todzhikiston*, Killed
The body of Suyari, a correspondent for the government magazine *Todzhikiston*, was found in Kurgan-Tiube at the end of March. It is suspected that he may have been killed by members of the progovernment National Front because he is from the Garm area.

MARCH 23
Mirbobo Mirrakhimov, *Tajikistan State Radio and Television*, Imprisoned, Legal Action
Akhmadsho Kamilov, *Television*, Imprisoned, Legal Action
Khayriddin Kasymov, *Television*, Imprisoned
Khurshed Nazarov, *Television*, Imprisoned

Mirrakhimov and Kamilov were charged with "conspiracy to overthrow the government through the mass media" and with slandering the former Speaker of the parliament. Kasymov and Nazarov were also charged with the same conspiracy charges as well as for the possession of videotapes allegedly showing human rights abuses by progovernment forces. All four journalists were held by the Tajikistani authorities.

APRIL 22
Staff, *Dzhavoni Todzhikiston*, Harassed
The entire staff of the newspaper *Dzhavoni Todzikiston* was fired by the newspaper's founder, the Youth Council of Tajikistan (formerly the Konsomol). The council was reportedly unhappy with the newspaper's independent line.

MAY 5
Igor Rotar, *Nezavisimaya Gazeta*, Attacked, Expelled
Rotar, a correspondent for the Moscow-based newspaper *Nezavisimaya Gazeta*, was forced to leave Tajikistan after being threatened by law enforcement officials. Early in the morning of May 5, according to the journalist, police officers entered his hotel room in Dushanbe. On the grounds that he had violated curfew, they beat him up, threatened him, and forcefully took him to a police station, where he was required to pay a fine of 10,000 rubles.

APRIL 28
Pirimkul Sattori, *Khatlon*, Killed
Sattori, a correspondent for the Kurgan-Tiube newspaper *Khatlon*, was arrested in that city by unidentified persons in military uniform. Several days later, his body was found in a cotton field. The reason for his killing is unknown.

SEPTEMBER 10
Vecherny Dushanbe, Censored
The September 10 issue of *Vecherny Dushanbe* newspaper was censored by the Tajikistani government. Apparently, the government did not want the paper to publish the interview withthe prosecutor of Tajikistan.

OCTOBER 21

Tabarali Saidaliev, *Ba Pesh*, Killed

Saidaliev, editor of *Ba Pesh* newspaper, was kidnapped on October 21, and his body was found three days later. It is suspected that the progovernment National Front is responsible for the killing.

Yugoslavia

The Federal Republic of Yugoslavia is comprised of the republics of Serbia and Montenegro. Serbia is the dominant partner in this federation. Throughout the war in Bosnia, the government of Serbia has kept a tight control of information. Both domestic and foreign media have been carefully watched, and those that appeared to step out of line became the targets of legal action. The few Serbian media outlets that try to maintain their independence face punitive legal and financial measures and threats of violence from the nationalist government of Slobodan Milosovich. One such outlet is the independent radio station *B92*, whose director Veran Matic was awarded CPJ's 1993 Press Freedom Award. CPJ has been able to confirm that two Serbian publications and several Albanian-language publications have been censored when the government took over Rilindja publishing house. Foreign journalists in Serbia were not immune to the government pressure on media. Four foreign journalists have been attacked, and one of them was briefly imprisoned.

JANUARY 12

Dragan Kojadinovic, *Studio B*, Threatened

Studio B, Harassed

Kojadinovic, director of the independent Belgrade television station *Studio B*, and two employees were threatened by four men armed with guns in the evening. They were waiting at the Hungarian border to take professional materials back to the station in Belgrade. After threatening the three journalists, the four armed men also set the truck with the equipment on fire.

FEBRUARY 21

Zeljko Radovanac, *Attacked*, Threatened

Radovanac, an openly gay man who hosts a weekly radio program in which he takes calls from gay men and lesbians, was taken from his home at about 10 at night by two Belgrade police officers, on the grounds that he was listening to Croatian music. At police headquarters, however, an interrogator demanded the names of all the members of Arkadia, the gay and lesbian lobby of Belgrade. He refused to give any names. During interrogation, he was beaten severely by two policemen, sustaining bruises on his legs and chest. His face became swollen. Radovanac was released at about 11:30 p.m. Two days later, the same interrogator called him and demanded the names of Arkadia members, threatening to apply Article 110 of the Serbian Penal Code (antisodomy law). Radovanac refused to cooperate.

MAY 20

Bujku, Censored

Zeri, Censored

Albanian-Language Media, Censored

The publishing house Rilindja, which had printed several Albanian-language publications, was transformed into a new organization, Panorama, which is under the control of the Serbian government. Panorama decided that it would stop printing the daily newspaper *Bujku*, the magazine *Zeri*, and other Albanian-language periodicals unless they accepted the management of Panorama. Panorama reportedly had the power to determine editorial policy and appoint editors.

205

The Middle East and North Africa

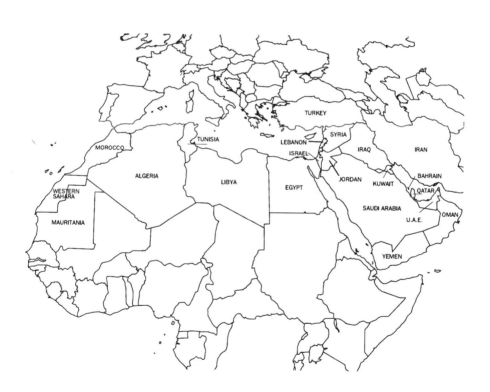

The Middle East and North Africa

by Avner Gidron

The Middle Eastern media did not share in the euphoria felt by the West over "The Handshake" between Israeli Prime Minister Yitzhak Rabin and Palestine Liberation Organization chairman Yasser Arafat. Although prospects for a settlement of the Arab-Israeli conflict improved in 1993, the year will also be remembered as one of the deadliest for journalists in the region. The assassination of 14 local journalists is an ominous reminder that ending the conflict between Israel and the Arab states will not stop political violence in the region.

The possibility of "peace" has emerged, not simply because of the end of the Cold War or the outcome of the Gulf War, but rather because local governments fear growing domestic discontent caused by decades of political repression and deteriorating economic conditions. Armed rebellions have intensified in three of the region's most important states. The press was in greatest danger in countries where a relatively free press has come under siege from both government and rebel forces. Whether these rebellions are spearheaded by populist religious movements (Algeria and Egypt) or by separatist groups (Turkey), press freedom and journalists' rights are among the principal casualties. Elsewhere in the region,

swift and cruel repression of all dissent, generous social welfare programs or a combination of the two, have so far succeeded in staving off open rebellion. In these countries, government censorship and outright ownership of the media remain in place, keeping journalists in line. And in a few countries, prescient leaders have staked their survival on implementing democratic reform and expanding press freedom.

Nine journalists were slain in Algeria between May and December 1993, an unprecedented toll in North Africa. The assassins have not been apprehended in most of the cases. It is suspected that armed fundamentalist groups fighting the secular regime targeted the journalists because of their profession. Ever since the army interrupted the electoral process in January 1992 to prevent a victory by the fundamentalist Islamic Salvation Front (FIS) in parliamentary elections, the government has made it extremely difficult for Algerian journalists to work freely and independently. Combined with the assassination campaign begun in 1993, it has become practically impossible for journalists to go about their work.

The conflict in Turkey's southeast between Kurdistan Workers' Party (PKK) rebels intent on carving out a Kurdish state and government forces determined to crush the rebellion has created extraordinarily difficult working conditions for journalists. The experience of the pro-Kurdish newspaper *Özgür Gündem* is a good example. Three of the four journalists killed in Turkey in 1993 worked for *Özgür Gündem*, bringing to seven the number of journalists from the newspaper who have been killed since it first appeared in May 1992. The killing has been accompanied by a government campaign of legal and administrative measures through which authorities have imprisoned *Özgür Gündem's* owner, editors and staff, and have confiscated countless issues. Not only Kurdish papers are under siege. Leftist and religious publications regularly bear the brunt of the government repression. Nor is the government the only source of oppression for the press. Muslim fundamentalists have claimed responsibility for the murder, in January 1993, of Uğur Mumcu, a prominent investigative journalist, and have attacked leftist writers. And the PKK, late in 1993, warned Turkish journalists to cease their reporting (which it perceives as pro-government) from the southeast. Following through on that threat, the PKK, early in 1994, began kidnapping journalists who did not obey the ban. Consequently the press and its readers must rely on propaganda, whether from the government or the PKK, for news about the war.

The Israel-PLO declaration of principles, signed September 13, has yet to tangibly improve the working conditions for journalists covering disturbances in the West Bank and Gaza. Soldiers continue to abuse and harass Palestinian and other journalists in the course of their work. If the Israeli army does begin its withdrawal from Gaza and Jericho in 1994, we will learn whether a Palestinian self-governing authority will show greater respect for journalists' rights than the occupying power has done.

Among Israel's Arab neighbors the peace process remains a sensitive topic. After years of bombarding their populations with propaganda about the "Zionist enemy," many regimes are now in the awkward position of having to prepare their citizens for the prospect of normalizing relations with Israel. In countries such as Lebanon and Jordan, where the press is sufficiently independent to challenge government dictates on this topic, news outlets overly critical of the negotiations have found themselves at odds with authorities.

In much of the Middle East there is no independent press that can get into trouble. In Syria, Iraq, Saudi Arabia, and Libya government propaganda dominates the printed page as well as the airwaves. When journalists do dare to take a stand, the consequences range from dismissal to long-term imprisonment and torture. CPJ has documented (53) journalists imprisoned in the Middle East and North Africa, as of February 1994— the largest number for any region.

Two countries that have attacked each other through their media in 1993 cracked down on dissent in their own press. The government of the Islamic Republic of Iran seems determined to further narrow the confines of permissible political discourse. Journalists and papers with impeccable Islamic and revolutionary credentials have discovered that the regime has become less tolerant of criticism from within. And Egypt's government, as it battles an insurgency by Muslim fundamentalists (whom it claims are funded by Iran), has become more sensitive to attacks from secular, as well as Islamist, opposition papers.

Press freedom has made some gains in a few countries. In 1993 Yemen's lively press continued to flourish under one of the region's most liberal press laws. And newspapers seem to have weathered politicians' attempts to make them scapegoats as catalysts of the country's political crisis. Jordan's press law was liberalized in May, though it remains far from ideal. And the free and fair (by regional standards) elections held in the fall reduced the power of the Islamists in parliament. Morocco's opposition papers have benefitted from their coverage of the trial of a police commissioner accused of raping hundreds of women. But their reporting remains constrained by restrictions on reporting about several vital political topics, including the monarchy and the status of Western Sahara.

Private broadcasting is still rare in the Middle East. There is a private television station in Morocco, but it is owned by King Hassan's son-in-law. Lebanon has by far the greatest number of private stations. But the public was reminded of the stations' precarious status by the government's eight month closure of the opposition ICN. Officially they are still illegal and passage of a law to license and regulate the broadcast media has been delayed because of political disputes within the government. Israel's experiment with private broadcasting began last fall. Whether the substance of news coverage will differ from that of state television remains to be seen.

Throughout the Middle East many people still rely on international radio broadcasts such as *BBC*, *VOA* and *Radio Monte Carlo* for information. These have proven to be the most difficult sources of news for governments to control. Crude techniques such as jamming have been used by Iraq in the past. Saudi Arabia, which already controls most of the pan-Arab print media and a satellite television and radio network, further expanded its control in 1993 by purchasing outspoken Arabic papers in Europe and using financial inducements to convince international broadcasters, including *Radio Monte Carlo*, to censor themselves.

Avner Gidron, *Program Coordinator for the Middle East and North Africa, joined CPJ in November 1991. He has lived and studied in Egypt, Jordan and Israel, and led a CPJ fact-finding mission to Lebanon last May. He is a contributing editor to* **World Press Review**. *He holds a Master's Degree in Middle East Studies and International Economics from Johns Hopkins University's Paul H. Nitze School of Advanced International Studies and is a graduate of Vassar College. Gidron is fluent in Arabic and Hebrew.*

Martha Hammond, *a freelance translator and consultant, contributed to this section and* **Yalman Onaran,** *a research associate at CPJ, wrote the Turkey section of this report.*

Middle East

The Middle East and North Africa

Algeria

Life for Algerian journalists has become a nightmare. Many no longer live with their families. They change residences frequently. Newsrooms receive threats every day. Nine journalists were killed between May and December, and at least two have survived assassination attempts. All the murders appear to be the work of armed religious extremists.

Ever since the army interrupted the electoral process in January 1992 to prevent a victory by the fundamentalist Islamic Salvation Front (FIS) in parliamentary elections, the government has made it difficult for Algerian journalists to work freely and independently. The replacement of hardline Prime Minister Belaid Abdessalam with the more moderate Redha Malek in the summer brought some improvements. But some publications remain closed.

The story of Omar Belhouchet, director of the independent French-language daily *El Watan* and 1993 CPJ Press Freedom Award laureate, is emblematic of the problems facing Algeria's independent press. In January *El Watan* was suspended and Belhouchet and five colleagues from the paper were taken into custody and charged with "publishing false information." The suspension and charges stemmed from *El Watan's* "premature" publication of a report about the murder of five policemen by fundamentalists. Belhouchet and his colleagues were released a week later but their trial is still pending. The suspension of *El Watan* was lifted after 10 days. Proceedings

were brought against Belhouchet and journalist Cherif Ouazani in April for publishing an interview with the secretary general of the leftist Ettahaddi movement that was harshly critical of the Algerian judiciary and government. In May, an Algiers court banned Belhouchet from "exercising any journalistic activity or making statements to other press organs" due to the charges against him. Later that month, Belhouchet narrowly escaped an assassination attempt, apparently by Muslim fundamentalists, when unidentified gunmen fired at his car while he was driving his children to school. This attack was the first attempt on the life of a journalist since the interruption of the electoral process. And on June 9 he and his colleagues were convicted of "insulting the judiciary and attacking a state institution" and given two-month suspended sentences. In October, Belhouchet was sentenced to a year in prison for an article in *El Watan* about the acquittal of a suspected terrorist. The case is being appealed.

The Algerian conflict has claimed at least 2,000 lives. But the journalists killed since May have all been deliberately targeted in a concerted campaign to assassinate secular intellectuals and professionals. Journalists make up the largest bloc of victims within this group. Tahar Djaout, editor and founder of the literary and cultural magazine *Ruptures*, was shot on May 26 and died on June 2. Television journalist Rabah Zenati was killed outside his home on August 3. Six days later Abdelhamid Benmeni, a reporter for the news weekly *Algérie-Actualité*, was killed in his home. On September 10, Saad Bakhtaoui, a reporter for an organ of a small party, was kidnapped and shot to death. Abderrahmane Chergou, a journalist and official of the leftist PAGS party, was stabbed to death outside his home on September 28. One week later, Djamel Bouhidel, a photographer for the weekly *Nouveau Tell,* was killed. On October 14, Mustafa Abada, former director of Algerian state television, was shot and killed. Four days later, his colleague Smail Yefsah, assistant news director of Algerian state television, was stabbed and then shot to death outside his home. And on December 27, poet and journalist Youcef Sebti was killed.

It is unclear how much control exiled FIS leaders have over the armed struggle carried out by groups such as the Armed Islamic Group and Armed Islamic Movement. But rather than condemning the murder of intellectuals and other civilians, statements made by exiled leaders Rabah Kebir and Anouar Haddam often justify the killing. Kebir accuses some slain journalists of collaboration with the regime and implies that their killings were justified: "If a journalist is associated with the process of informing [the authorities], he ceases to become a journalist and becomes, in effect, a combatant." But Kebir does not offer any evidence to suggest that any of the murdered journalists were informants.

JANUARY 2
El Watan, Censored
The French-language daily *El Watan* was suspended by order of the ministry of culture and communications for having "prematurely revealed" information about a "criminal action"

perpetrated in a closed military zone. The suspension stemmed from the paper's publication of a report on January 2 that Muslim fundamentalists murdered five policemen the previous day at a police station near Laghouat. The paper was allowed to resume publishing on January 13.

JANUARY 2
Omar Belhouchet, *El Watan,* Imprisoned
Abderrazak Merad, *El Watan,* Imprisoned
Omar Berbiche, *El Watan,* Imprisoned
Tayeb Belghiche, *El Watan,* Imprisoned
Ahmed Ancer, *El Watan,* Imprisoned
Nacera Benali, *El Watan,* Imprisoned
Belhouchet, *El Watan's* director; Merad, the managing editor; and Berbiche, Belghiche, Ancer, and Benali, reporters for the paper, were arrested. On January 5, they were charged with "publishing false information that harms the security of the state and the unity of the country, revealing information that compromises national defense, obstructing a criminal investigation, making public, without proper authorization, military information that harms national security, and undermining the morale of the armed forces." The charges stem from the paper's publication of a report on January 2 that Muslim fundamentalists murdered five policemen the previous day at a police station near Laghouat. The journalists were released on January 9 and are still awaiting trial.

JANUARY 13
Anne Dissez, *Radio France Internationale,* Expelled
Dissez, a correspondent for *Radio France Internationale,* was forced to leave Algeria after authorities refused to renew her work permit. No explanation was given for the refusal.

MARCH 18
John Baggaley, *Reuters*, Imprisoned,
Legal Action

Baggaley, a correspondent for *Reuters*, was charged with spreading false information and attacking a state institution (the gendarmerie). He had incorrectly reported that the sports minister had been assassinated, attributing the story to a telephone conversation with the gendarmerie. *Reuters* had printed the government's denial. Baggaley was held by the gendarmerie for nearly 24 hours. After he questioned Baggaley on March 20, an examining magistrate refused the prosecutor's request that he be held in custody. The case against him was never pursued.

APRIL 7
Abdelhamid Benzine, *Alger Républicain*,
Imprisoned

Benzine, director of the independent daily *Alger Républicain*, was arrested and detained for three hours at Serkadji Prison before he was conditionally released. The arrest was made on orders of the Examining Magistrate of Algiers, and the charge leveled at him, that of "attacking an official body," stems from the publication of a March 28 editorial that criticized the government ministries for making "dangerously childish" statements and the courts for handing down unsatisfying verdicts in terrorist cases. Some reports indicate that on April 29 Benzine was placed under judicial supervision, which hampered his journalistic pursuits.

APRIL 25
Omar Belhouchet, *El Watan*, Legal Action
Cherif Ouazani, *El Watan*, Legal Action

Belhouchet, director of the independent French-language daily *El Watan*, and Ouazani, a journalist with the paper, were charged with "harming national unity, inciting violence and conspiring against the security of the state." The charges stem from an interview with

Hachemi Cherif, leader of the leftist Ettahaddi Party, containing statements the government considered libelous. On May 4, Belhouchet and Ouazani were placed under judicial supervision and barred from working in their profession. The court used a heretofore little used article of the Code of Penal Procedure that allows a judge to order defendants "to refrain from certain professional activities when the infraction was committed while exercising, or at the time of exercising, these activities, when there is reason to fear that a new infraction will be committed." The ban was lifted on June 9 when they each received a two-month suspended sentence.

APRIL 28
Abderrahmane Mahmoudi, *L'Hebdo Libéré*,
Legal Action

A judge barred Mahmoudi, director of the independent weekly *L'Hebdo Libéré*, from practicing journalism while he was being investigated on charges of undermining national unity, endangering state security, and attacking state institutions. The ban was lifted in January 1994.

MAY
Ali Drâa, *Al-Jazair al-Youm*, Harassed

At the end of May, Drâa, director of the daily *Al-Jazair al-Youm*, discovered that there was a court order prohibiting him from leaving national territory. The reasons behind the interdiction are unclear.

MAY 17
Omar Belhouchet, *El Watan*, Attacked

An assassination attempt was directed at Belhouchet on the morning of May 17 as he was driving his children to school. According to eyewitnesses, at least two men fired shots at his car. Belhouchet escaped without injury. It is suspected that the attack was carried out by Muslim fundamentalists.

MAY 26
Taher Djaout, *Ruptures*, Killed
Djaout, editor-in-chief of the weekly cultural publication *Ruptures*, was shot outside his home near Algiers by Islamic militants on May 26. He died of his wounds on June 2. Djaout, who won the prestigious Prix Méditerranée in 1991 for his novel *Vigiles*, had received several death threats. His magazine, founded in January 1993, expressed views strongly opposed to Islamic fundamentalism.

JULY 31
Merzak Baghtache, Attacked
Baghtache, a freelance journalist and writer who is a member of the National Consultative Council (CCN), was shot and wounded on July 31 by unknown gunmen near his home in Bab el-Oued, Algiers. The motive behind the attack is unclear, but it is suspected that fundamentalists were involved.

AUGUST 1
Al-Jazair al-Youm, Censored
The Arabic daily *Al-Jazair al-Youm* was suspended indefinitely by order of the ministry of culture and communications for publishing information that "undermines public security and the higher interests of the state." No offending articles were specified in the order, but press reports link the suspension to the paper's publication, the previous day, of an advertisement of the Algerian Islamic Solidarity Association. The text of the notice warned the government of the consequences of executing 140 Islamists condemned to death for participating in acts of terrorism. The case is still pending.

AUGUST 3
Rabah Zenati, *Algerian Television*, Killed
Zenati, a reporter for Algerian state television, was killed by unknown assailants on August 3 outside his parents' home in a suburb of Algiers.

Some reports have attributed Zenati's murder to statements he made on television while covering a march against terrorism that took place on March 22. According to one report, family members said that Zenati had received death threats in the mail from members of an Islamic resistance movement.

AUGUST 9
Abdelhamid Benmeni, *Algérie-Actualité*, Killed
Benmeni, a reporter who held an administrative position at the French-language weekly magazine *Algérie-Actualité*, was killed by three unknown assailants on the night of August 9 at his home in Eucalyptus, Algiers. Some reports indicate that Benmeni's assassins were disguised as policemen. The motives for the murder are unclear, but it is suspected that Islamic extremists were involved.

SEPTEMBER
Ali Draâ, *Al-Jazair al-Youm*, Legal Action
Bachir Hammadi, *Al-Jazair al-Youm*, Legal Action
Abdallah Bechim, *Al-Jazair al-Youm*, Legal Action
An Algiers court banned Draâ, director of *Al-Jazair al-Youm*, and Hammadi and Bechim, two of its editors, from practicing their profession while they are being investigated on charges of attacking state institutions and decisions of the judiciary. The Arabic-language daily was suspended at the beginning of August.

SEPTEMBER 10
Saad Bakhtaoui, *El-Minbar*, Killed
Bakhtaoui, formerly a reporter with *El-Minbar*, organ of the Popular Association for Unity and Action (APUA), was kidnapped on September 10. His body was found on September 11 or 12 in Larbaa, near Algiers. Bakhtaoui had been shot to death. It is suspected that Islamic extremists were involved.

SEPTEMBER 27
Ammi Marengo, Attacked

Marengo, a newspaper vendor in Algiers, was found dead with his throat slashed.

SEPTEMBER 28
Abderrahmane Chergou, Killed

Chergou, a former journalist and official of the leftist PAGS party, was stabbed to death outside his home in the Algiers suburb of Mohammedia. Muslim fundamentalists are believed to be responsible for the killing.

LATE OCTOBER
Omar Belhouchet, *El Watan,* Legal Action

Belhouchet, director of *El Watan*, was sentenced to a year in prison for defaming the judiciary. The charges stem from an article in the French-language daily about public reaction to the acquittal of a suspected terrorist. The sentence is being appealed.

OCTOBER 5
Djamel Bouhidel, *Nouveau Tell,* Killed

Bouhidel, a photographer with the weekly *Nouveau Tell*, was killed in Blida, west of Algiers. Religious extremists are suspected of having carried out the murder.

OCTOBER 6
Mustapha Sadouki, *ENAMEP,* Attacked

Sadouki, a driver for *ENAMEP* (*l'Entreprise nationale des messageries de la presse*), was killed the night of October 6-7 near the Algiers suburb of Oued-Smar while next to his vehicle.

OCTOBER 14
Mustafa Abada, *Algerian Television,* Killed

Abada, former director of Algerian state television (replaced in August 1993), was shot and killed in Ain Taya, near Algiers, presumably by Muslim fundamentalists.

OCTOBER 18
Smail Yefsah, *Algerian Television,* Killed

Yefsah, assistant news director of Algerian state television, was stabbed and then shot to death outside his home in Bab Ezzouar in Algiers. Algerian newspapers held a one-day strike after his murder to protest the ongoing terror campaign against journalists.

DECEMBER 15
Hamid Laribi, *L'Événement,* Imprisoned
Mourad Termoul, *L'Événement,* Imprisoned
Aissa Khelladi, *L'Événement,* Imprisoned

Laribi, director of the weekly *L'Événement*, Termoul, its editor-in-chief; and Khelladi, a journalist with the paper, were questioned by the police. They appeared before an examining magistrate on December 18 and were placed under a committal order. Laribi was immediately granted a conditional release for health reasons. Termoul and Khelladi were held in Serkadji Prison before they, too, were conditionally released. They were charged with "slander and defamation of the armed forces," apparently because of an article by Khelladi about a letter sent by imprisoned Islamic Salvation Front (FIS) leader Ali Belhadj to the Commission for National Dialogue. The article was entitled "Belhadj Threatens the Generals."

DECEMBER 27
Youcef Sebti, Killed

Sebti, a poet and journalist, was murdered at night in his room at the National Institute for Agronomy in El Harrach where he taught and resided. He was found the next morning with his throat slit and, according to one report, two bullets in the abdomen. His killers have not been identified, but it is assumed that he was targeted by Islamist extremists. Sebti was a frequent contributor to Algerian publications, including the independent daily *El Watan*.

Bahrain

Bahrain's geography and demographics explain a lot about its rulers' insecurity. This geopolitical sensitivity manifested itself in at least one violation of press freedom last year: *Akhbar al-Khalij,* one of three dailies, was temporarily shut down for publishing an "erroneous" map. Maps are a sensitive issue for this tiny nation. Bahrain lies in the Persian Gulf between its domineering neighbor, Saudi Arabia, to which it is connected by a causeway, and Qatar, with which it has territorial disputes.

Iraq's invasion of Kuwait in 1990 intensified the Emirate's feeling of vulnerability. And Iran has historical claims to Bahrain, a majority of whose population is Shiite Muslim. The Shiite opposition makes the autocratic government edgy. A United Arab Emirates-based magazine was banned because its correspondent in Bahrain refused to suppress an interview with a Shiite opposition leader.

Bahrain's government did make a symbolic move toward democratization last January when the Emir, Shaykh Isa bin Salman al-Khalifah, created a consultative council. But the council's powers are limited to offering the Emir its opinions on proposed legislation.

JANUARY
Ahmad al-Shamlan, *Al-Watan, Al-Khaleej,* Exit denied
Shamlan, a columnist who writes for the Kuwaiti daily *Al-Watan* and the UAE daily *Al-Khaleej,* was denied permission to leave the country.

JUNE
Al-Shorouq, Censored
The Bahrain office of the UAE-based magazine *Al-Shorouq* was closed by the government. The magazine's bureau chief had refused to provide the original transcript of an interview with a Shiite opposition figure.

JULY 18
Akhbar al-Khaleej, Censored
The daily newspaper was suspended for three days by the ministry of information after publishing a map that showed the disputed Hawar Islands to be within the borders of Qatar.

Egypt

The February 1993 bombing of the World Trade Center in New York City brought to international attention the government's war with Islamic militants. Egyptian authorities, unprepared, overreacted to press scrutiny. Egypt was visited by an atypical number of Western journalists who suddenly discovered desperation, poverty, and human rights abuses. Foreign journalists traveling to Upper Egypt, where the conflict is most intense, were placed under hotel arrest. Some reporters were held for questioning. If anything, these moves made Western news reports less sympathetic to the government.

The Egyptian press (excepting broadcast media, which are state-owned) continued to be at odds with an increasingly besieged and sensitive administration. In October, shortly after President Muhammad Hosni Mubarak won a referendum supporting him for a third term, the government cracked down on *Al-Shaab,* organ of the pro-Islamist Labor Party. Reporters and party leaders were

Middle East

217

detained and questioned about several articles deemed insulting to the government and harmful to state security. In November, the government banned interviews with leaders of "terrorist" organizations. However, the Egyptian Journalists' Syndicate thwarted government proposals for a law that would categorize writers according to work experience and make their writing subject to review by special committees.

At the same time, press freedom was under constant threat from Islamic extremist groups. According to the London-based, Saudi-owned Arabic-language daily *Al-Hayat*, three press establishments in Cairo received bomb threats on March 23. Other Egyptian journalists reported receiving threatening messages from fundamentalists.

In early 1994, the Minister of Culture, Farouq Husni, unveiled plans to ease censorship by creating a committee of intellectuals to oversee the state censor. Testing the waters, *Rose al-Yousef,* a weekly magazine, published excerpts of Salman Rushdie's *Satanic Verses* as well as previously banned works of fiction by Nobel laureate Naguib Mahfouz.

MARCH 18
Al-Hayat, Censored
An issue of the London-based Arabic daily *Al-Hayat* was banned by the authorities because it contained an interview with Shaykh Omar Abdul-Rahman, exiled spiritual leader of the radical Islamic group Al-Gam'a al-Islamiyya, in which the Shaykh reportedly defended attacks on tourists and policemen (in Egypt).

APRIL 2
Al-Majalla, Censored
An edition of the Saudi magazine *Al-Majalla* was seized because it published an article on

a financial scandal known as the "Lucy Artine affair." Artine was the reputed mistress of a senior official in the administration who was caught in an indiscretion with a judge who had increased her alimony. On March 20, the information ministry had banned all press references to the scandal.

JUNE 20
Mohamed Sid-Ahmad, *Al-Ahram/Al-Ahali,* Harassed
Sid-Ahmad, prominent member of the leftist Tagammu' Party and columnist for both that party's weekly newspaper *Al-Ahali* and the semiofficial daily *Al-Ahram,* and retired Brigadier General Mourad E. Dessouki were summoned for questioning before military prosecutors for their statements that were reported in an article by Peter Waldman in the *Wall Street Journal* on June 14. Sid-Ahmad was quoted as saying "You have a dissatisfied military that is very sensitive to whether their status is respected." Neither has been charged, but both are under investigation for revealing military secrets.

JULY 30
Al-Hayat, Censored
Security agencies seized an edition of the London-based Arabic daily *Al-Hayat,* apparently because its front page featured a statement by a group called "Those Delivered from the Fire" that threatened revenge on the Egyptian government should harsh penalties be handed down to certain defendants.

OCTOBER 7
Hilmi Murad, *Al-Shaab,* Imprisoned
Salah Budaiwi, *Al-Shaab,* Imprisoned
Ali Al-Qammash, *Al-Shaab,* Imprisoned
Adil Hussein, *Al-Shaab,* Imprisoned
Magdi Hussein, *Al-Shaab,* Imprisoned
Ibrahim Shukri, *Al-Shaab,* Imprisoned
Shortly after the October 4 referendum reelecting President Mubarak, security agencies came

down hard on *Al-Shaab*, semiweekly organ of the moderate Islamist Labor Party. Murad, deputy chairman of the party and a columnist for *Al-Shaab*, and Budaiwi and al-Qammash, journalists with the paper, were arrested on the night of October 7-8 and detained at a police station for interrogation through the next day. They were then released on bail, while Adil Hussein, Labor Party secretary-general and the paper's former editor-in-chief, and Magdi Hussein, *Al-Shaab*'s editor-in-chief, were summoned for questioning. State Security prosecutors interrogated them for two days. On October 10, they detained Shukri, Labor Party leader and chairman of *Al-Shaab*'s board of directors. He was questioned and then released on October 13 without bail. On October 14, Murad, Budaiwi, al-Qammash, and Adil Hussein appeared again before the State Security prosecutors for questioning. The six men face charges that include publishing false information, slander, promoting terrorist ideas, and endangering social peace and national unity. The charges stemmed from numerous articles including a column of Murad's entitled "The Aftershocks of the Referendum, Like Those of the Earthquake, Will Continue to Be Felt," a report of Budaiwi's entitled "The Greatest Act of Sabotage Against Agriculture with Egyptian Hands and Zionist-U.S. Planning," and one by al-Qammash called "The State Security Intelligence Is Behind the Criminal Prisoners' War Against Political Prisoners at Abu Za'bal Prison."

LATE NOVEMBER
Mahmoud al-Maraghi, *Al-Arabi*, Harassed
Al-Maraghi, editor of *Al-Arabi*, was interrogated by prosecutors about an interview that was published in the November 22 edition of the weekly organ of the Arab Democratic Nasserite Party, conducted by fax, with Ayman al-Zawahiri, a leader of the Islamic Jihad organization who lives in exile in Switzerland.

Al-Maraghi was not charged, but he was placed under investigation for propagating "terrorist ideology." On November 28, Interior Minister Hassan al-Alfi ordered a ban on all press interviews with extremists, based on provisions of 1992's "antiterrorism" amendments to the penal code.

Iran

Since Iraq's defeat in the Gulf War, Iran has become the dominant power in the Gulf. It has normalized relations with most of the region's governments and has demonstrated its determination to expand its sphere of influence beyond the Gulf to the Levant and North Africa. Many in the Middle East look upon the Islamic Republic as a successful Islamic democracy. It is true that in some ways (e.g., universal adult suffrage) Iran is more democratic than many of its neighbors, such as Iraq, Saudi Arabia, or Syria. Iran has a lively and faction-ridden press. But since President Hashemi Rafsanjani's reelection in June, the government seems to have become less tolerant of the press of the "loyal opposition."

Worsening economic conditions and widespread public discontent with a body of officialdom riddled with corruption make the Rafsanjani government very sensitive to criticism in the press. Factional fighting between President Rafsanjani and his radical opponents resulted in several legal cases against newspapers and journalists in 1993. In March the publisher of *Abrar*, a daily aligned with the radicals, was summoned to court on libel charges. In April the Special Clerical Court ordered the suspension of *Rah e-Mojahed*. The magazine,

Middle East

known for its support of Ayatollah Montazeri once Khomeini's designated spiritual successor but now considered an opponent of Iran's clerical leadership, had published statements by aides to Montazeri decrying an attack on his home by Revolutionary Guards. In August the editor of *Salam,* another radical daily, was arrested, and the paper's publisher, Hojatoleslam Kho'iniha, was summoned to Special Clerical Court to face libel charges. *Salam* had reportedly angered the government with its coverage of the hospitalization of Ayatollah Montazeri. Also in August, the editor of Iran's leading daily, *Keyhan,* was summoned to the prosecutor's office after publishing articles deemed critical of Ayatollah Mohammad Yazdi, the head of Iran's judiciary.

Referring to a letter sent by CPJ requesting information about the three aforementioned cases, Ayatollah Yazdi, in a Friday prayer sermon, implied that charges against *Salam's* editor would be announced after he had been tried. He criticized CPJ and other Western human rights organizations as being hypocritical. But in December *Salam's* editor was convicted and sentenced to a year in prison, and the charges still were not made public.

JANUARY
Ava-ye Shomal, Censored
The ministry of culture and Islamic Guidance suspended the weekly magazine *Ava-ye Shomal,* based in Rasht, after it published the picture of a "half-nude" woman. Apparently, the picture was connected to the screening of the American film *Basic Instinct.*

MARCH
Ghafur Garshassbi, *Abrar,* Legal Action
Garshassbi, owner of the the radical daily *Abrar,* was summoned to Tehran's Magistrate's Court for allegedly publishing libelous material.

According to Middle East Watch a press release from the court charged that *Abrar* repeatedly published "unscupulous allegations against persons sometimes followed by either subsequent denials or corrections by way of apology or reminder to readers or explanation." The identity of the plaintiffs and the outcome of the trial are unknown.

MAY
Ettela'at, Building Attacked
A bomb exploded in the Tehran headquarters of the conservative daily *Ettela'at.* No one claimed responsibility for the attack but some connect it to an earlier attack on its subsidiary weekly magazine, *Ettela'at-e Haftegi,* after it had published an article titled "Why Have I Become Psychologically Ill?" next to a photo of an Islamic Revolutionary Guard who died in the war with Iraq.

APRIL
Rah e-Mojahed, Censored
The Special Clerical Court ordered that the publication of *Rah e-Mojahed* be stopped, after it had printed criticism of the February arrest of several aides to dissident religious leader Ayatollah Hossein Ali Montazeri.

AUGUST 26
Abbas Abdi, *Salam,* Imprisoned
Abdi, editor-in-chief of the radical daily *Salam,* was arrested by order of the prosecutor of the Islamic Revolutionary Court. The charges are unclear, but they reportedly stem from a published report about the opposition of government officials to the hospitalization of dissident religious leader Ayatolloah Hossein Ali Montazeri. In his Friday prayers sermon on September 13, the head of the judiciary, Ayatollah Mohammad Yazdi, referred to a letter sent by CPJ that inquired about the specific charges against Abdi. In the sermon, Yazdi claimed that the charges would be publicized at the end of the trial. On December 22, the Tehran Islamic Revolutionary Court sentenced

Abdi to one year in prison and a suspended sentence of 40 lashes. The government still has not announced the charges on which he was convicted.

AUGUST 28

Mehdi Nassiri, *Keyban*, Legal Action

Nassiri, editor-in-chief of Iran's leading daily, *Keyban*, was summoned to court for questioning about recent articles he had published criticizing the head of Iran's judiciary, Ayatollah Mohammad Yazdi, after Yazdi filed a complaint against him. Nassiri was released pending trial on slander charges. According to some reports, several other lawsuits have been filed against him since Yazdi's initial complaint.

AUGUST 29

Mohammad Musavi Kho'iniha, *Salam,*

Legal Action

Hojatoleslam Kho'iniha, a cleric and publisher of *Salam*, was summoned for questioning before a clerical court in a slander suit. This came in the wake of the arrest of *Salam's* editor-in-chief, Abbas Abdi, on August 26. Kho'iniha's case will reportedly be tried before a jury in the press courts. The Iranian government claims that there is no connection between the two cases.

OCTOBER 15

Manouchehr Karimzadeh, *Farad*, Legal Action

Karimzadeh, a cartoonist, was sentenced to 10 years in prison after he was retried by order of the Supreme Court. He had been arrested in April of 1992 after a piece of his appeared in the science magazine *Farad*. It portrayed a soccer player with an amputated arm and wearing a turban. Authorities took the image to be a caricature of the late Ayatollah Khomeini and tried both Karimzadeh and *Farad's* editor-in-chief, Nasser Arabha, in a revolutionary court. In September of 1992, Karimzadeh was sentenced to one year in prison and Arabha was sentenced to six months. It is believed that Arabha was acquitted in the retrial.

Iraq

There is virtually no press freedom in Iraq. The media is controlled directly or indirectly by the ruling Baath party.

The stranglehold on the press has been tightened by the continuing United Nations embargo against Iraq, which has caused severe newsprint shortages, forcing newspapers to reduce their size and circulation. A column that appeared in the daily army organ last July regrets that "unlicensed vendors" take advantage of the situation by charging many times the (already inflated) official prices. One story the press in Baghdad has been following in recent months is a lawsuit against *Voice of America (VOA)* by former correspondent Omar Jumah, who claims that he was wrongfully dismissed from his job during the Gulf War. Jumah alleges that he was fired after protesting the way in which his reports were edited to downplay Iraqi civilian casualties.

In UN-protected Iraqi Kurdistan, newspapers and radio and television broadcasting continue to enjoy considerable independence. However, tension between the Iraqi Kurdish government and the Kurdistan Workers' Party (PKK), which has been fighting a secessionist war against the Turkish army for nine years, has caused problems. There are reports that the Kurdish government has placed technical printing-related obstacles before the mouthpiece of the Iraqi Communist Workers' Party known to be a pro-PKK publication. A journalist with the paper charged that a colleague of his was tortured and assassinated in August; CPJ has been unable to confirm this.

JANUARY 17

Peter Brinkmann, *Bild Zeitung,* Attacked

Brinkmann, a reporter for the German daily *Bild Zeitung,* was wounded when a cruise missile fired by the U.S. Navy hit Baghdad's Al-Rashid Hotel. The missile was meant for an Iraqi nuclear facility outside Baghdad. Brinkmann lost two teeth and had minor facial injuries.

JULY 1

Rob Reynolds, *CNN,* Expelled

Jeremy Bowen, *BBC,* Expelled

Reynolds, *CNN* correspondent in Baghdad, was ordered out of the country. Iraqi authorities gave *CNN* some time to assign a replacement before his actual expulsion. *CNN* appealed the decision and the appeal was denied. The reasons for the expulsion order are unclear. Bowen, correspondent for the *BBC,* and his four-member television crew were ordered out by that evening. Bowen told the *Associated Press* that the authorities were angered by a report that "included words that said it was clear that Saddam is channeling resources to the military." Bowen also appealed the decision to no avail.

Israel and the Occupied Territories

Middle East

Despite the signing of the Israel-PLO accord, Palestinian journalists in the West Bank and Gaza continue to suffer censorship and intimidation at the hands of the Israeli army. The interim self-government accord may eventually improve working conditions for journalists on both sides of the green line. When the Israeli army withdraws from Gaza and Jericho, we will see if the PLO does a better job of protecting journalists' rights. However the pullout will not directly affect the center of the Palestinian press, East Jerusalem, which was annexed by Israel after the 1967 war.

The closure of the Occupied Territories in March made journalists' work that much more difficult. Those living in the West Bank and Gaza needed special permits to travel to East Jerusalem, where most papers and magazines are based. By some accounts, getting the required permits became easier in late 1993. The army now uses administrative detention against journalists more sparingly, but several Palestinian journalists remain behind bars for nonviolent offenses. *Al-Fajr's* Mousa Qous, arrested in 1991 and convicted of instructing others to write graffiti, remains in prison because he is affiliated with a faction of the PLO that does not support the Gaza-Jericho agreement.

Two Palestinian dailies, *Al-Fajr* and *Al-Shaab,* closed down this year for financial reasons. An experiment in Palestinian television news was launched in the summer with European financing. A Palestinian television station, based in the West Bank town of Ramallah, is expected to begin broadcasting in 1994.

The prospect of peace with the Palestinians—perhaps Syria and Jordan, as well—may enhance the freedom of Israel's media. In November the government's monopoly over local television news finally ended when the commercial *New Second Channel* hit the airwaves. The channel's director-general is a former Army spokesperson. However it is still too early to know how readily the government will part with the draconian powers it wields over the press under the British

Mandate-era Emergency Defense Regulations. The modus operandi of Israel's mainstream press is still dictated by the increasingly anachronistic editors' agreement with the ministry of defense, according to which editors of the major papers practice self-censorship in security matters in exchange for privileged information. Besides being discriminatory to all news organizations that are not parties to the agreement, this institution has slowed progress on developing guarantees of press freedom by limiting the number of court cases challenging censorship.

One paper that did defy the censors, *Hadashot,* closed at the end of 1993 for financial reasons. Shortly after it was founded in 1984, the maverick daily published the photos of Palestinian hijackers killed by members of the security services after they had been captured. The General Security Service (GSS) had claimed that all the hijackers were killed when rescuers stormed the bus. The paper exposed a coverup that eventually led to the resignation of the chief of the GSS. *Hadashot* was suspended by the army for three days, and its editors were sued by the censor. In January the Tel Aviv District Court overturned the conviction of *Hadashot's* editors for failing to submit the disputed article to the censors. This decision may serve as a precedent, preventing censors from construing the term "threat to national security" too broadly.

JANUARY 12
Paul Kern, *Sygma*, Attacked, Imprisoned, Threatened
Kern, a photographer working for the Paris-based *Sygma* photo agency, was threatened and beaten in the Shati refugee camp in Gaza. He was photographing children with slingshots when an army jeep arrived. Soldiers got out and chased Kern and two other reporters into a store. When Kern refused to surrender his film, one soldier threatened him by pointing a loaded M-16 rifle at his head while another removed lenses from his camera. The two soldiers beat him with gun butts. He was loaded onto a jeep, taken to a police station and held for three hours. An army spokesman apologized for the incident the next day.

JANUARY 15
Marwan al-Ghoul, *Reuters Television*, Threatened, Harassed, Imprisoned
Al-Ghoul, a cameraman working for *Reuters Television*, was briefly detained by an army officer in Jabalya refugee camp in the Gaza Strip. The officer took him to an army camp and held him for two hours. He broke al-Ghoul's video camera and confiscated his videotape. As he drove al-Ghoul out of Jabalya, the officer threatened to kill him if he ever returned.

JANUARY 28
Amir Chai, *Israel Television*, Attacked
An Israeli soldier threw a percussion grenade at a crowd in the West Bank town of Hebron as Chai, an *Israel TV* correspondent, was interviewing Palestinians about their reaction to a High Court ruling that upheld the deportation of 400 Palestinians to Lebanon. An army statement claimed that the grenade was thrown after the crowd, that had gathered around the television crew and was blocking traffic, refused to disperse.

FEBRUARY 6
Majdi al-Arabid, *Worldwide Television News (WTN)*, Attacked
Al-Arabid, a cameraman with *WTN*, was shot in the leg and lightly wounded while filming clashes between soldiers and Palestinian demonstrators in Jabalya refugee camp in the Gaza Strip.

Middle East

FEBRUARY 7

Taher Shriteh, *CBS; Reuters,* Imprisoned
Marwan al-Ghoul, *Reuters Television,* Imprisoned
Ashraf al-Ghoul, *Reuters Television,* Imprisoned
Shriteh, a cameraman for *CBS* and *Reuters;*
Marwan al-Ghoul, a cameraman for *Reuters TV;*
and Ashraf al-Ghoul, Marwan's brother and
assistant, were detained in Gaza City while
filming kids throwing stones at Israeli soldiers.
An officer ordered them to stop filming and
leave. When they refused, they were forced into
a jeep, and their video cameras were forcibly
removed. While in the jeep, the officer filled
out a form declaring the area a closed military
zone. They were taken to Ansar II detention
center and released the next day.

LATE MARCH

Palestinian Journalists Working in East Jerusalem,
Entry Denied
The closure of the Occupied Territories in late
March made it illegal for Palestinians in the
West Bank and Gaza to enter Israel, including
annexed East Jerusalem. Because the Palestinian
media is based in East Jerusalem, the closure
hit journalists particularly hard. Palestinian
journalists living in the West Bank and Gaza
were required to apply for special permits to
travel to East Jerusalem. Journalists report that
this was a frustrating and a time-consuming
process. According to Middle East Watch,
restrictions were relaxed on October 22, and
permits became easier to obtain.

MARCH 31

Al-Zahara Press Service, Censored
The army sealed off *Al-Zahara Press Service,*
in the West Bank town of Hebron. It was
ordered closed for six months.

JUNE 14

Bassam Abdallah, *Reuters Television,* Imprisoned,
Harassed
Abdallah, a stringer for *Reuters TV,* was
detained by soldiers as he was attempting to
film the aftermath of a grenade attack near

his home in the Rafah refugee camp. He was
beaten and his equipment was confiscated.
Abdallah was released early the next morning,
and his equipment was returned. In a July 28
letter to CPJ, a counselor from Israel's Embassy
in Washington explained that Abdallah's "suspicious and timely proximity to the attack raised
questions about his possible involvement."

JUNE 19

Ahmad Jadallah, *Reuters,* Attacked, Harassed
Jadallah, a photographer with *Reuters,* was
assaulted by a group of soldiers after he had
photographed them beating up a taxi driver
in Gaza City. The soldiers beat Jadallah,
confiscated his camera, and returned it to him
without his film, despite the fact that he had
identified himself as a journalist and had shown
them his press credentials. In a July 28 letter
to CPJ, a counselor at the Israeli Embassy in
Washington wrote, "This charge [that soldiers
had beaten Jadallah] is being investigated and
if it is found that the soldiers acted in a manner
contrary to their instruction then legal procedures will be implemented against them."
CPJ was never informed about the outcome
of the investigation.

JUNE 21

Majdi al-Arabid, *Worldwide Television News,*
Attacked
Al-Arabid, a cameraman for *Worldwide
Television News (WTN),* was shot in the leg by
an Israeli officer as he was filming a confrontation between soldiers and demonstrators in
Shati refugee camp. According to al-Arabid,
the same officer had earlier ordered him to stop
filming, but he refused since the camp had not
been declared a closed military area. Al-Arabid
claims that when he ignored the warning, the
officer threatened to shoot him in the head if he
persisted. Al-Arabid filed a complaint with the
army the same day. This was the fourth time he
had been shot by soldiers in a five-month

period. In a July 28 letter sent in response to a protest by CPJ, a counselor at the Israeli Embassy in Washington promised an immediate investigation into al-Arabid's shooting. But CPJ was never informed of its outcome.

JUNE 22

Talal Abu Rahma, *CNN,* Imprisoned, Attacked
Abu Rahma, a stringer for *Cable News Network (CNN),* was detained by members of an undercover army unit during a raid on his apartment building in Gaza City. He was held for six days in an interrogation cell in Ansar 2 and released on June 27 without charges. Abu Rahma was barefoot at the time of his arrest, and he was never given shoes. He was handcuffed the whole time, even during meals. He was beaten and forced to stand or kneel for prolonged periods. When he complained to a guard that the hot floor was burning his bare feet, the guard replied, "You better get used to it, because you're going to hell." A July 28 letter from a counsellor at the Israeli Embassy in Washington to CPJ explained that "Mr. Abu Rahma was one of several individuals present in a building [his apartment building] in which a number of terrorists were apprehended. An investigation was conducted to examine the relationship between Mr. Abu Rahma and the terrorists, after which he was released."

JULY 16

Taher Shriteh, *Reuters/CBS,* Attacked
Shriteh, a reporter for several international news organizations including *Reuters* and *CBS,* was filming an army patrol driving through Shati refugee camp when an army officer fired at him. The last vehicle in the patrol stopped, and an officer got out and aimed an M-16 rifle at Shriteh's head. Shriteh immediately dropped his video camera. As the officer continued to aim at him, Shriteh jumped behind a wall. The officer fired at his head and missed. Shriteh reports that the officer then let out a loud

laugh, got back into his vehicle and drove off. In a letter to CPJ, a counselor at Israel's Embassy in Washington promised that the incident would be investigated and that CPJ would be informed of any developments. CPJ received no further communication on this matter.

JULY 17

Taher Shriteh, *Reuters/CBS,* Attacked
Shriteh, a reporter for several international news organizations including *Reuters* and *CBS,* tried to film a group of soldiers surrounding a Palestinian lying on the ground in Gaza City's Sheikh Radwan neighborhood. Several soldiers and border guards pounced on Shriteh as soon as he had taken out his camera. Though he showed them his press card, the soldiers and border guards persisted in their attempts to remove his video camera. An officer then presented Shriteh with a paper declaring the area a closed military zone and ordered him to leave.

NOVEMBER 30

Fayez Noureddine, *Agence France-Presse,* Attacked, Harassed
Patrick Baz, *Agence France-Presse,* Attacked, Harassed
Israeli soldiers attacked Noureddine, a Palestinian photographer with *AFP,* and Baz, the agency's chief photographer (a Lebanese-French national), in Jabalya refugee camp in the Gaza Strip. The two were taking photos as some youths threw stones at a military outpost in the camp. About 20 soldiers and their officer emerged from the outpost and rushed toward the two photographers. Two soldiers dragged Noureddine by his hair and punched him in the face, while others beat Baz. One soldier wearing a steel helmet head-butted Baz. Afterwards, the officer confiscated all their film, claiming that they had entered a closed military zone. But he never showed the two photographers any official papers declaring Jabalya off limits.

Middle East

225

NOVEMBER 30

Jerome Delay, *Associated Press*, Attacked

Delay, an *AP* photographer, was wounded while covering clashes in Khan Younis, in the Gaza Strip. Israeli soldiers opened fire on demonstrators protesting the killing of a leader of the Fatah Hawks, the military wing of the mainstream Fatah movement of the PLO. Delay was hit in the leg by a rubber bullet when soldiers fired at a home where he and other reporters had taken cover.

DECEMBER 4

Awad Awad, *Agence France-Presse*, Attacked, Harassed, Imprisoned

An Israeli army officer beat Awad, an *AFP* photographer, as he was covering clashes between Palestinian demonstrators and Israeli soldiers in the West Bank town of Ramallah. The officer clubbed Awad on the head to prevent him from taking pictures. He then took the photographer to the Ramallah police station. Awad was released after five hours. His film was confiscated.

Jordan

As Jordan continued on its path toward democratization, the government softened some legal restrictions on the press's activities. But journalists fear that the new Press and Publications Law, supposedly enacted to protect them, still provides the authorities with the power to silence the press. Enacted in May, the Press and Publications Law eliminated the government's unlimited punitive powers over the press, provided journalists with the right to due process when charged with violations, and granted political parties the right to publish newspapers. But journalists are concerned about several regressive articles in the law. For instance, only the official media may cover matters pertaining to the army, the royal family, and national security. Also, harsh antidefamation statutes make criticism of the heads of Arab, Muslim, or friendly states off-limits. And journalists must reveal their sources if asked to do so by the courts and must join the Jordan Press Association (JPA). Last summer the government attempted to impose a "code of honor" on Jordanian journalists. But the JPA protested the move, stating that its members already adhere to the code of ethics of the Arab Journalists Union and that upon admission into the JPA, each member takes an oath vowing loyalty to the nation and the King and promising to practice the profession in good faith.

MAY 24

Al-Hayat, Censored

An issue of the London-based daily *Al-Hayat* was censored by Issa al-Jahamani, director of the Press and Publications Department of the Information Ministry, for publishing a distorted account of King Hussein's remarks at a meeting with editors of local (Jordanian) newspapers. The article in question, which was written by *Al-Hayat* correspondent Salamah Ni'mat, was entitled "King Hussein: I Cannot Continue to Support Saddam."

AUGUST 17

Al-Bilad, Censored

Nayef al-Tawara, *Al-Bilad*, Legal Action
Raed Salha, *Al-Bilad*, Legal Action

Police raided the printing house of the daily *Sawt al-Shaab* where the new independent weekly *Al-Bilad* is published, confiscated all copies of *Al-Bilad's* edition featuring a report on the suspects arrested in connection with a fundamentalist plot to assassinate King Hussein, and prevented the paper's 10 employees from leaving the building for a while. On the same day, al-Tawara, *Al-Bilad's* managing director, and Salha, its editor-in-chief, were summoned to appear before Amman's public prosecutor, Isam Brayk, to answer to a government charge that *Al-Bilad* had violated the Press and Publications Law in a number of its recent stories. According to *Al-Bilad*, one of the contested stories was a report about southern Jordan. Two other charges of violating the Press and Publications Law had already been lodged against the paper.

SEPTEMBER 26
Ramadan Rawashdeh, *Al-Ahali*, Harassed, Imprisoned
Rawashdeh, a reporter for *Al-Ahali* weekly, organ of the leftist Jordanian People's Democratic Party (the Jordanian branch of the Hawatmeh wing of the Democratic Front for the Liberation of Palestine) was arrested in front of the courthouse in Marka where 10 people accused in an assassination plot against King Hussein were being tried. The arrest occurred after Rawashdeh, who had been stripped of his entry permit the previous day, attempted to enter the courthouse. Major Mohammad Hijazi, the prosecutor in the above trial and the party who ordered Rawashdeh's arrest, told the *Jordan Times* that he was charged on four counts: "slandering the judicial authority," "publishing news, information and criticism affecting judges, witnesses and public opinion," "publishing minutes of the trial which the court had prohibited," and "violating Article 42 of the Press and Publications Law which prohibits the printing of minutes of such trials." Rawashdeh had published an article in *Al-Ahali* on September 20 that was subtitled: "Court delays referring defendants to doctors." It referred to a defense request that the defendants be examined for signs of torture. Rawashdeh was released on bail on September 30. His editor-in-chief, Jamil al-Nimri, was also indicted in the case.

OCTOBER 30
Nayef al-Tawara, *Al-Bilad*, Imprisoned
Raed Salha, *Al-Bilad*, Imprisoned
Mohammad Tomalie, *Al-Bilad*, Imprisoned
Al-Tawara, the managing director of the weekly tabloid *Al-Bilad*, Salha, its editor-in-chief, and Tomalie, a journalist with the paper, were arrested and brought before the public prosecutor's office on charges of publishing information that was "harmful to national security, defamatory toward the prime minister and the chamber of deputies, and injurious to an Arab state and an Arab chief of state." Apparently, the charges stemmed from three articles printed in *Al-Bilad's* most recent edition: one signed by Tomalie that criticized Prime Minister Abd al-Salam Majali, one about human rights violations in Saudi Arabia, and a piece by al-Tawara criticizing PLO chief Yasser Arafat for having made an autonomy agreement with Israel. The three were supposed to be held for 14 days but were released on bail after four hours of interrogation.

Kuwait

Only China has more imprisoned journalists than Kuwait, where 18 journalists remained incarcerated for allegedly collaborating with Iraqi occupation forces. The journalists worked on a newspaper published during the Iraqi occupation. The government's spate of lawsuits against journalists with the leading opposition daily, *Al-Qabas,* in 1992 was not repeated in 1993. By midyear *Al-Qabas's* editor-in-chief, Muhammad al-Saqr, and a reporter with the paper, Khodeir al-Oneizi, were cleared of violating national security in a lawsuit filed by the military in April 1992. The biggest blow to the quality of the press is the "restructuring" of the coun-

try's population, that is, the systematic expulsion of non-Kuwaiti residents, among them many leading journalists. In the 1970s and '80s, Arab expatriates with alternative ideals, Palestinians in particular, sought refuge in Kuwait, invigorating the political discourse of a society where only male citizens over 21 who can trace their family roots in Kuwait before 1920 are enfranchised. The Iraqi invasion and the al-Sabah regime's postliberation policy of nationality cleansing put an end to the days when Kuwait lured such talents as the cartoonist Naji al-Ali, who contributed to *Al-Qabas,* and the writer and novelist Ghassan Kanafani.

FEBRUARY 1
All Media, Legal Action
The chief prosecutor barred the local press from publishing reports on financial scandals without his prior authorization.

DECEMBER 8
Sami Al-Munayes, *Al-Taleea,* Imprisoned, Legal Action
Ahmad Al-Nafisi, *Al-Taleea,* Imprisoned, Legal Action
Ahmad Al-Dayeen, *Al-Taleea,* Imprisoned, Legal Action
Al-Munayes, owner and publisher of *Al-Taleea,* the weekly mouthpiece of the leftist Kuwait Democratic Forum (KDF);Al-Nafisi, *Al-Taleea's* editor-in-chief; and Al-Dayeen, the magazine's managing editor, were detained by the public prosecutor's office and interrogated with regard to a complaint filed by Ahmed al-Jarallah, editor-in-chief of the *Arab Times* and *Al-Siyassah* newspapers. The complaint charged two of the men with defamation for publishing a gossip item on September 22 about an arrangement between an unnamed editor-in-chief of a local paper and Spanish millionaire Javier de la Rosa. The piece alleged:

"An editor-in-chief of a local newspaper has received half a million dollars to interview de la Rosa and boost his image concerning involvement in the scandal of Kuwaiti investments in Spain." Al-Dayeen was released later that day since he was not charged in the case. Al-Munayes and al-Nafisi refused to pay a bail of KD 100 each and were detained overnight. They were released the next day against " personal guarantees."

Lebanon

Lebanon's boisterous media faced new challenges from a government that seems determined to assert control over its Fourth Estate. In May Prime Minister Rafiq Hariri's government suspended *Al-Safir,* one of the country's most influential papers, for a week because it published an Israeli working paper presented to the Lebanese delegation to the peace talks in Washington. But many, including the paper's editor-in-chief, believe that the real reason for the suspension was the paper's outspoken criticism of Saudi Arabia's human rights record. Hariri, a billionaire who made his fortune in Saudi Arabia, is a Saudi citizen.

In April, the government closed the *Independent Communications Network (ICN)* and suspended its sister newspaper, *Nida' al-Watan,* after they accused the prime minister of buying up the property of Christians in what was described as an attempt to "Islamicize" the country. The station and paper are owned by Maronite businessman Henri Sfeir, a political opponent of the prime minister.

Concerned about the crackdown, which coincided with an ongoing cam-

(continued on page 232)

Beirut's Embattled Media

by Avner Gidron

Lebanon's freewheeling media, once renowned as "the parliament of the Arabs," faces a crackdown that many fear will turn it into another muzzled Fourth Estate.

Just last month Prime Minister Rafiq Hariri's government suspended for one week the influential daily *As-Safir* because it leaked a confidential Israeli working paper presented to the Lebanese delegation at the peace talks in Washington. But editor-in-chief Talal Salman says the real reason was the paper's outspoken criticism of Saudi Arabia's human rights record, and its negative assessment of the Lebanese government which Salman describes as "a collection of Hariri's employees and business associates."

The suspension followed two other recent closures of media outlets and coincides with a new effort by the government to regulate the country's overcrowded airways.

The broadcast media flourished during the chaos of Lebanon's 15-year civil war. By war's end there was a station for almost every armed faction. Today, in addition to the official state television, there are between 35 and 60 unofficial television stations and at least three times that many radio stations.

In April the government closed Independent Communications Network (ICN), its most vocal critic, after the station accused the prime minister of buying up the property of Christians in an attempt to "Islamicize" the country.

ICN is owned by Maronite millionaire businessman Henri Sfeir, widely viewed by local journalists as a demagogue who used the station merely to further his own political ambitions. The lone television station to stand up for ICN was Al-Manar, the voice of the militant Islamic Hizballah. "We don't agree with Mr. Sfeir's politics," said Sheikh Khodr Nour al-Dine. "But we believe ICN was closed as a warning and because it is the weakest politically. We support ICN because it expressed the fears of Lebanon's Christians."

SPECIAL REPORT: Lebanon

As the voice of the Muslim opposition Al-Manar has its own reasons to fear a government crackdown on the media. Hizballah opposes the peace process and uses Al-Manar to disseminate its views.

"In Lebanon, anything about the peace talks is taboo. It is like this throughout the region, although in Israel the press can write what it wants. It can bring a government down," complains Al-Manar's Nour al-Dine, who believes the government will use financing rules to shut down his station. He denies widespread rumors that his station receives money from Iran.

Minister of Information Michel Samaha predicts that a new law he is drafting to regulate licensing of broadcast media based on strict financial and technical requirements will shut down all but seven or eight of the current 46 stations on the air. But he denies the motives are political. In fact, Lebanon's congested airways do interfere with broadcasts of neighboring countries and are in violation of international law.

But Samaha also defends the government's right to suspend a news organ when it stirs up confessional discord. "We are coming out of a civil war whose wounds have not yet completely healed. We cannot allow a TV station or newspaper to reignite these passions."

Sensitivity about discord among religious groups is natural given the traumatic civil war that at times pitted Christians against Muslims, Christians against Druze, Muslims against Muslims, and Christians against Christians. Fifteen years of fighting shattered the delicate balance that had been maintained since independence by the National Pact of 1943. An unwritten supplement to the constitution, the pact delineates what is called a "confessional" mode of power sharing among the country's various religious and ethnic communities. It reserves the presidency of the republic, command of the army and internal security for the Maronites. It designates that the prime minister must be a Sunni Muslim, and the speaker of parliament a Shi'ite Muslim. A new agreement, hammered out by Lebanese leaders at the Saudi resort of Ta'if in 1989, gave the Muslims greater political power but was boycotted by some Christian factions who believed it would grant Syria hegemony in Lebanon.

Last summer the Christian-owned *Lebanese Broadcasting Company (LBC)*, the first private television station and by far the most popular, campaigned against parliamentary elections which were widely boycotted by Christian voters. Its director, Pierre al-Daher, says his station has since toned down its opposition to the government. "I am not confident that even *LBC* can survive (regulation)," al-Daher confided. "This government is so weak it needs to make a show of force—like sending soldiers to occupy ICN's building. If *LBC* can't survive, no private station can."

Many journalists, like al-Daher and Sheikh Nour al-Dine, openly blame the Lebanese government for the media crackdown, but few are willing to publicly point the finger at Syria. Muhammad Moghrabi, a lawyer specializing in human rights, is an exception. He believes Syria ordered its "stooges"—his term for the Lebanese government—to close ICN and its sister publication *Nida' al-Watan*.

"It's illogical for Syria to allow its satellite more freedom than itself," Moghrabi explains. "Pre-1975 Lebanon set a bad example for its dictatorial neighbors. Its liberalism and pluralism were its main sins. The years of organized terrorism and crime mostly took care of that. Now it's time for them to finish off all that remains."

*Avner Gidron traveled to Lebanon in May and June 1993 for the Committee to Protect Journalists. A version of this article was published by the **Pacific News Service** on June 29, 1993.*

SPECIAL REPORT: Lebanon

paign by the government to regulate the Arab world's only private broadcast media, CPJ sent a delegation to Beirut in May to discuss journalists' concerns and meet with Lebanese officials. We found Lebanon's broadcast media flourished during the chaos of the civil war. By war's end there was a station for almost every faction. Today there are, by various counts, between 35 and 60 television stations and at least three times as many radio stations. And while nearly all the militias, with the notable exception of Hizballah (which is fighting Israel's occupation in the south), have been disarmed, their television and radio stations are still on the air. The first private television station, the *Lebanese Broadcasting Company (LBC)*, owned by a Christian militia known as the Lebanese Forces, remains the most popular. Officially, state television *(Télé-Liban)* is the only legal one. Others include those owned by Prime Minister Hariri, the Communist Party, Shi'ite fundamentalist Hizballah, and an assortment of deputies and ministers. The majority of existing stations have limited reach, and nearly all offer pirated programs. The most popular, like the *LBC*, offer foreign news broadcasts, such as *CNN* and *BBC*, in addition to their own news programs. Entertainment—imported movies, game shows, sitcoms, serials—predominates.

The government is proposing a new licensing system for broadcast media that will condition the granting of licenses on compliance with strict financial and technical requirements. In a meeting with Information Minister Michel Samaha, CPJ conveyed the concern of many Lebanese journalists that the government could use this opportunity to close opposition-controlled television and radio stations.

Crucial to the success of Lebanese reconstruction and national reconciliation, Hariri's government believes, is the media's respect of certain taboo subjects including the peace process, the growing power of Muslims in society, criticism of Saudi Arabia, and, of course, criticism of Syria.

The proposed law on the broadcast media, which Samaha had told CPJ would be enacted by the summer's end, has been held up by intra-government fighting. Some members of parliament and cabinet ministers have personal interests at stake; they are shareholders in private television stations. In fact, the prime minister owns *Future Television (FTV)* and 49 percent of *Télé-Liban*. Fears that Hariri's business interests guide his policy making proved valid when, in December, he pushed a draft law through the cabinet that would have given *FTV* a monopoly in satellite broadcasting. After President Elias Hrawi refused to sign it, the law was amended to limit satellite broadcasts to state television until the audio-visual media law is passed.

APRIL 29
Independent Communications Network, Censored
On April 29 security forces entered the headquarters of *Independent Communications Network (ICN)*, a Beirut-based television station owned by Henri Sfeir, and ordered its employees to evacuate the premises. This occurred after an order was issued by the public prosecutor closing *ICN* indefinitely. *ICN* is accused of broadcasting material that "inflames confessional passions and incites conflict among the nation's various sects." On December 23, a Beirut court ordered the reopening of the station, and it has resumed broadcasting.

APRIL 30
Nida' al-Watan, Censored
The government suspended *Nida' al-Watan*, a daily newspaper owned by Henri Sfeir, and removed copies of its April 30 edition from newsstands. The suspension apparently stemmed from the paper's publication of an article that accused Prime Minister Rafiq Hariri of "carrying out a plan to turn Lebanon into a Muslim country and buy properties owned by Christians." *Nida' al-Watan* was permitted to resume publication on June 7.

MAY 12
Al-Safir, Censored
The daily *Al-Safir* was suspended for one week. The closure stemmed from the publication, in the paper's May 11 issue, of an article that included the text of a working paper handed to the Lebanese delegation by the Israeli delegation at the bilateral peace negotiations in Washington, DC, Beirut's public prosecutor, Fawzi Abu Mrad, ordered that the paper be closed for one week, in accordance with Article 25 of the Press Code, because it printed "a document that disclosed information that should have remained secret to safeguard the security of the state." The leftist paper was able to circumvent the weeklong suspension by publishing under another masthead.

MAY 28
Al-Sharq, Censored
The Beirut public prosecutor banned the May 28 issue of the pro-Syrian daily *Al-Sharq* and ordered the paper suspended for one week for having published a caricature "attacking the dignity of the head of state." The suspension order was rescinded later that day.

JULY 26
Ahmed Haidar, *Al-Manar Television*, Killed
Haidar, a 27 year-old cameraman with the Hizbollah-owned television station *Al-Manar* in Beirut, was killed by shelling while covering the Israeli military's massive incursion into southern Lebanon in July.

Morocco

Two events in 1993 were of particular consequence to the Moroccan press. First there was the story of a police commissioner, Mohammed Mustapha Tabet, who raped more than 1,500 women at a studio that he kept in his precinct between 1990 and February of 1993, when he was caught. The story was gruesome. Over 500 assaults were documented by Tabet on videotape. The trial, which began at the end of February, was closed to the public (and press) after the second day. Government papers reported little on the so-called Tabet affair; the sales of opposition papers skyrocketed as a result of their coverage.

The editor-in-chief of a leading opposition daily says the episode revealed a hunger for investigative journalism from a public fed up with a party-dominated press where, due to government imposed constraints, opinion and commentary prevail to the detriment of information. The scandal and the negative light it shed on the government could have spelled a victory for the opposition in the parliamentary elections that were held in June and September 1993, but though the opposition parties did very well, no party or coalition of parties won enough seats to form a government. King Hassan decided to appoint a government on his own, offering a limited number of minor cabinet posts to the opposition, who declined them.

The frustration of the opposition was expressed in its newspapers. The angry

words printed in the nationalist Istiqlal Party's *L'Opinion* resulted in the director and editor being called in for questioning, showing that even the limited freedom of opinion enjoyed by the Moroccan press is still being contested by the government.

JANUARY 20
Abdelkarim Ghallab, *Al-Alam,* Legal Action
Ghallab, director of *Al-Alam,* organ of the nationalist opposition party Istiqlal, and the paper's correspondent in Tangier were sued for libel by Mohammed Ziane, attorney, parliamentarian, and businessman. Ziane also claimed 10 million dirhams in damages. The article in question appeared in *Al-Alam* in July 1992 and stated that the vehicle of a government attorney had been seized in Tangier along with 120kg of a concentrated form of cannabis. The outcome of the suit is unknown. Ziane represented the government in its 1992 defamation case against labor leader Noubir Amaoui.

FEBRUARY 27
Ahmed el-Kohen Lamrhili, *Al-Assas,* Exit Denied
El-Kohen, editor and publisher of the French-language monthly *Al-Assas,* was stopped at the airport by security and prevented from traveling to Paris to be with his wife. Although he carries a valid passport, he has not been allowed to leave the country since 1979. At that time *Al-Assas* published an article about the failure of the army to protect a town from a Polisario guerilla attack. Authorities have never offered an explanation for the travel ban.

APRIL 14
Fiammetta Rocco, Harassed
Rocco, a freelance journalist on assignment for London's *The Independent on Sunday,* was in Casablanca to research an article about the trial of a senior police commissioner sentenced to death for raping several hundred women. On the afternoon of April 14, Rocco was visited in her hotel room by two men in plainclothes who told her they were policemen. They questioned her and searched her personal effects. On April 16, at airport customs, Rocco was approached by a man in plainclothes and two assistants. She was taken to an office where her notes, newspaper clippings, and personal items were removed from her bags. The three men refused to show her identification and told her that the items they had removed belonged to Morocco and would not be returned. They detained her for an hour, then escorted her to the departure lounge.

SEPTEMBER 25
Asrar, Censored
The director of *Asrar,* a weekly satirical magazine, was summoned to National Security in Rabat where he was informed that the prime minister had issued an order suspending the publication of *Asrar* until further notice. The authorities have not given any reasons for the ban despite the requests of the Moroccan Press Syndicate and *Asrar's* management for an explanation.

OCTOBER
Abdelkader Chaoui, *Al-Alam,* Harassed
Chaoui, leftist author and journalist with *Al-Alam,* Arabic-language daily organ of the nationalist Istiqlal Party, was prevented from leaving the country by Rabat airport police. He was planning to travel to Paris at the invitation of Maison du Maroc, a Moroccan cultural center. According to Chaoui, this was the fifth time in four years that he was prevented from leaving the country. Chaoui, formerly a member of a banned Marxist organization, was imprisoned in 1974 for fifteen years for conspiring against the monarchy. He wrote a book about his experiences in prison that was both published and banned in 1987.

OCTOBER
Al-Maw'id al-Siyasi, Censored
Authorities seized an issue of the weekly review *Al-Maw'id al-Siyasi* for reasons that are unclear.

NOVEMBER 17
Mohamed Idrissi Kaitouni, *L'Opinion,* Harassed
Khaled Jamai, *L'Opinion,* Harassed
Kaitouni, director of the French-language weekly organ of the nationalist Istiqlal party *L'Opinion,* and Jamai, the paper's editor-in-chief, were called in for questioning by the state ministry for the interior and information about an article Jamai had signed entitled "The Moroccan Political Landscape: The Real Stakes," which the paper had published the previous day. The authorities considered the article to be "virulent and subversive." In it Jamai takes the government to task, particularly with regard to recent parliamentary elections. He claims that the administration "fabricated" parties, confounding the electoral system and resulting in a hung parliament.

Saudi Arabia

The Saudi royal family continues to silence dissenting voices at home and abroad. Though the press in Saudi Arabia is privately owned, it is one of the most restricted in the Middle East. King Fahd must approve the hiring of editors and may fire them at his will. In 1993 the Jeddah-based English-language daily *Arab News* saw two successive editors-in-chief dismissed. They also barred the press from discussing financial scandals. In May the government cracked down on the newly founded, Islamist-oriented Committee to Defend Legitimate Rights (CDLR), arresting its officials and firing other members and supporters from their government jobs. After a brief interlude, necessitated by Operation Desert Storm, the Saudis have returned to their long-standing policy of rejecting most visa applications from Western journalists. At the end of 1993, King Fahd finally inaugurated the long-promised *majlis al-shura,* or "Consultative Council." Its 60 members, who have been hand picked by the King, are to advise him and the Council of Ministers on issues referred to it. Its recommendations are nonbinding. Outside the kingdom, the Saudis were able to convince Shiite opposition figures to close down two publications critical of the Saudi regime, the London-based *Al-Jazirah al-Arabia* and the Washington-based *Arabia Monitor.* In exchange the Saudi government released some political prisoners and allowed four exiled leaders to return to the country. An agreement was signed in August by the Saudi information minister and the director of the Middle East Division of *Radio Monte Carlo,* in which the latter agreed to publicize the government's "great achievements during the reign of King Fahd, Custodian of the Holy Places. *Radio Monte Carlo,* based in France, has a very large audience in Saudi Arabia and elsewhere in the Middle East. And an adviser to the royal court is reportedly negotiating a deal for the takeover of three Arabic-language European publications: the London-based *Al-Arab* and *Sourakia* and the Paris-based *Al-Muharrar.* In 1993 *Al-Arab* serialized an Amnesty International report on the oppression of Shi'ites and Christians in Saudi Arabia. Members of the royal family already own the influential dailies *Al-Hayat* and *Al-Sharq al-Awsat,* the wire service *UPI,* and the *Middle East Broadcasting Company (MBC),* a worldwide satellite television and radio network. It has become virtually impossible to find any criticism of the Saudis in the international Arabic-language media.

Middle East

FEBRUARY 15

Khalid Maeena, *Arab News,* Harassed

Maeena, editor-in-chief of the English-language daily *Arab News,* was forced to resign after the paper printed a wire story about a *Wall Street Journal* interview with Shaykh Omar Abdul-Rahman who was quoted as saying that, "the Egyptian people will not accept being whipped and robbed by the corrupt Mubarak regime." The Saudi government was reportedly embarrassed by this criticism of one of its allies.

JULY 11

Sivaram Balaram, *Arab News,* Imprisoned
Farouq Luqman, *Arab News,* Harassed

Balaram, editor of the comics page of the English-language daily *Arab News,* was arrested on July 11, two days after Luqman, the paper's editor-in-chief, was briefly detained and interrogated. The cause of the arrest was the printing of a "B.C." cartoon on March 7 in which the main character says, "God, if you're up there, give me a sign." Then, after it starts to rain on him, he adds, "Well, we know two things. He's up there, and he's got a sense of humor." The authorities apparently thought the cartoon was questioning the existence of God. Balaram was released in late August or September and returned to India. Luqman, a native of Yemen and a naturalized Saudi citizen, had taken over the paper after its former editor-in-chief, Khalid Maeena, was forced to resign in February.

Syria

The Baath regime of President Hafez al-Assad has all but eradicated professional journalism in Syria, which was once an intellectual and literary center of the Arab world. All the dailies are government-run and staffed by government bureaucrats.

The slightest transgression by a reporter or editor will, at the very least, cost him his job. Journalists are well aware of the possible consequences of criticizing government policies. Prolonged imprisonment and torture can result. Consequently, the dogmatic newspapers have very low circulation figures, especially given Syria's relatively large literate population. In addition to internal censorship, Syria has aggressively exported censorship (most notably to Lebanon). Syria continues to hold most of the long-term imprisoned journalists in the Middle East. Syria carried out a policy, begun in 1992, to try secular political prisoners who had been held without charge or trial in State Security Courts. Information about these trials has been very difficult to verify. But observers have reported that the trials do not meet minimum international standards of fairness. The trials of five imprisoned journalists began this summer: Abdallah Muqdad, a journalist with the *Syrian Arab News Agency (SANA)* was arrested in 1980 on suspicion of membership in a rival wing of the Baath Party. Ahmad Swaidan, a reporter for *Kifah al-Ummal al-Ishtiraki,* has been held since January 1982 on suspicion of membership in a rival wing of the Baath Party. Samir al-Hassan, a Palestinian editor of *Fatah al-Intifada,* was arrested in April 1986 and accused of membership in the banned Party for Communist Action (PCA). Anwar Bader, a reporter for Syrian radio and television, was arrested in December 1986 and accused of membership in the PCA. Salama George Kila, a Palestinian journalist and CDF member, was arrested in March 1992. The State Security Court concluded the trials of three other journalists: Faisal Allush, a journalist and political writer held since 1985, was sentenced in June to 15 years in prison for membership in the PCA; and Ibrahim Habib, a freelance journalist arrested in 1987, was sentenced in July to three years in prison. Ahmad Hasso, a Kurdish writer and journalist and member of the Committees for the Defense of Democratic Freedom and Human Rights in Syria (CDF), was arrested in March 1992. He was sentenced to two years in prison.

JUNE 29
Faisal Allush, Legal Action
Allush, a journalist and political writer who has been imprisoned since 1985, was sentenced by the State Security Court to 15 years in prison for membership in the banned Party for Communist Action (PCA).

JULY
Ibrahim Habib, Legal Action
Habib, a freelance journalist and an activist with the Committees for the Defense of Democratic Freedoms and Human Rights in Syria (CDF), was sentenced to three years in prison by the State Security Court. According to Amnesty International, Habib has been in prison since 1987, and it is possible that he was released after he was sentenced.

Turkey

Four journalists were killed and government pressure and attacks against the press and journalists intensified during 1993. The Kurdish insurgency in the southeast remained the main issue which inflicted the heaviest toll on freedom of the press. The government used legal and extralegal measures in its attempt to silence Kurdish news organizations sympa-

thetic to the insurgency. The PKK (Kurdistan Workers' Party) banned all Turkish journalists from working in the Southeast and Turkish newspapers from getting distributed in the region. Several small left-wing publications were targets of government prosecution as well as attacks by fundamentalist mobs. The killings of three journalists were documented by CPJ; and one, missing since August, is presumed dead. Three of the journalists were working for the pro-PKK daily *Özgür Gündem*, which faced more legal and extralegal harassment than any other news organization in the country. The fourth murder was of a very prominent Turkish journalist and was claimed by fundamentalist groups. The death-toll in 1993, though a marked improvement over 1992, when 11 journalists were killed, is still one of the worst in Turkey's recent history. As in 1992, most of the journalists killed were covering the Kurdish conflict. The murderers have not been apprehended in any of the cases. But many Kurdish journalists suggest that security forces were involved in some of the murders. The high death-toll, along with the increased government restrictions on coverage and the PKK ban, made journalists more reluctant to cover the fighting first-hand this year. In some ways the press has enjoyed new freedom. The constitution was amended this year to allow private broadcasting for the first time. Publishing in the Kurdish language is no longer a crime. Extreme left wing, fundamentalist and Kurdish publications have proliferated in large numbers in the last few years. However, despite allowing these publications to exist, the government has put every possible pressure on them to prevent them from spreading their

Middle East

(continued on page 245)

Turkish Journalists Pressured from All Sides

by Yalman Onaran

On July 2, 1993, a mob of fundamentalists chanting "death to infidels" attacked a hotel in Sivas where a group of Turkish intellectuals had gathered. The threat became reality: they set the hotel ablaze, and 37 people died. Among the survivors was the main target of the attack, Aziz Nesin, one of Turkey's most prominent Turkish journalists.

Nesin had openly defied Islamic fundamentalists two months earlier by publishing excerpts from Salman Rushdie's *Satanic Verses* in his newspaper, *Aydinlik*. Reviled by the extreme religious right, Nesin, 78, has also been harassed throughout his career by the secular authorities in Ankara, who resent his criticism of corruption and human rights abuses. Nesin's plight is symbolic of what many journalists in Turkey face—pressure form all sides.

Assaults on journalists and the freedom of the press mirror Turkey's severe internal political conflicts. The increasingly fierce rebellion by Kurdish guerrillas in the Southeast has claimed more than 10,000 lives since 1984. Clashes between Muslim fundamentalists and secular-minded intellectuals have increased in the last few years. The Turkish military, although it has not intervened in the political system directly since 1980, remains a powerful force.

Uğur Mumcu, a prominent investigative journalist, was killed by a car bomb in January 1993. Muslim fundamentalist groups claimed responsibility. More than 100,000 people attended his funeral, shouting slogans such as "Turkey will not be another Iran." Secular Turks were furious at the killing for it exposed their vulnerability to fundamentalist violence.

In separate incidents, two reporters for Turkey's only Kurdish-language daily were killed; the newspaper, *Özgür Gündem*, accuses the government of involvement in the crimes, a charge that officials in Ankara vigorously deny. A third reporter for the same paper has been missing since August, and is presumed dead.

In 1992, CPJ documented 11 murders of journalists in Turkey—the highest toll ever there and more than in any other country that year. In 1993, the Committee confirmed four deaths of journalists in circumstances that appeared related to their journalistic work. But it would be wrong to assume that press conditions are improving. First of all, the lower death-toll was largely due to decreased coverage of the fighting in the Southeast. Restricted by the government and the PKK rebels, journalists have stopped covering the conflict first-hand. Still, the 1993 toll was one of the worst in recent years.

More importantly, the conditions journalists and news organizations faced were as bad as ever, if not worse, in 1993. Many journalists were imprisoned for alleged crimes related directly to their writing. Scores of publications were shut down by court order. Publishers paid hundreds of thousands of dollars in fines. Hundreds of cases against news organizations remained pending in courts.

Despite all these pressures from the government and segments of the public, the Turkish press has become more diverse, colorful, aggressive and outspoken. Many new publications have emerged in the last few years, representing almost every possible ideology. Although the government shut down private radio stations briefly last year because private broadcasting was in violation of the Turkish constitution, it wasn't much later that the political parties in the parliament joined forces to amend the constitution. Now legal for the first time, radio and TV stations have proliferated over the airwaves. Nationally distributed dailies (based in Istanbul) still exert the greatest influence over public opinion. However, broadcast journalism is gaining importance as more and more people watch TV, and news documentaries produced by prominent print journalists gain popularity.

One of the signs of the positive change from the recent past is the the existence of pro-Kurdish publications. But, even though they are allowed to exist, they are targets of government prosecution because they are perceived as supportive of the banned Kurdistan

Workers' Party, (PKK), which is waging a separatist war. Even mainstream Turkish publications face legal action when, once in a while without realizing, they run articles that officials assert publicize the rebels' views. These are simply news articles about the fighting in the Southeast, and usually a PKK commander is quoted. To escape legal harassment, the mainstream press has been simplifying its coverage more and more. Reports about the region generally do not go beyond simple numbers of "terrorists" and soldiers killed.

The PKK's recent ban on Turkish journalists in the region has caused the coverage of the conflict to deterioriate further. On October 19, all news bureaus in the Southeast were shut down following a threat by the PKK. Most Turkish journalists have left the region since then, and reporting of the clashes is even less trustworthy.

The PKK banned distribution of Turkish newspapers in the region as well. As a result, Turkish police, accustomed to confiscating newspapers, ended up distributing them in Diyarbakir and other cities of the region when the government ordered breaking through the ban.

Meanwhile, distribution of the pro-Kurdish daily *Özgür Gündem* is regularly prevented by pro-government thugs, and by the police, the newspaper claims. *Özgür Gündem* has been the main target of an undeclared government campaign to silence opposition to its policy regarding the Kurdish problem. There are currently 246 cases pending against the newspaper. Most of these are in the State Security Courts, which are less independent from the executive branch. The courts have already sentenced the newspaper's former editors to a total of more than 13 years in prison and $250,000 in fines. They also ordered that the paper be closed for 5 months. These decisions are being appealed.

Government harassment of *Özgür Gündem* is not limited to legal action. During a raid of its Istanbul headquarters and most local bureaus last December, the police rounded up so many staff members for questioning that the paper was forced to stop publishing for three days. The police justified the raid with a search warrant based on suspicion that some *Özgür Gündem* employees belong to the outlawed PKK.

The biggest fear its staff feels day to day is the possibility of being killed. In 1993 alone, three of its reporters were murdered. Since May 1992 when *Özgür Gündem* started publishing, seven of its journalists have been killed.

The colleagues of the killed journalists blame the government for at least two of the three deaths. Both Ferhat Tepe, the Bitlis correspondent, and reporter Aysel Malkaç disappeared when there was heavy police presence around. The newspaper claims that they were both taken into custody by the police and died under torture.

There is no evidence to implicate the government in the killings. Soon after Tepe had disappeared, someone called *Özgür Gündem* and claimed that he was being held by the "Ottoman-Turkish Revenge Brigade," a previously unknown organization. His body was found a week after his disappearance in a lake near the city of Elazığ.

Nothing has been heard from Malkaç since she disappeared on August 7. A prisoner who was being interrogated at Istanbul police headquarters on August 8 and 9 claims to have seen Malkaç there. But nothing has come out of this claim. Kemal Kiliç, the third *Özgür Gündem* journalist killed last year, was shot by unidentified gunmen in a village near Urfa.

Journalists who follow the incidents in the Southeast closely suspect these assasinations are being carried out by counter guerilla forces originally formed by the government to fight the PKK on a different level, now out of government control. Ultra-religious and ultra-nationalist groups which have been getting more organized and stronger in the region are also possible suspects.

Ultra-religious groups are suspected even more in the killing of the fourth Turkish journalist last year, the only one who did not work for the regularly attacked Kurdish daily. Several Islamic groups claimed responsibility for Mumcu's death.

Although the majority of the Turkish public is strongly committed to secularism, the ideological clash between the religious right and the secular, Western-educated elite has been prevalent since the last decades of the Ottoman Empire. The balance of power tipped in favor of the Western-oriented elite with the foundation of the modern republic in 1923. Resurgences of religious fundamentalism have occurred in cycles since then but the religious parties could never muster more than 10 percent of the vote.

However, due to recent democratization, although limited and imbalanced, financial and moral support from the Islamic regimes in Iran and Saudi Arabia, and dissatisfaction with mainstream left and right-wing parties, the religious right has gained more vigor than ever before in the last few years. During fall 1992 elections for mayor in some municipalities, the religious Welfare Party received almost 30 percent of the total votes, becoming the second party after the main opposition party. It is expected to receive an even larger chunk of the votes in the nationwide mayoral elections coming up this spring. Most recent opinion polls have put it in the lead in Istanbul and as the second highest nationwide.

This strengthening of the religious right has intensified the clash between secularists and fundamentalists. And while in the past, the religious right had not questioned the secularism of the Turkish state, the contemporary movement clearly criticizes the founder of modern Turkey, Kemal Atatürk, for secularizing the state and the social structure in 1923 and openly advocates an Islamic state similar to that of Iran or Saudi Arabia.

Like Mumcu, who was a staunch defender of secularism, many intellectuals come under fire from the religious right, some going as far as threatening lives. The Sivas incident, where 37 writers, poets and other intellectuals were killed, was another culmination of this Islamic resurgence, its grasp on a large segment of the population and the new brevity with which some far-right groups carry out their threats.

After Nesin escaped the hotel fire that killed his colleagues, a Turkish businessman announced that he would give a reward of $25,000 to anyone who would assassinate the journalist. *Aydinlik*, where Nesin is the senior columnist, has come under physical attack several times by religious mobs raiding the newspaper's offices, destroying presses and threatening its journalists.

Kurdish and left-wing publications are prosecuted regularly under the infamous "Anti-terror" law which makes illegal the spreading of separatist propaganda or "insulting the Prophet [Mohammed]."

On the other hand, an ultra-religious press flourishes undisturbed by the government prosecutors because the government uses different standards for far right publications. With the support of the main opposition party, it has blocked the addition of a new clause to the anti-Terror law that would make anti-secularist propoganda a crime as well. The government's junior coalition partner pressed for this new clause without success.

Another section of the Anti-terror law makes it a crime to insult the military. Many left-wing publications have been prosecuted under this clause. This clause has also resulted in arrests of mainstream journalists. Even Mehmet Ali Birand, the prominent Turkish television journalist who is believed to have strong backing inside the government, was summoned in January to testify about his feature on draft resisters and charged with "insulting the military."

The Turkish military has always had a central role in Turkish politics. It seized power in three coups in the last 30 years. Despite the recent economic and political liberalization, civilian leaders still feel the looming power of the military. Tansu Çiller, Turkey's first female prime minister and a former economics professor, is no exception. Çiller's recent switch from advocating a political solution for the Kurdish problem to the old recipe of a military victory over the PKK is generally attributed to her acknowledgement of this power.

The military's influence affects press freedoms more directly, too. The office of the Joint Chiefs of Staff filed more than 200 complaints about the press with prosecutors last year. Then in November, the office announced that it was not satisfied with the prosecution of these cases. The following months became a legal nightmare for journalists when the courts started processing their trials faster.

In the Southeast, where a continuing state of emergency puts the military directly in charge of civilian security, roadblocks by soldiers are a common sight. The military usually denies journalists access to certain towns where fighting between the PKK and the army is intense.

Being a foreign journalist in southeastern Turkey is in most cases better than being a local journalist. Turkish journalists who might venture into the region despite the PKK's ban risk abduction by the guerrillas and subsequent punishment. Kurdish journalists are constantly harassed by the police and face legal problems. Foreign journalists, on the other hand, can usually travel in the region freely, especially if they have informed the PKK beforehand of their visit. The PKK has said that its ban does not apply to foreign journalists, but they should get permission first. Turkish authorities do not bother foreign journalists if they have proper credentials. However, Turkish translators accompanying foreign journalists are not immune from trouble. Often, they end up in custody once articles by the foreign journalist they accompanied are published and reprinted by the Turkish press.

While foreign journalists enjoy some form of immunity from the problems of press in Turkey, local journalists continue to struggle with the powers that be: the government, the PKK, the military and fundamentalists. The killing of journalists continues; hundreds of trials proceed in courts; harassment carries on.

As Turkey advances on its course toward full democracy, journalists are asked to take the back seat where the bumps on the road feel worst.

Yalman Onaran *is a research associate at CPJ and the New York Bureau Chief for the Turkish weekly* **Nokta.** *He has written about the Middle East, Eastern Europe and Central Asia for American periodicals as well. Onaran has received an MS from Columbia University's School of Journalism and an MIA from the School of International and Public Affairs.*

ideas. **Writing that advocates ethnic or ideological separatism draws government harassment in the form of confiscations, legal action in the courts, mistreatment by the police, detention, heavy prison sentences and temporary closure by court order.**

JANUARY-DECEMBER
Özgür Halk, Censored
Haydar Demir, *Özgür Halk*, Legal Action
Riza Erdoğan, *Özgür Halk*, Legal Action
Hasan Tepe, *Özgür Halk*, Legal Action
İlhan Özdemir, *Özgür Halk*, Legal Action
Hüseyin Bora, *Özgür Halk*, Legal Action
Özgür Halk, a monthly left-wing magazine, has been under constant legal pressure by the government. Ten of the 12 issues published in 1993 were confiscated and resulted in court actions, most still in progress. The editor-in-chief at the time, Hasan Tepe, was sentenced to two years in prison and a $14,000 fine for the January 1993 issue. The owner, Haydar Demir, was also fined $14,000 for the same issue. In another court case finalized this year but based on an issue published last year, former editor Riza Erdoğan was sentenced to five months in prison. All the confiscations and court cases are based on the Anti-terror Law. Diyarbakir correspondent Huseyin Bora was arrested by the police in November and is being tried for a press release he wrote while under arrest. Adana correspondent İlhan Özdemir was arrested in October and was still in custody at the end of 1993. Erdoğan and Tepe are currently in hiding.

JANUARY-DECEMBER
Azadi, Censored
Zana Sezen, *Azadi*, Imprisoned
Sedat Karakaş, *Azadi*, Legal Action
İkramettin Oğuz, *Azadi*, Legal Action
Hikmet Çetin, *Azadi*, Legal Action
The pro-Kurdish weekly newspaper *Azadi*

has been under constant legal harassment since it started publishing in May 1992. In 1993, 40 issues were confiscated, and trials were launched against the newspaper for each issue. In trials resolved in 1993, the editor Sedat Karakaş was sentenced to three and a half years in prison and fined $42,000 altogether. Karakaş has fled the country to avoid serving these sentences. Most of these sentences were for issues published in 1992. In these cases, former owner Hikmet Çetin was fined $16,000; current owner İkramettin Oğuz was fined $35,000 and sentenced to one and a half years in prison. Oğuz's prison sentence is being appealed. Zana Sezen, the editor-in-chief, has been in prison since October 18 and is being tried for her responsibility as the editor for articles published. Only three cases were resolved with acquittal in 1993.

JANUARY-DECEMBER
Emeğin Bayrağı, Censored, Legal Action
Bülent Genç, *Emeğin Bayrağı*, Legal Action
The weekly left-wing newspaper *Emeğin Bayrağı* has had its share of government harassment. In 1993, of the 21 issues published, 18 were confiscated. In a trial concluded this year, former editor Bülent Genç was sentenced to two years in prison and a $25,000 fine. In this trial, based on an article calling on the workers of the world to unite and another about the conflict between right- and left-wing ideologies, the magazine was ordered shut down for three days as well. For the 21 issues published this year, 40 separate actions have been taken in court by prosecutors. The prosecutors are requesting a total of 500 years in prison for the editors and over $125,000 in fines in the court cases still in progress.

JANUARY-DECEMBER
Gerçek, Censored
Yücel Özdemir, *Gerçek*, Legal Action
Kemal Tekin Sürek, *Gerçek*, Legal Action
The pro-Kurdish weekly magazine *Gerçek* has literally had to pay a high price for freedom

of the press. The former owner of the weekly, Kemal Tekin Sürek, was fined $94,000 as a result of court decisions resolved in 1993. The former editor-in-chief, Yücel Özdemir, was fined $80,000 and sentenced to a total of seven years and 11 months in prison. He is currently in hiding. Twenty issues were confiscated during the year. While five trials ended in acquittal, among the ones still in progress, four demand the temporary closure (15 days in each case) of the magazine.

JANUARY-DECEMBER
Aydinlik, Censored, Legal Action
The left-wing newspaper *Aydinlik* has been the target of government harassment since it started publishing on May 1, 1993. Since that date, 31 issues have been confiscated. Among these, the first 13 were seized because they contained excerpts from Salman Rushdie's novel *The Satanic Verses*. The case launched after these confiscations accuses the newspaper of "insulting the Prophet," a crime in Turkish law. Seven of the other confiscations have also resulted in court actions, some for "separatism" and some for "insulting the military." Because it is a relatively new paper and trials are a long process in Turkey, no decisions have been reached against *Aydinlik* in 1993. But many are expected to be resolved in 1994 while new trials will be launched based on other issues that have been confiscated but not taken to court yet, according to Hale Soysü, the editor-in-chief.

JANUARY-DECEMBER
Deng, Censored
Kamil Ermiş, *Deng*, Legal Action
Ermiş, former editor of pro-Kurdish monthly magazine *Deng*, was sentenced to three years in prison and fined $15,000 for articles published in the magazine. He has fled the country to avoid serving his term. Various issues of the magazine were confiscated.

JANUARY-DECEMBER 1993
Mücadele, Censored
Sakine Fidan, *Mücadele*, Imprisoned
Gülten Şeşen, *Mücadele*, Legal Action
Namik Kemal Cibaroğlu, *Mücadele*, Legal Action
Editors at the left-wing weekly *Mücadele* complain of regular harassment by the police. They claim that their Istanbul headquarters and 14 bureaus around the country have been raided by the police many times, without any reasons given. The Diyarbakir representative Sakine Fidan was arrested during one of these raids recently and is still in custody. Of the 38 issues published in 1993, 34 were confiscated. In trials based on these confiscations, the magazine has been ordered to shut down for 16 days. The owner of *Mücadele*, Gülten Şeşen, was fined $75,000, while the former editor, Namik Kemal Cibaroğlu, was sentenced to serve six months in prison and pay a $37,500 fine. These sentences are currently being appealed.

JANUARY-FEBRUARY
Özgür Gündem, Legal Action
Yaşar Kaya, *Özgür Gündem*, Legal Action
Ocak Işık Yurtçu, *Özgür Gündem*, Legal Action
Davut Karadağ, *Özgür Gündem*, Legal Action
İsmail Beşikçi, *Özgür Gündem*, Legal Action
Ertan Aydin, *Özgür Gündem*, Legal Action
Doğan Güzel, *Özgür Gündem*, Legal Action
Sati Kaya, *Özgür Gündem*, Legal Action
Ercan Kanar, *Özgür Gündem*, Legal Action
Kamil Çelikten, *Özgür Gündem*, Legal Action
Özgür Gündem, a pro-Kurdish newspaper, and its editors currently face 246 trials in Istanbul courts, most of them at the State Security Court (DGM). In 1993, verdicts were reached in 73 cases; 41 guilty, usually for "separatist propaganda" deemed criminal under the infamous anti-terror law. As a result of the trials concluded in 1993, the newspaper's owner, Yaşar Kaya, was fined a total of $170,000. Former editor-in-chief Ocak Işık Yurtçu was sentenced to 11 1/2 years in prison and fines

totaling $70,000; another former editor, Davut Karadağ, was sentenced to two years and three months and fined $8,750. Writers İsmail Beşikçi and Ercan Kanar, cartoonists Ertan Aydin and Doğan Güzel, reporter Sati Kaya, and another former editor, Kemal Çelikten, were each sentenced to 10 months in prison. In five of these trials, the newspaper was also sentenced to temporary closure for a total of five months. All these cases are being appealed.

JANUARY 19
Orhan Karaagar, *Özgür Gündem,* Killed
Karaagar was a distributor of the newspaper *Özgür Gündem.* He was fatally stabbed by unknown assailants while going to his home in Van.

JANUARY 22
Stephan Waldberg, *Radio Dreyeckland,*
Legal Action
Waldberg, a freelance journalist for Germany's *Radio Dreyeckland* was arrested on October 23, 1992, after crossing the Iraqi border. On a previous visit to Turkey, Waldberg collected information on the political situation in southeastern Turkey and northern Iraq. While in Iraq, he interviewed members of the Kurdistan Workers' Party (PKK). During detention resulting from his October 1992 arrest, Waldberg was threatened with physical violence and was made to listen to the sounds of detainees under torture. On January 22, the Diyarbakir State Security Court found him guilty of violating Article 169 of the Criminal Code, providing assistance and shelter to an armed gang. He was sentenced to a prison term of three years and nine months. While in prison, Waldberg lost consciousness and suffered a head injury during a raid by police and soldiers to end a hunger strike at the prison. Waldberg was pardoned by the Turkish president and released on December 23.

JANUARY 24
Uğur Mumcu, *Cumhuriyet,* Killed
Mumcu, a reporter and columnist for *Cumhuriyet,* was in his car outside his home in Ankara when a bomb in the car exploded. The identity of those responsible for the attack has not been determined, but among groups that have claimed responsibility are the Islamic Liberation Organization, the Raiders of Islamic Great East, and Islamic Jihad. Mumcu, who reported on Islamic fundamentalism, drug and gun smuggling, and the Kurdish separatist movement, among other subjects, was a staunch supporter of the secular principles of Kemal Atatürk. Before his death, he had been researching the alleged connection between the Kurdistan Workers' Party (PKK) and Turkish intelligence. He had reportedly received numerous death threats.

FEBRUARY 25
Kemal Kiliç, *Özgür Gündem,* Killed
Kiliç was shot and mortally wounded by unknown assailants in Külünçe village, near the city of Urfa. He had been questioned by police about a news release he had put out on the difficulties distributors were facing in selling the newspaper *Özgür Gündem* in Urfa province.

MARCH 31
All Private Radio and Television Stations,
Censored
All private radio and television stations were ordered by the Turkish government to cease broadcasting on March 31. This move silenced all private radio stations that were established in recent years but were considered illegal because Article 133 of Turkey's constitution granted the state a monopoly over broadcast media. Private Turkish television stations were not affected because they are based outside Turkey. The article was amended by the Turkish parliament on July 8 to allow private broadcasting. Private radio stations started broadcasting after three months of silence.

Middle East

JUNE 14
Eşref Yaşa, *News Kiosk*, Attacked, Imprisoned
Haşim Yaşa, *News Kiosk*, Killed
According to a report by Amnesty International, in 1992 police warned news kiosk owner Eşref Yaşa to stop selling leftist publications. On January 15, 1993, an unknown gunman opened fire on him on a street in Diyarbakir, seriously injuring him. His uncle, Haşim Yaşa, who subsequently took over the newsstand, was shot and killed by unknown assailants. After his uncle's funeral, Eşref Yaşa was detained briefly and assaulted by police. He was reportedly told, "You survived last time, but you should have been finished off. We will kill you next time."

JULY 13
Tacettin Demir, *Özgür Gündem*, Imprisoned
Demir, a correspondent for *Özgür Gündem*, was detained on July 13 after investigating the aftermath of clashes between the army and the PKK (Kurdistan Workers' Party) guerrillas in Diyadin. Authorities, who had denied holding Demir, released him on July 22.

JULY 14
Davut Karadağ, *Özgür Gündem*, Imprisoned, Legal Action
Karadağ, the editor of *Özgür Gündem*, was remanded into custody as he appeared in a state security court in Istanbul to testify in a case against his newspaper. In a separate trial for an article that appeared in *Özgür Gündem* on May 2-3, Karadağ was sentenced to five months in prison and a $6,000 fine. The decision was reached on November 18. The court also ordered that the paper be suspended for 15 days. The decision is being appealed.

JULY 19
Nezahat Özen, *Özgür Gündem*, Attacked, Imprisoned, Legal Action
According to Amnesty International, Özen, an *Özgür Gündem* correspondent, was detained by police in Mardin on July 16, where she was researching a story about a girl who was tortured and raped by an officer at the gendarmerie station in Derik. On July 19, Özen, who was seven months pregnant, had to be transferred from police headquarters to a hospital because she had been severely tortured. Amnesty International reports that since then Özen was taken out of the hospital by police, brought before a judge, and imprisoned. She was released just before she gave birth.

JULY 20
Mehmet Yazici, *Özgür Gündem*, Imprisoned
Özgür Gündem correspondent Mehmet Yazici was taken into custody by the police and held for longer than two months.

JULY 28
Ferhat Tepe, *Özgür Gündem*, Killed
On August 8, a body found near the city of Elazığ was identified as being that of *Özgür Gündem's* Bitlis correspondent, Ferhat Tepe. The body was found in Lake Hazar, but the cause of death was not determined. Tepe had disappeared on July 28. He reportedly was forced to get into a car after he left his father's shop in the center of Bitlis. Although several teams of police were seen patrolling the streets at the time, they denied any knowledge of the incident. On July 29, a caller claimed that Tepe was being held by a group called the Ottoman Turkish Revenge Brigade. The journalist is said to have received death threats in the past.

AUGUST 3
Ahmet İçge, *Özgür Gündem*, Imprisoned
İçge, the Ağri and Doğubeyazit correspondent for *Özgür Gündem*, disappeared. Authorities in Ağri subsequently confirmed that they were holding him. It is not known on what charges he was detained. He was later released.

AUGUST 7
Aysel Malkaç, *Özgür Gündem*, Killed
Malkaç, a correspondent for *Özgür Gündem*,

disappeared after leaving the newspaper's main office in Istanbul. Staff members suspect that she was taken by the police because there was a heavy police presence around the building. A prisoner who was being interrogated at Istanbul police headquarters on August 8 claims to have seen Malkaç. Since she has been missing for longer than seven months and no news has been forthcoming about her whereabouts, her colleagues and friends presume Malkaç is already dead.

AUGUST 17
Salih Tekin, *Özgür Gündem*, Imprisoned, Attacked, Legal Action
Tekin, a reporter for *Özgür Gündem*, was detained. He was formally arrested on September 10, 1993. He wrote a letter from prison claiming that he was subjected to torture. Tekin was released on November 18 after the first hearing of the trial demanding five years in prison for Tekin. He is being tried without being in custody.

SEPTEMBER 12
Özgür Gündem, Attacked
The Batman bureau of the Turkish newspaper *Özgür Gündem* was bombed by unknown attackers. The property inside the bureau was damaged, but no one was injured.

SEPTEMBER 12
Aslan Saraç, *Özgür Gündem*, Imprisoned
Hasan Yildiz, *Özgür Gündem*, Imprisoned
Özgür Gündem's Van correspondent, Saraç, and his translator, Yildiz, were arrested by the police on their way to meet a group of European parliamentarians in a Van hotel. They were released several days later without any reasons given for their detention.

SEPTEMBER 28
Mustafa Kaplan, *Beklenen Vakit*, Legal Action
Kaplan, a reporter for the pro-Islamc newspaper *Beklenen Vakit*, was sentenced to eight

months in prison for an article he wrote. He is currently serving his term.

SEPTEMBER 28
Zülküf Akkaya, Killed
Newspaper distributor Zülküf Akkaya was killed by unidentified gunmen in Diyarbakir. The newspaper *Özgür Gündem* claimed that he was killed for distributing their newspaper among others because he was threatened many times for selling *Özgür Gündem.*

SEPTEMBER 30
Newroz, Censored
Doğan Karakuzu, *Newroz*, Legal Action
The monthly pro-Kurdish magazine *Newroz* was shut down for a month by the Istanbul State Security Court for publishing articles deemed to be separatist propaganda. Editor-in-chief Karakuzu was sentenced to two months in prison and fined $5,000. At the time of this decision, there were 24 other cases against the magazine pending in courts. Every single issue published this year was confiscated and resulted in court action against reporters, editors, and the owner of the magazine.

OCTOBER 9
Adil Başkan, Killed
The only news distributor in the Nusaybin district of Mardin was killed by armed men. The distributor, Adil Başkan, was 28 years old. The newspaper *Özgür Gündem* claims that earlier he was threatened for distributing *Özgür Gündem* and that is why he was killed. Başkan distributed all the newspapers in Nusaybin.

OCTOBER 19
All News Bureaus in Diyarbakir, Censored
All the Turkish news bureaus in Diyarbakir were shut down following a threat by the Kurdistan Workers' Party (PKK). Journalists left the region fearing PKK attacks, and the flow of news coming out of the region declined drastically. The PKK has also prevented the

Middle East

distribution of Turkish newspapers in the region. The ban is still in effect. Although distribution of newspapers resumed on November 15 after negotiations between news distributors and the PKK, it has been interrupted for brief periods on and off due to disagreements. News bureaus remain closed.

OCTOBER 22
Ferit Demir, *Milliyet*, Kidnapped

Milliyet newspaper's Tunceli correspondent, Demir, was kidnapped by the Kurdistan Workers' Party (PKK) for disobeying the PKK ban on news organizations and journalists in southeastern Turkey. Demir was released on October 26 after he agreed to stop working in the region as a journalist.

NOVEMBER 25
Tercüman, Censored

The right-wing daily *Tercüman's* November 25 edition was confiscated by the police for a news article on the PKK's targeting a right-wing political party. No trial was launched.

NOVEMBER 27
Adnan Işık, *Özgür Gündem*, Killed

Işık, one of *Özgür Gündem's* distributors in Van, was killed in an armed attack. No one claimed responsibility. Işık's coworkers claim that his attackers fled the scene in cars belonging to the Van police.

DECEMBER 3
Musa Duru, Killed
Yahya Çilligöz, Killed

Duru and Çilligöz, two newspaper distributors in Batman, were killed by unidentified gunmen. No one claimed responsibility for the attack.

DECEMBER 7
Ekonomik Panorama, Censored

The mainstream weekly economics magazine *Ekonomik Panorama* was confiscated by the authorities for an interview with a PKK leader published in the December 7-13 issue. A trial was not initiated against it.

DECEMBER 9-11
Özgür Gündem, Attacked, Censored
Gurbetelli Ersöz, *Özgür Gündem*, Imprisoned, Legal Action
Ferda Çetin, *Özgür Gündem*, Imprisoned
Gülten Kişanak, *Özgür Gündem*, Imprisoned

The Istanbul headquarters and nine local bureaus of *Özgür Gündem* were raided by the police during a three-day operation ordered by the Istanbul State Security Court. More than 100 staff members, most of them reporters and editors, were arrested during the raids. The editor-in-chief, Gurbetelli Ersöz; the deputy editor, Ferda Çetin; and a news editor, Gülten Kişanak, were among those arrested during the raids and were still in custody at the end of 1993 while many others were released after a few days. Because of the massive arrests, the publication of the newspaper was halted for three days for the lack of staff to publish it. The police said they found guns and gas masks in the Istanbul and Diyarbakir offices. The newspaper's lawyers say those were kept in case of possible attacks on the newspaper's offices. Such attacks have occurred in the past. The Turkish government, in its second response to 14 letters CPJ has sent during the year, claimed that the raid on the newspaper's offices was not a violation of press freedom because the courts suspect that the newspaper has links to the outlawed PKK organization. As an indication of how "deeply entrenched" freedom of the press is in Turkey, government spokesperson Yildirim Aktuna pointed to the fact that *Özgür Gündem* is still being published. However, Aktuna failed to mention the three days the newspaper had to cease publication because of the police raid and more than 100 court cases opened by government prosecutors that demand the closure of the newspaper. By the end of 1993 four trials ended with the court calling for the closure of the paper: two of them for 15 days, two for a month. If appeals fail, *Özgür Gündem* will be suspended for two months.

DECEMBER 12
Esma Turan, *Taraf,* Legal Action
Kazim Albayrak, *Taraf,* Legal Action
The Islamic monthly *Taraf* has been the target
of legal actions by the government for many
articles published this year. In the only trial
that was concluded in 1993, the editor-in-chief,
Esma Turan, was sentenced to one year in
prison and a $25,000 fine, while the owner,
Kazim Albayrak, was fined $10,000. The judg-
ment was for an article about an Islamist underground organization and charged that "illegal
organizations and armed acts were praised."
Numerous issues of *Taraf* were confiscated in
1993, mostly for spreading "antisecularism."
Taraf openly advocates the establishment of
an Islamic state in Turkey.

DECEMBER 14
Erhan Akyildiz, *HBB TV,* Imprisoned,
Legal Action
Ali Tevfik Berber, *HBB TV,* Imprisoned,
Legal Action
Television journalists Akyildiz and Berber were
arrested. The two journalists had interviewed a
member of the Association of Persons Against
War on the show "Anten" on *HBB TV* on
December 8. Based on this interview, they have
been charged with "provoking the population
against the army," a violation of the criminal
code. Unusually, they are being tried by a military court. They were released on December 20
to be tried under bail. They were then sentenced by the military court to two months
in prison. The decision is being appealed.

DECEMBER 14
Zuhat Tepe, *Özgür Gündem,* Killed
A distributor of the newspaper *Özgür Gündem*
in İskenderun was found dead near his house.
Twenty-seven-year-old Zuhat Tepe's throat
was slashed by unidentified assailants.

DECEMBER 23
Celal Başlangiç, *Cumhuriyet,* Legal Action
Aydin Engin, *Cumhuriyet,* Legal Action
Engin, a reporter with the mainstream daily
Cumhuriyet, and Başlangiç, its editor-in-chief,
were each sentenced to a year and three months
in prison for an interview published in the
newspaper. The court ruled that Müslüm
Gürbüz, the leader of a religious sect in eastern
Turkey, had "insulted Atatürk," the founder
of modern Turkey, during the interview.
According to Turkish law, insulting Atatürk
is a crime. Gürbüz received the same sentence
as the two journalists. Their sentences were
commuted to a $230 fine by the judge.

Yemen

**Since unification, Yemen has boasted one
of the Arab world's freest presses. While
the broadcast media remain under state
control, the print media have flourished.
All but a handful of the over 100 papers
and periodicals accept a government
stipend, yet a wide array of political views
is represented. The press escaped the
political crisis that rocked Yemen relatively unscathed. But fears of reprisal from
both official and unknown parties linger.
Parliamentary elections in April were won
by the General Peoples Congress (GPC),
the ruling party in the former North
Yemen. Since unification, the GPC has
ruled in an uneasy alliance with the
Yemeni Socialist Party (YSP), the ruling
party of pre-unification Marxist South
Yemen. After the elections the tradition-
ist Islah Party joined the coalition. The
crisis began when the vice president,
Ali Salem al-Baidh of the YSP, refused to
leave his former capital of Aden, where**

he has been since August, to be sworn in in Sanaa, until his party's grievances are addressed. Al-Baidh's grievances include the lack of progress in investigating the assassination of at least a dozen YSP officials, political and economic discrimination by the central government against YSP members and southerners, and the slow pace of integration of parallel government structures—most importantly the armed forces. The Dialogue Committee set up to resolve the crisis asked that the press be more closely surveilled. Many politicians claim that irresponsible reporting has perpetuated the crisis. In December, the offices of the weekly *Sawt al-Ummal* were fired on by unidentified gunmen after the paper published a report on an alleged assassination attempt on the vice president. In a victory for press freedom, a lawsuit filed by the press prosecutor against the English-language weekly *Yemen Times* was thrown out by the courts in August because the case was initiated by the ministry of information rather than the allegedly slandered party, Presidential Council chairman Ali Abdullah Saleh. The Yemeni Journalists' Syndicate chief, Abdul-Bari Taher, commented: "In societies which declare themselves to be democratic and accept freedom of the press, there is no need for a ministry of information—because this ministry tries to justify its existence by harassing journalists."

OCTOBER 3
Ray Shillito, *Clark Television* (London), Imprisoned
Abdullah Hassan Mohammed, *Clark Television* (London), Imprisoned
Shillito and Mohammed, journalists with *Clark Television* on assignment for Britain's *Channel 4*, entered Yemen on September 29 to research a story on visa fraud. On October 3 the two journalists were detained by authorities. They were kept in jail at first, then moved to a hotel, where they were held under house arrest. Shillito was charged with "aggression" against the Yemeni people and attempting to obtain documents illegally. Mohammed was never charged. Both men were prohibited from leaving the country. On December 9 the journalists announced that their passports were returned to them and that they were scheduled to leave Yemen the next day.

DECEMBER 11
Sawt al-Ummal, Attacked
Unidentified assailants opened fire on the Sanaa offices of the weekly organ of Yemen's trade unions, *Sawt al-Ummal*. The paper's most recent edition, which was absent from the newsstands, published a report about an alleged plot to assassinate Vice President Ali Salem al-Baidh. The article named army officers supposedly involved in the conspiracy. *Sawt al-Ummal* is closely associated with al-Baidh's party, the Yemen Socialist Party.

Index (alphabetical by country)

Donors

The Committee to Protect Journalists gratefully acknowledges the news organizations, foundations, companies, and individuals whose contributions make our work possible. In 1993, CPJ received over $960,000 in gifts and grants, which has allowed CPJ to work on all of the cases listed in this volume of *Attacks on the Press*. To find out how you or your company can help, see pages 258-59.

$50,000 and above
The Ford Foundation
The Freedom Forum
The John D. and Catherine T. MacArthur
   Foundation

$25,000-$49,999
Goldman, Sachs & Co.
The Joyce Mertz-Gilmore Foundation
NBC
Newark Star Ledger
Smith Barney Shearson
Time Warner Inc.
Viacom International Inc.

$10,000-$24,999
Blockbuster Entertainment Corporation
Castle Rock Entertainment
CBS Broadcast Group
The New York Daily News
Dow Jones & Company
The Hearst Corporation
The John Roderick MacArthur Foundation
The John Merck Fund
Morgan Stanley & Co.
The New York Times Company
The New Yorker
QVC Network, Inc.
The Scherman Foundation
Televisa
Marlo Thomas & Phil Donahue

Time
Turner Broadcasting System
The Washington Post

$5,000-$9,999
Allen & Company Incorporated
Franz & Marcia Allina
American Lawyer Media/Courtroom
   Television Network
Baker & Hostetler
The Bank of New York
Bear, Stearns & Co., Inc.
Bresnan Communications Company
Comedy Central
Debevoise & Plimpton
Donaldson, Lufkin & Jenrette, Inc.
Furman Selz Incorporated
General Electric
Drue Heinz Foundation
Jack Hilton Incorporated
Kekst and Company Incorporated
Kroll Associates, Inc.
Macmillan, Inc.
MCA Inc.
The Menemsha Foundation
New Line Cinema Corp.
New York Newsday
Newsweek
Ogilvy Adams & Rinehart
Paramount Communications Inc.

Major support helped the Committee with many new initiatives. An expanded training and outreach program was sponsored by the Freedom Forum. The John D. and Catherine T. MacArthur Foundation supported an upcoming anthology on the relationship between freedom of the press in Mexico and NAFTA. The Joyce Mertz-Gilmore Foundation sponsored a major upgrade of CPJ's computer and communications equipment. Mead Data Central provided its Lexis and Nexis research services so CPJ can respond more quickly to attacks on the press. And the Ford Foundation, CPJ's earliest major funder, continued its core support.

People
Price Waterhouse
Random House, Inc.
Reuters America Inc.
Robinson, Lake & Lerer
Simpson Thatcher & Bartlett
Times Mirror
Tribune Broadcasting Company
TV Guide, New York Post and News America Publishing, Inc.
Twentieth Century Fox Film Corporation
Weil, Gotshal & Manges

$1,000-$4,999
Arent Fox Kinter Plotkin & Kahn
BHC Communications, Inc.
The Boston Globe
James E. Burke
Cablevision Systems Corporation
The Chase Manhattan Bank
The Coca-Cola Company
Mr. & Mrs. Marshall S. Cogan
Continental Cablevision, Inc.
Helen K. Copley
Cowles Media
The Discovery Channel
Discovery Networks
Stuart & Rivian Glickman
Harper's Magazine
Mark Asset Management Corp.
New York Review of Books
The Samuel I. Newhouse Foundation
Donald A. Pels
Philip Morris Companies
Playboy
Steven Rattner & Maureen White
Spelling Entertainment
Stichting: European Human Rights Foundation
TeleCable Corporation
Tishman Speyer Properties
A. Robert Towbin
Katrina vanden Heuvel
Vogue
Whittle Communications
James D. Wolfensohn Incorporated

IN-KIND SERVICES
The Associated Press
Brook Trout Technology
cc:Mail, a division of Lotus

Mead Data Central
New York Newsday
Optus Software
Reuters America Inc.

Contributing News Organizations
American Lawyer Media/Courtroom Television Network
The Associated Press
The Boston Globe
Capital Cities/ABC
CBS Broadcast Group
Cowles Media
The Discovery Channel
Dow Jones & Company
Harper's Magazine
The Hearst Corporation
Macmillan, Inc.
NBC
The New York Daily News
New York Newsday
New York Review of Books
The New York Times Company
The New Yorker
Newark Star Ledger
Newsweek
People
Playboy
Random House
Reuters America Inc.
Televisa
Time
Time Warner Inc.
Times Mirror
Tribune Broadcasting Company
Turner Broadcasting System
TV Guide, New York Post & News America Publishing Inc.
USA Today
Viacom International Inc.
Vogue
The Washington Post
Whittle Communications

Ways to Help CPJ

	Journalists	Everyone
Become a Member *Starting at $35*	Show your support for your colleagues and stay informed about press conditions by becoming a member of CPJ. Gift memberships are also available.	Show your support for freedom of the press and stay informed about press conditions by becoming a member of CPJ. Gift memberships are also available.
Buy CPJ's publications. *Members receive a 50% discount*	CPJ's reports on press conditions and safety manuals for journalists are an invaluable tool for reporters. Buy them for your newsrooms and help defray the cost of this important service. (CPJ will provide its publications at no charge to any journalist who cannot afford them).	CPJ's reports on press conditions around the world shed light on emerging political developments. They are essential reading for anyone interested in freedom of expression or human rights.
Attend the International Press Freedom Awards Dinner *November 9, 1994* *New York City*	The International Press Freedom Awards Dinner honors the struggle of journalists who risk their lives to report the news. It is a major gathering of journalists and media companies, and it raises more than half of CPJ's operating funds. Show your support for freedom of the press by attending this important event.	The International Press Freedom Awards Dinner honors the struggle of journalists who risk their lives to report the news. It is a major gathering of journalists and media companies, and it raises more than half of CPJ's operating funds. Show your support for freedom of the press by attending this important event.
Provide Information on Cases	We need information. Whenever a colleague or news organization is threatened, harassed, or attacked, we need reliable information fast..	We need information from as many sources as possible. If you have information about a journalist or news organization being threatened, harassed, or attacked, contact CPJ immediately.
Support our Campaigns	Letters from journalists in support of their colleagues under attack do make a difference. Stay on top of current cases by subscribing to CPJ's quarterly newsletter, *Dangerous Assignments* and to CPJ's electronic alert system. Call CPJ for details.	There is strength in numbers. Letters of protest from the business community concerning the cases CPJ is working on adds to the international pressure of news organizations and human rights groups. Stay on top of current cases by subscribing to CPJ's quarterly newsletter *Dangerous Assignments*, and to CPJ's electronic alert system. Call CPJ for details.
News Coverage and Letters to the Editor	Freedom of the press is a barometer of social and political upheaval. Coverage of the problems faced by independent journalists in developing countries is the best way of furthering the cause of press freedom worldwide.	Write letters to the editor of your local news organization expressing your concern for the cases that CPJ is working on.

	News Organizations	**Companies**
Become a Corporate Member *Starting at $1,000*	CPJ works on behalf of journalists everywhere. Your organization's membership sends a powerful message that journalists everywhere are looking out for the rights of their colleagues.	Companies rely on the up-to-the-minute information that news organizations provide. And news organizations rely on advertising revenue. This close working relationship makes freedom of the press vitally important to all businesses. Your company's membership contribution is a symbolic message that says Freedom of the Press is Everybody's Business.
Buy CPJ's publications **Members receive a 50% discount**	CPJ's reports on press conditions and safety manuals for journalists are invaluable tools for reporters. Buy them for your newsrooms and help defray the cost of this important service. (CPJ will provide its publications at no charge to any journalist who cannot afford them.)	CPJ's reports on press conditions around the world shed light on emerging political developments. This information can be extremely useful for international businesses.
Support our Membership Campaign	Encourage your employees to become members of CPJ by distributing our membership materials at work. Your company can also match employee contributions to CPJ.	Encourage your employees to become members of CPJ by distributing our membership materials at work. Your company can also match employee contributions to CPJ.
Buy a table at the International Press Freedom Awards Dinner *November 9, 1994* *New York City*	The International Press Freedom Awards Dinner honors the struggle of journalists who risk their lives to report the news. It is a major gathering of media companies and journalists, and it raises more than half of CPJ's operating funds. Show your company's commitment to CPJ's work by purchasing a table for 1994.	The International Press Freedom Awards Dinner honors the struggle of journalists who risk their lives to report the news. It is a major gathering of media companies and journalists, and it raises more than half of CPJ's operating funds. Show your company's commitment to CPJ's work by purchasing a table for 1994.
Donate products and services	CPJ is well-known for its solid research. You can help keep us informed by joining the many news organizations around the world that donate their newspapers, magazines, wire services, and other information services.	Your company can keep our costs down by providing products and services we need, such as publicity, graphic design, advertising, long-distance telephone, printing, travel, video, photography, computers, software, cameras, office furniture. You name it, we need it.

Staff

William A. Orme, Jr.
Executive Director
(212) 465-1004 (x102)
E-Mail: orme@cpj.igc.apc.org

Anne Newman
Director of Publications
(212) 465-1004 (x108)
E-Mail: anewman@cpj.igc.apc.org

Todd Wiener
Director of Development
(212) 465-1004 (x113)
E-Mail: twiener@cpj.igc.apc.org

Program Coordinators

Avner Gidron
Senior Researcher
Middle East and North Africa
(212) 465-1004 (x105)
E-Mail: middleeast@cpj.igc.apc.org

Ana Arana
Americas
(212) 465-1004 (x106)
E-Mail: latinamerica@cpj.igc.apc.org

Ahamat Omran
Africa
(212) 465-1004 (x103)
E-Mail: africa@cpj.igc.apc.org

Vikram Parekh
Asia
(212) 465-1004 (x109)
E-Mail: asia@cpj.igc.apc.org

Leonid Zagalsky
Eastern Europe (including the republics of the former Soviet Union)
(212) 465-1004 (x104)
E-Mail: europe@cpj.igc.apc.org

Administration

Nicole Cordrey
Administrative Assistant
(212) 465-1004 (x115)
E-Mail: ncordrey@cpj.igc.apc.org

Kari Corwin
Membership and Event Coordinator
(212) 465-1004 (x107)
E:Mail: kcorwin@cpj.igc.apc.org

Fiona Dunne
Administrative Assistant
212 (465)-1004 (x100)
E-Mail: fdunne@cpj.igc.apc.org

Sunsh Stein
Business Manager
(212) 465-1004 (x116)
E-Mail: sstein@cpj.igc.apc.org

Board of Directors

CPJ Publications

Publications are presented as a public service. All members receive a 50% discount and publications are provided free to journalists who cannot afford them. Visa, Mastercard, American Express, check and money orders are accepted. To order any titles listed below, please call (212) 465-1004.

Attacks on the Press, $30
A comprehensive annual survey of attacks against journalists and news organizations around the world.
1993 Edition, Preface by Charlayne Hunter-Gault
1992 Edition, Preface by Terry Anderson
1991 Edition, Preface by Walter Cronkite
1990 Edition, Preface by Loren Ghiglione
1989 Edition, Preface by Mary McGrory
1988 Edition, Preface by Anthony Lewis
1991 and 1990 editions are available in Spanish.

Dangerous Assignments Quarterly, $10
CPJ's newsletter focuses on international press conditions and attacks on the press. Free to members.

Silenced by Death, $10
Journalists Killed in the United States (1976-1993)
A study of journalists killed in the United States reveals that when foreign-born journalists are killed, their cases are rarely solved. July 1993.

Journalists' Advisory on Yugoslavia, $10
How to Survive and Still Get the Story
This easy-to-carry booklet provides advice from journalists for journalists on everything from where to get flak jackets, and insurance and rental cars to tips on avoiding sniper fire in Sarajevo. It includes a list of important phone numbers.
March 1993.

Don't Force Us to Lie, $20
The Struggle of Chinese Journalists in the Reform Era
A detailed study of the determined efforts of Chinese journalists to speak and write freely throughout the 1980s and early 1990s. With a foreword by Dan Rather and contributions by China scholar Anne Thurston, this 167-page book is one of the most comprehensive accounts available of how journalism works in the world's most populous country. January 1993.

Bouch Pe, $10
The Crackdown on Haiti's Media Since the Overthrow of Aristide
An exposé on the brutal suppression of Haiti's journalists by the military leaders who ousted the country's first democratically elected president. Bouch Pe comes from the Creole saying, "Se je we, bouch pe: Your eyes can see, but your mouth can't speak." September 1992.

Frontline Reports, $10
Yugoslavia, East Timor, Russia, Southeast Asia, Pakistan
Expert analysis of press conditions in five regions: Slavenka Drakulic on Yugoslavia, Kamran Khan on Pakistan, Allan Nairn and Amy Goodman on East Timor, Martin Walker on Russia, and James Clad on Southeast Asia. January 1992.

In The Censor's Shadow, $10
Journalism in Suharto's Indonesia
A comprehensive account of media repression in Indonesia despite the government's avowed

policy of openness. It includes eyewitness accounts by two American reporters of the Army massacre in Dili, East Timor. November 1991.

The Soviet Media's Year of Decision, $10

Pulitzer-prize winning journalist Hedrick Smith analyzes the press in Gorbachev's Soviet Union and events leading up to the attempted coup of August 1991. This report includes a comprehensive guide to media organizations, primarily in Russia.

Dangerous Assignments, $10

A Study Guide

Designed to stimulate classroom discussion of press freedom issues, *Dangerous Assignments* describes the dangers that reporters face in Latin America, Southeast Asia, and Africa. Also available is a companion 60-minute television documentary featuring U.S. network anchors. Fall 1991.

Killing the Messengers, $10

Lithuania and Latvia, January 1991

Martin Walker reports on an investigative mission to the Soviet Union sponsored by CPJ. June 1991.

Enforced Restraint, $10

Press Conditions in Turkey

A report on the harassment of foreign journalists and the repression of local journalists attempting to cover the Kurdish separatist movement in southeastern Turkey. December 1990.

Journalism Under Occupation, $20

Israel's Regulation of the Palestinian Press

CPJ and Article 19 argue that the control Israel exercises over the Palestinian press goes well beyond what might be justified to avert clear threats to security. October 1988.

Becoming a CPJ Member

CPJ helps journalists fight: •**Wrongful Imprisonment** • **Assaults** • **Harassment** • **Censorship**
Your membership includes a subscription to CPJ's newsletter, *Dangerous Assignments,*
and a 50% discount on all other CPJ publications.

"CPJ often is the only thing keeping a journalist alive, the only thing that offers hope of release
from prison or persecution."

Terry Anderson

Member Profile

I want to join as a:
- [ ] Member $35
- [ ] Student........................$15
- [ ] Contributor...............$100
- [ ] Supporter $500
- [ ] Benefactor..............$1,000

I work as a:
- [ ] Reporter
- [ ] Photographer
- [ ] Editor/Producer
- [ ] Publisher
- [ ] Other:

Name

Company

Address

City   State   Zip

Work Phone   Home Phone

Fax   E-Mail

PAYMENT INFORMATION

[ ] Visa   [ ] Mastercard   [ ] American Express   [ ] Check Enclosed

Card Number   Expiration Date

Name On Card   Amount to Charge

Signature

All contributions are tax-deductible

---

330 Seventh Avenue, 12th Floor, New York, NY 10001, USA
(212) 465-1004 • Fax: (212) 465-9568 • E-Mail: cpj@igc.apc.org

Becoming a CPJ Member

**CPJ helps journalists fight: •Wrongul Imprisonment • Assaults • Harassment • Censorship
Your membership includes a subscription to CPJ's newsletter, *Dangerous Assignments*,
and a 50% discount on all other CPJ publications.**

"CPJ often is the only thing keeping a journalist alive, the only thing that offers hope of release
from prison or persecution."

Terry Anderson

Member Profile

I want to join as a:
[ ] Member $35
[ ] Student.......................$15
[ ] Contributor..............$100
[ ] Supporter.................$500
[ ] Benefactor.............$1,000

I work as a:
[ ] Reporter
[ ] Photographer
[ ] Editor/Producer
[ ] Publisher
[ ] Other:

Name

Company

Address

City   State   Zip

Work Phone   Home Phone

Fax   E-Mail

PAYMENT INFORMATION

[ ] Visa   [ ] Mastercard   [ ] American Express   [ ] Check Enclosed

Card Number   Expiration Date

Name On Card   Amount to Charge

Signature

All contributions are tax-deductible

---

330 Seventh Avenue, 12th Floor, New York, NY 10001, USA
(212) 465-1004 • Fax: (212) 465-9568 • E-Mail: cpj@igc.apc.org

Becoming a CPJ Member

CPJ helps journalists fight: •**Wrongul Imprisonment** • **Assaults** • **Harassment** • **Censorship**
Your membership includes a subscription to CPJ's newsletter, *Dangerous Assignments*, and a 50% discount on all other CPJ publications.

"CPJ often is the only thing keeping a journalist alive, the only thing that offers hope of release from prison or persecution."

Terry Anderson

Member Profile

I want to join as a:

[ ] Member $35
[ ] Student.......................$15
[ ] Contributor...............$100
[ ] Supporter.................$500
[ ] Benefactor..............$1,000

I work as a:

[ ] Reporter
[ ] Photographer
[ ] Editor/Producer
[ ] Publisher
[ ] Other:

Name

Company

Address

City   State   Zip

Work Phone   Home Phone

Fax   E-Mail

PAYMENT INFORMATION

[ ] Visa   [ ] Mastercard   [ ] American Express   [ ] Check Enclosed

Card Number   Expiration Date

Name On Card   Amount to Charge

Signature

All contributions are tax-deductible

---

330 Seventh Avenue, 12th Floor, New York, NY 10001, USA
(212) 465-1004 • Fax: (212) 465-9568 • E-Mail: cpj@igc.apc.org

How to Report an Attack on the Press

CPJ needs accurate, detailed information in order to document abuses of press freedom and effectively help journalists in trouble. CPJ corroborates the information and takes appropriate action on behalf of the journalists and news organizations involved.

What to report:

Journalists who are:
- Missing
- Killed
- Arrested or kidnapped
- Wounded
- Assaulted
- Threatened
- Harassed
- Wrongfully expelled
- Wrongfully sued for libel or defamation
- Denied credentials
- Censored

News Organizations that are:
- Attacked, raided or illegally searched
- Materials confiscated or damaged
- Editions confiscated or transmissions jammed
- Closed by force
- Wrongfully sued for libel or defamation
- Censored

Information Needed:

CPJ needs accurate, detailed information:
- Journalists and news organizations involved
- Date and circumstances of incident
- Background information

Who to call:

Anyone with information about an attack on the press should call CPJ:

Call collect if necessary.
(212) 465-1004

Or send us a fax at:
(212) 465-9568

Africa: Eleanor Bedford,
(212) 465-1004 (x103)
E-Mail: africa@cpj.igc.apc.org
Americas: Ana Arana,
(212) 465-1004 (x106)
E-Mail: latinamerica@cpj.igc.apc.org
Asia: Vikram Parekh,
(212) 465-1004 (x109)
E-Mail: asia@cpj.igc.apc.org
Eastern Europe (including the republics of the former Soviet Union): Leonid Zagalsky,
(212) 465-1004 (x104)
E-Mail: europe@cpj.igc.apc.org
Middle East and North Africa:
Avner Gidron,
(212) 465-1004 (x105)
E-Mail: middleeast@cpj.igc.apc.org

What happens next:

Depending on the case, CPJ will:
- Confirm the report.
- Pressure authorities to respond.
- Notify human rights groups and press organizations around the world: *IFEX, Article 19, Amnesty International, Reporters Sans Frontieres, PEN, International Federation of Journalists, Human Rights Watch and others.*
- Increase public awareness through the press.
- Publish advisories to warn other journalists about potential dangers.
- Send a fact-finding mission to investigate.